Global Modernization

Global Modernization

Rethinking the project of modernity

Alberto Martinelli

Sage Studies in International Sociology
Sponsored by the International
Sociological Association/ISA

SAGE Publications
London ● Thousand Oaks ● New Delhi

© Alberto Martinelli 2005

First published 2005

SAGE Publications Ltd
1 Oliver's Yard
55 City Road
London EC1Y 1SP

SAGE Publications Inc.
2455 Teller Road
Thousand Oaks, California 91320

SAGE Publications India Pvt Ltd
B-42, Panchsheel Enclave
Post Box 4109
New Delhi 110 017

British Library Cataloguing in Publication data

A catalogue record for this book is available
from the British Library

ISBN 0 7619 4799 X

Library of Congress Control Number: 2004099513

Typeset by C&M Digitals (P) Ltd., Chennai, India
Printed in Great Britain by The Cromwell Press, Ltd, Trowbridge, Wiltshire

For Barbara

Contents

Introduction

The concepts of modernization and modernity have a peculiar fate: their popularity in the everyday language of mass media, political discourse and educated public opinion appears almost inversely proportional to their position in comparative social sciences research. Not a week passes in which one does not hear or read about the necessity of modernizing public administration, modes of transportation or schools in this or that country. A week does not pass without reading or hearing news and comments on the modernization program of the UK Labour government or the Chinese Communist Party. In the past few years, the concepts have not wavered in popularity and are still very widespread, both in the general sense of various attempts at reforming political and institutional frameworks, as well as in the specific sense of the study of economic and social transitions of countries that until not too long ago were defined as the 'Third World'.

On the other hand, in the scientific debate, the concepts have experienced changing fortunes: modernization enjoyed great popularity in sociology and political science in the 1950s and 1960s mostly with regard to developing countries, then a decline in the subsequent 20 years as a result of various criticisms the theory provoked, and, in the last decade of the twentieth century, found a lively revival of interest in the problems of modernity, mostly in the sense of an exploration of multiple modernities, that is of the different paths toward and through modernity. Since the varying fortunes of these concepts are closely linked to the chief historical processes of the second half of the twentieth century, it is necessary to trace them with a few broad strokes.

It should nevertheless be remembered, first, that the study of modern society's formation process is at the center of sociology's classic analysis, and is the sociological topic *par excellence*, but the classics prefer to employ concepts such as that of capitalism and industrial society instead of the concept of modernization.

The concept of modernization established itself in the social sciences in the political-ideological climate of the years after the Second World War, marked on the one hand by de-colonization and associated hopes for rapid development of post-colonial countries and, on the other, by the competition between the United States and the Soviet Union to attract such countries into their sphere of influence. In this context, numerous North American sociologists and political scientists devoted themselves to studying the problems that 'backward' Third World countries had to face in order to acquire the characteristics of modernity as it appeared in the developed countries of the West (we will define the studies of this period as making up the classic theory of modernization).

Subsequently, the disappointments deriving from the difficulty and the failures of efforts at economic growth and social transformation in Third World countries, and the crisis of American hegemony in the 1960s following the Vietnam War, fostered many epistemological as well as ideological criticisms of the classic theory. These criticisms not only nourished alternative approaches but also brought on a decline in interest in the next 15 to 20 years (and often the abandonment of the concept of modernization as too closely identifiable with the theory that was criticized).

Starting in the mid-1980s, the debate resumed with vigor – with the word 'modernity' often preferred to the more ideologically loaded modernization – as a result of the combined effect of the vast processes at the end of the millennium that we can summarize into three groups. The first concerns the transformations of capitalism, manifested in the globalization of the economy, in the unfolding of the *post-industrial* society, in the passage from the organization of labor in large assembly-line factories (of the Fordist–Taylorist type) to automatic and flexible forms of labor, and in the increasing centrality of consumption with respect to production. These transformations stimulated the reflections of *postmodern* sociology (according to which developed countries have by now entered into a new historical phase distinctly different from the modern one), and the reactions of many who maintain, instead, that the process and the project of modernity are far from being accomplished and that we still live in the epoch of *late* or *radical modernity*.

The second type of process is represented by the rapid and strong economic development of Asian countries (at first, the four 'Asian Tigers' of the Far East – South Korea, Taiwan, Singapore and Hong Kong – but more and more also China, India, Thailand and Malaysia), and some countries in Latin America, that are following different routes to modernity which, however, share the effort of building an alliance between economic liberalism and state authoritarianism. The economic success of these countries throws into difficulty neo-Marxist theories of dependence and the growing gap between dominant central countries and the underdeveloped peripheries, as well as liberal theories that support the reciprocal strengthening of economic growth and political democracy.

At the end of the 1980s, the third process revealed itself, with a series of traumatic events in large measure unexpected by world public opinion and not foreseen by the majority of scholars: the fall of the Soviet Union, the reunification of Germany and the start of a difficult economic and political transformation for the post-Soviet and post-Communist countries of Eastern Europe. This process had far-reaching consequences, first of all, for global politics, leaving the United States as the only superpower, facilitating the enlargement of the European Union to the East, and creating new constraints and opportunities for modernizing countries outside the West.

These profound and often traumatic changes revived interest in the theory of modernization at the end of the twentieth century and at the beginning of the twenty-first. They stimulated the attention of scholars who, never having abandoned the argument, proposed revisions and updates of the theory of the 1950s and 1960s. These major shifts also kindled a critical reflection on the concept of modernity, re-examining the processes of modernization to affirm the persisting centrality, as well as the decline of this characterization of contemporary societies. The new theories about reflexive and global modernization, insofar as they shift attention from a somewhat static notion of cultural modernity back to modernization as a process in time, are particularly promising in the field of history and can help a fruitful dialogue developing between sociologists and historians in the near future. As Nolte (2001) argues, the idea of modernization has weathered many storms and changed its appearance, but it seems that it still offers an indispensable clue to the historical and sociological analysis of long-term changes in society and culture.

The recent dramatic changes also generated new interpretations of economic modernization in non-Western countries, such as the study of the new *political economy* and the comparative analysis of cultures, with particular attention to the newly industrialized countries of East Asia and to Chinese modernization, one of the most significant phenomena of our time. Finally, they stimulated monographic studies on individual societies' pathways to modernization, and introduced the concept of *multiple modernities*.

Today, the study of modernization and modernity is a very vital and promising field in sociology and political science that offers indispensable tools for analyzing the routes taken by developed countries and the transformations and rapid and tumultuous crises of many Asian and Latin American countries, as well as the transition of the post-Communist countries of Eastern Europe.

These are, in short, the reasons that induced us to write a book on modernization and modernity in which critical reflection on the theories is the key to understanding the most important problems and the fundamental choices that face countries that modernize, preferring such concepts (cleansed of their ethnocentric connotations) to synonyms such as 'development' or 'growth' that are limited by their economic dimension, or such as 'social change' that seems, on the other hand, too general.

In the face of the deep and thorough social transformations occurring in the age of globalization, sociological imagination often gives the impression of lagging behind and being inadequate to confront the scope of transformation. We should follow Rabelais' warning to avoid 'the building of the new with dead stones'. Beck exaggerates in pointing out that most contemporary sociologists work with 'zombie concepts', but it is true that we have to modify our perspective and work out new concepts, new theories, and new narratives, based on increased comparative research. I am also convinced, however, that theoretical innovation not only requires imagination and innovation, but also a careful reassessment, updating, refining, and transformation of past concepts and theories. We have to avoid a frequent bad habit in social science of just inventing new names for old bottles. We should take time selecting and assessing which old bottles still contain good wine, as in the case of some parts of modernization theories.

Overview of the book

The book is composed of five chapters. In Chapter 1 the concepts of modernization and modernity are defined and the distinctive characteristics of the modernization process are re-established, based on the varied experience of both modern and modernizing countries and the contribution of the classics of social theory. The various dimensions of the transition to modernity are assessed, paying special attention to the culture and the institutional arrangements of modernity.

Chapter 2 discusses the principal contributions of that theory, which we define as the classic theory of modernization, worked out mostly in the United States in the 1950s and 1960s to study the 'backward' countries of the Third World. This literature, which has been too hastily dismissed as theoretically obsolete and ideologically biased, is analyzed in terms of the unit of analysis chosen: the fundamental characteristics of the types of societies that begin to modernize (in particular, the presence of structural and cultural preconditions and obstacles, constraints and opportunities, to the agency of individual and collective actors); the factors, mechanisms and processes that explain the transformation from one type of social entity into another or the transition from one phase to another; the form, sequence and direction that the process of change assumes; the critical thresholds of political and social development; the types and characteristics of the various actors (with their objectives, resources, strategies, values); and the duration, and the intended and unintended consequences of the process.

Chapter 3 reviews the main criticisms that were directed at the classic theory and the principal strains of research that developed from that criticisms, both in the analysis of the origins and the roads to modernization taken by developed countries in the West, as well as in the current processes of modernization in non-European countries. These strains are historical sociology and political development approaches, and the neo-Marxist approaches of *dependencia* and the world system. The chapter concludes with a recognition of the contemporary studies of *political economy* and the comparative analysis of cultures of modernizing societies (especially East Asia) and with a synthesis of the key aspects of a critical theory of modernization.

Chapter 4 examines current trends in Western developed countries in light of the renewed interest in the themes of modernity and modernization. First, we outline the main features and develop a critique of the post-modernity approach, then, we briefly assess the theoretical contributions of Berman, Habermas, Touraine and Wagner, who share, although with different reasoning, the idea that modernity is still an incomplete process, and, finally, we examine more deeply Giddens's interpretation of radical modernity and Beck's concept of the risk society.

Chapter 5 analyzes the relationship between modernization and globalization: first, it delineates globalization as a multi-faceted process, where tendencies toward homogenization and diversification co-exist and conflict with each other, allowing for at least a partially autonomous paths toward and through modernity. Second, it makes a critical appraisal of the literature on multiple modernities, arguing that different paths toward and through modernity are taking place in the contemporary world because of the different structural arrangements and cultural codes of modernizing countries and because of the position they hold in the world economy and in the international power system. Then it shows that multiple modernities are possible also because globalization erodes nation-states' sovereignty, but not to the point of preventing governments from being proactive agents of development and modernization. And, finally, it argues the potentialities of relatively specific modernization projects are more likely to be realized in a context of democratic global governance such as the one outlined in the final section – rather than in a unipolar world system.

The first four chapters of the volume are the English translation by Amy Carden Suardi, whom I thank for her excellent work, of my book *La modernizzazione*, published by Laterza in 1998, and in its seventh edition in 2004, with some necessary updating. Chapter 5 was written expressly for the English edition.

1

Modernization and Modernity

The concepts of modernization and modernity

By modernization we mean the sum of the processes of large-scale change through which a certain society tends to acquire the economic, political, social and cultural characteristics considered typical of modernity.

The concept of modernization implies, therefore, the concept of modernity in the meaning it acquired in the eighteenth century, even though its origins go back many centuries. The late Latin term *modernus* derives from *modo*, which means 'now, recently', and dates back to the end of the fifth century AD. It was used in an antinomic sense compared to *antiquus*, particularly by St Augustine to contrast the new Christian era with pagan antiquity. More generally, it was used as a means of describing and legitimizing new institutions, new legal rules, or new scholarly assumptions. Thus, from its very inception, the term modern has been carrying some normative implications, insofar as it implied a depreciation of the old and traditional.

The coming of Christ marks a radical break that divides historical time into a 'before' and an 'after' and introduces, guided by the Hebrew Messianic tradition, the message of redemption. Despite the emphasis on the Messianic anticipation of the second coming of Christ and universal judgement, especially intense among millenarist movements, that orientation toward the future and valorization of the new that are typical of modernity are not, however, part of medieval thought. On the contrary, the sharp distinction between sacred time and profane time and the City of God and the City of Man encourages devaluation of the new as an expression of superficiality and vanity. And at the same time, the daily experience of the population, the great majority of whom live in the rural countryside, keeps the naturalistic notion of the ancient world alive, a notion which conceives time through the cycle of birth and death, the changing of the seasons throughout the year, and the alternating of day and night.

Humanism and the Renaissance re-evaluate secular time and open new, broad geographic and cultural horizons to European civilization. They introduce the concept of the medieval period being between the ancient era and the modern one and distinguish between 'ancient' states and societies and 'modern' ones. The new epoch is seen as a rebirth and a radical shift after the stagnation and what Petrarch called the 'barbarisms' of the Middle Ages; but the new reawakening is nonetheless conceived upon the model of classic antiquity.

Renaissance culture reassesses its interest in mundane affairs and reaffirms its autonomy, and develops a new trust in critical reason and human creativity. Machiavelli, for example, does not believe in any ordering design – natural or divine – in politics, and thinks that it is actually the task of politics to create order in the world. Real political relations – defined as the struggle to win, utilize and contain power – are ascribed a pre-eminent position in social life as the main constituent elements of society. But he searches in the eternal canons of Greco-Roman antiquity for legitimation of his own audacious innovations. Because of the instability of all singular constitutional forms, he suggests the model of ancient Rome's mixed government, combining elements of monarchy, aristocracy and democracy. The Renaissance offers, therefore, an essential contribution to the formation of the concept of modernity, that is still incomplete, however, due to the persistent dominance of the classical model.

A subsequent fundamental passage is represented by the Reformation which stressed the conception of the person as an individual. In the teachings of Luther and Calvin, the individual was conceived as alone before God, directly responsible for the interpretation and enactment of God's will. The major consequences of these doctrines for the development of modern culture and institutions were, first, the fostering of the notion of the individual agent as 'master of its destiny' which implies the release of the believer from the institutional support and control of the Church; and, second, the sanctioning of the separation between State and Church and of the autonomy of secular activity in all domains which did not directly conflict with moral and religious practice.

An essential aspect of the claim of modern culture is made by the philosophy of the seventeenth century and in particular by the Cartesian theory of reconstructing knowledge based on human reason alone, which implies a rejection of the preceding philosophical systems. In this intellectual climate, fueled by the great advances of Galilean and Newtonian science, the conviction grows that the tyranny of ancient thinkers should be abolished. In the late seventeenth-century dispute between the ancients and the moderns, the latter come out winners. Anticipating the dispute, to the traditional opinion, according to which the ancients are the most wise, both Bacon and Descartes genially counter that we moderns are 'the true ancients' since we are able to have a greater experience of things and to benefit from a long history of the world and since, if truth is the daughter of time, we must be closer to the truth. A new faith develops in the progressive education of humanity and in the great inventions of modern times that transform the world (the printing press, gunpowder and the compass, according to Bacon). Nevertheless, the notion of progress is not yet fully developed and remains mingled with the deep-rooted conviction that decadence and degeneration are at least as much innate to the fate of humanity as progress in what are defined by Vico as the 'courses and recourses' of history; an idea that will continue for a long time to be hegemonic in non-Western cultures.

It is exactly this concept of time and of history that is modified in Western culture in the course of the next century, by virtue of the great political and industrial transformation that alters the concept of revolution and gives concrete substance to the notion of progress. It is only then that the concept of modernity establishes itself completely.

With the Enlightenment the fundamental identification of the modern with the *here and now* is established, and from then on *modern society is our society*, the society in which we live, whether we are citizens of the late eighteenth century or citizens of the early twenty-first century. Modern society does not negate history, because comparison with the past is necessary, but it sees neither particular patterns in the past to imitate nor particular lessons to learn. The greatest Ciceronian expression, *historia magistra vitae*, exemplifies the pre-Enlightenment idea of history as a rich repository of examples to orient human action and implies a concept of human experience fundamentally uniform and immutable, marked by recurrent events, in which special value is attached to experience. With the Enlightenment historical thinking incorporated the key notion of rupture and shifted from cyclical to progressive models. Since then and after the American and French Revolutions, the modern world was considered a world open to the future, and the term modern carried the normative implication of a depreciation of the old or traditional.

The traditional notion of history and time is gradually modified in the second half of the eighteenth century, opening the way toward a conception of modernity with the idea of *progress* at its core, elaborated by Kant, Condorcet and Turgot. The modern world is a world that in a radical way is open to a better future to be attained by a natural progression in the cultural path of mankind. As Tuveson (1964) and Koselleck (1985) observe, Christian millenarianism is secularized, liberated from the 'moral terrorism' of the apocalyptic anticipation of the end of the world, and transformed into the idea of scientific and rational progress for the human race.

The past no longer offers life lessons, its authority is rendered powerless, but it helps us to understand what we have become, and for this reason it is continually reinterpreted in the light of the present. A radical formulation of this attitude, with specific reference to the revolution of modernity, is found in *Democracy in America* (1835–1840) in which de Tocqueville writes:

> Although the revolution that is taking place in the social condition, the laws, the opinions, and the feelings of men is still very far from being terminated, yet its results already admit of no comparison with anything that the world has ever before witnessed. I go back from age to age up to the remotest antiquity, but I find no parallel to what is occurring before my eyes; as the past has ceased to throw its light upon the future, the mind of man wanders in obscurity. (1945, vol. 2: 349)

Modernity is a process with no end that implies the idea of permanent innovation, of continual creation of the new. Living in the present, it is oriented towards the future, avid for novelty, promoting innovation. It invented, as Kumar (1995) observes, the *tradition of the new*.

The French Revolution and the connected (yet profoundly different) American War of Independence, embody the new notion of a mass political experience and of the new democratic state. The French Revolution is the first modern revolution, and it radically transforms the concept of revolution itself. New events require new words, and new meanings for old words. The astronomical concept of revolution as perpetual cyclical movement of heavenly bodies gives life to the political concept of revolution. It shares the idea of capsizing, the 'upside down', but signifies the opposite of the astronomical concept as well, in so far as it represents a break with the existing and the creation of something new (a concept analogous with regard to the spatial dimension, but antinomic with regard to the temporal dimension).

If the French Revolution gave modernity its form and characteristic conscience, based on reason, the Industrial Revolution gave it its material substance. The Industrial Revolution's explosive development, the force of vapor and steel, the acceleration of economic transformations – all invested revolutionary proportions in the great processes of change, which were quite evident to contemporaries who experimented with them in their daily life.

And since Western societies show the greatest differences and contrasts with preceding societies in economic and social organization, political relations and cultural features, they become the symbol of modernity. Modernization tends to identify itself with Westernization, in the sense that Western society becomes world civilization (which creates, as we will see, complex interpretive and methodological problems).

Modernity also comes to signify, as Habermas argues (1985), the establishment of rights and freedoms. The modern project is a universalizing project of emancipation and, at the same time paradoxically, a legitimating ideology for the expansion of the first modern Western societies.

In light of this brief reconstruction of the concept of modernity, we define modernization in this work not in a broad or vague sense like any other progressive historic change, but as a historically determined process. Modernization is the specific sum of the large-scale social, economic, political and cultural changes that have characterized world history in the past 200 years and that originate from the multi-faceted revolution (economic, social, political, cultural) of the second half of the eighteenth century. It is a process that tends to be global in two senses: it affects all aspects of the involved societies, and it progressively extends to the rest of the world from its birthplace in Western Europe.

Modernization refers then to a process, or better, an ensemble of well-defined processes, and implies modernity. Nonetheless it is distinguished from modernity, which refers to the specific modalities of social life and culture that assert themselves in the course of such process.

The concept of modernization, though based on the historical experience of Western countries in Europe and North America, can also be applied to the rest of the world (the *Rest* versus the *West*), keeping in mind the diversity of time periods, the sequences of their development and the specificity of their institutions. While the technology-driven changes and the implications of the market globalization process indeed progressively involve the whole world, every country offers *specific and uneven responses*, resulting from the combination of their institutional and cultural inheritance, together with cultural models imported from abroad. These various responses manifest themselves in a context marked by the international division of labor and by international power relations. The concept of modernization establishes itself in the social sciences in the decades after the Second World War (taking the place of concepts of industrialization and capitalist development) in order to interpret, in a coherent and broad way, at first the common processes and then increasingly also the varying responses of different developing countries to the challenges of the global economy.

The study of the formation of modern society is a sociological topic *par excellence*, from the moment that the fathers of social science, from de Tocqueville to

Marx, from Weber to Durkheim, from Pareto to Simmel, focused their attention on analyzing the modern break and the contradictions and problems that spring from it.

This volume will not examine the classic theorists in detail, apart from what is necessary to define the essential characteristics of modernization and modernity in this first chapter. The present volume is instead focused on the theories of modernization elaborated by contemporary sociology and political science.

The essential aspects of the modernization process in the light of the classic thinkers of the social sciences

The concept of modernization adopted here is, as we have said, historically defined. The subject of modernization is indeed so vast and its meanings so varied that several choices of method and content have to be made. It does not signify any type of change, evolution or social progress (such as the invention of the wheel or the compass) but it defines the combination of social, economic, political and cultural large-scale changes that have characterized the past 200 years and that are by now taking over the entire world. Such changes originate from the two-fold revolution of the second half of the eighteenth century: the political-cultural revolution in its French and American versions and the economic-social revolution in its double aspect of the systematic introduction of industry and the development of the world market.

It has to do with a set of changes that were made over a period of many centuries (according to some scholars, starting from the proto-capitalist system of bankers in the twelfth century, according to others, from the great maritime explorers of the fifteenth century, and according to still others, from the great scientific discoveries of the seventeenth century) and that culminated in the revolutionary eighteenth-century processes.

The progressive formation of modern democracies (through the demand for natural rights and popular sovereignty) and of a world market (through intensifying long-distance commerce and European expansion in other continents) is a centuries-old process that precedes the technological and industrial revolution. The 'Glorious Revolution' that puts an end to the English civil wars of the 1600s with the first constitutional monarchy prepares and precedes the democratic revolution that takes place in France and in the United States at the end of the next century. Newton's science and Descartes's philosophy anticipate the modern scientific revolution. But it is in the eighteenth century that modern society reaches maturity and that the idea of modernity itself receives its binding formulation in the philosophical debates of the Enlightenment. In the following century modern society is strengthened, identifying itself with industrialism and with the rapid and profound changes associated with it. And in the twentieth century various non-Western countries, beginning with Japan, 'enter into modernity' and the process generalizes.

Common directions of modernization are those toward innovation and unceasing change through the processes of creative destruction, the growing structural differentiation of society (economic production and distribution that separate from family and community, politics separating from religion), and the formation of sovereign nation-states.

Its most characteristic trait is the totality of its double meaning. In one sense it concerns the economic, social, political and cultural aspects of the societies in which it manifests itself and involves all the spheres of action and life of its inhabitants. And in another sense, despite its direct reference to European societies, it progressively covers, with various rhythms and sequences, the entire world, inserting itself more or less forcefully into a unique global system, that appears today at the birth of the millennium strongly interdependent from an economic point of view and closely connected from a cultural one. As Berman writes:

> Modernity is a mode of vital experience – experience of space and time, of the self and others, of life's possibilities and perils – that is shared by men and women all over the world to-day. Modern environments and experiences cut across all boundaries of geography and ethnicity, of class and of nationality, of religion and ideology: in this sense, modernity can be said to unite all mankind. But it is a paradoxical unity, a unity of disunity, that pours us all into a maelstrom of perpetual disintegration and renewal, of struggle and contradiction, of ambiguity and anguish. (1983: 15)

The pervasiveness and the expansive thrust of modernization require that the process be studied with reference not only to the way modern Western societies are formed, but also to the transformations that have progressively involved the rest of the world. Such transformations produced outcomes that are partially different and plural according to the genetic code of the various societies involved, but they are influenced by a substantially univocal process that they try to imitate as well as oppose in several ways.

Recognizing the intrinsically globalizing character of modernization does not mean adopting a Eurocentric approach, or even less, suggesting a single blueprint for the transition to modernity. Instead it means recognizing the univocity of the process as well as the specificity of the different routes toward and through modernity.

The process of modernization connotes, in other words, the sum of interconnected changes from which emerges a distinctive type of social organization and civilization – the 'modern society'. The definition of this model, which necessarily draws upon the richness and variety of real social structures, can be based on a combination of analytical characteristics or shared essential aspects (in turn 'deduced' from similar but not identical historical processes) that distinguish it from models of 'traditional' or pre-technological societies.

The essential aspects of the modernization process in diverse historical experiences can be summarized briefly:

1. The development of science and technology, which takes place through a basic transformation of the nature of scholarly and scientific practices and institutions, becomes the primary source of economic growth and social change and increases our capacity for controlling the variability of the natural environment and population growth, and also changes our image of the universe, the place we occupy there, and our notions of biological evolution.
2. Industrialization, founded on the technology of machines and mechanical energy, which greatly increases the capacity to produce and exchange goods and services of increasing quantity and value.

3. The progressive forming of a global capitalist market and the intensification of economic interdependence between different nation-states and between the various regions of the world.

4. Structural differentiation and functional specialization in different spheres of social life (and in particular the accentuated division of labor between the classes and genders, and the separation of the public sphere from the private sphere) that create new forms of power and social struggles and imply new problems for integration and governing the social complexity.

5. The transformation of the class system and the increase in social mobility, of which the most salient features are the decline of the farm laborer, the growth of the bourgeoisie and the working class, and the expansion and diversification of the middle class.

6. Political development, meaning both the establishment of secular nation-states (equipped with vast public administrations, greater political and military efficacy and continually struggling to increase their political power), as well as the rise in the political mobilization of movements, parties and representative associations that fight to defend their interests and establish collective identities.

7. Secularization, seen as 'the disenchantment of the world', the emancipation of civil society and scientific knowledge from religious control, and the privatization of faith.

8. The establishment of values typical of modernity, in particular, individualism, rationalism and utilitarianism.

9. Demographic disturbances that uproot millions of people from their ancestral habitat and the concentration of the majority of the population in urban environments that are functionally complex, culturally pluralistic, socially heterogeneous if not chaotic.

10. The privatization of family life, its insulation from the social control of the community and the separation of the workplace from the home, and the liberation of women from patriarchal authority.

11. The democratization of education and the development of mass culture and mass consumption.

12. The development of the means of material and symbolic communication that embrace and unite the most disparate peoples and societies.

13. The compression of time and space and their organization according to the demands of industrial production and the world market.

The order in which these aspects are listed does not imply a scientific-technological or economic determinism. Among the various spheres of society there are, in fact, not as many relationships of cause and effect as there are influences and reciprocal conditioning that vary in each moment in history and each situation studied. Nonetheless, the order adopted does indicate that technological innovations and economic processes demonstrate the greatest homogeneity and synchronicity, spread more rapidly than the others, and impose themselves in the most uniform way in different contexts, whereas cultural, political and institutional responses are much more varied and provide the main sources of diversity.

We will organize these various processes with regard to the different dimensions (economic, social, political and cultural) of modernization and to the particular type of characteristic personality, and with reference to the classic sociological thought of de Tocqueville, Marx, Weber, Durkheim, Pareto, Simmel, Schumpeter and Polanyi. Variability is introduced by both the temporal dimension (ordering countries based on the time period in which the modernization process began, or when contacts with more developed countries started, and on the rhythms and sequences in which it unfolds) and by the historic specificity of the various societies. Consequently, we will underline the principal differences between Western modernization and the experience of other countries.

The economic and social dimensions of modernization

Economic modernization is generally understood as a system of industrial production that applies scientifically-based technology, replaces human and animal labor by inanimate and mechanical energy, develops a complex division of labor that reveals a hierarchy of specialized abilities acquired in formal education processes, produces commodities by means of commodities, and involves the vast commercialization of goods and services in a tendentially global market.

The organization of such an economic system pivots on the figure of the entrepreneur innovator, craftsman of the destructive creation of capitalism. This organization is inspired by rational principles, or the adequacy of the means to the ends and the resources for the objectives, and proves to be more efficient than traditional economies or mere subsistence, according to indicators of performance such as growth of gross national product and per capita income. The classical and neo-classical political economy represents a systematic attempt at understanding the new economic relationships that emerge from the Industrial Revolution and the development of the capitalist market.

An alternative view of the same processes is Marx's historical-materialist theory of social change, focusing on the contradiction between the transformation of the 'structure' of society (i.e. the evolution of the productive forces and the related changes in class relations), and the 'superstructure' of society (i.e. the changes in culture and in the legal and political institutions). The fundamental type of contradiction is the changing division of labor, which generates inequalities, as well as asymmetries of power and class conflict leading to historical ruptures. Capitalism, as any other phase in history, contains the germs of its own destruction, but the process of 'creative destruction' is by far more dynamic and encompassing. In Marx's 'grand narrative', the 'natural laws' of classical political economy are 'historicized', insofar as they are relevant only to one phase – that of bourgeois capitalism – in the sequence of historical phases through which human society passes. Marx's theory of capitalism can be considered the most influential nineteenth-century theory of modernization, as well as a bridge between the first explicit variants of modernization theories (those of the Scottish Enlightenment historians such as Ferguson and Millar) and the early twentieth-century contributions of the sociological classics, first of all, Weber and Durkheim.

Later interpretations of the economic modernization process generally distinguish several stages, starting from the initial preconditions, which are an accumulation of agrarian or mercantile capital, continuing with actual industrial take-off, economic maturity and mass consumption. Each of these stages is characterized by specific relationships between saving, consumption and investment; between private initiative and public intervention; and by diverse forms of nesting of economic activity in the social, institutional and cultural context.

The principal indicators used to describe and measure such changes by institutions such as the Inter-university Consortium for Political and Social Research and the World Bank (increases in energy consumption and production of iron and steel, growth of gross national income and per capita income, the value added and the distribution of the work force per economic sector) show the gap between the gross national income of developed countries and that of the rest of the world. They also show how the added value of the service industry grows more quickly, not only in more developed countries (at the expense of the added value in agriculture as well as in industry), but also in developing countries (where it grows together with the added value in the industrial sector at the expense of that in agriculture). This can entail, as we will see, serious social imbalances such as over-urbanization.

A historic alternative has existed alongside the dominant capitalist form of economic modernization – the planned economy – as seen in the Soviet Union and other transitional communist societies. While this form demonstrates some traits in common with capitalist modernization (for example, the centrality accorded to technology and industrial development as engines of modernization), it diverges on many other aspects (the collective ownership of the means of production, the replacement of the market by central economic planning as the standard for allocating factors of production, and the concentration of political and economic power in the hands of a single elite).

The social dimension of modernization is manifested in phenomena correlated to demographic change, urbanization, and the shifting position of women, and is primarily expressed in social differentiation and increasing individual autonomy. Profound modifications of the population structure take place, first, a severe decline in the infant mortality rate and then, a drastic drop in the birth rate and the prolongation of the average life. In addition, vast migratory processes uproot millions of people from their rural ancestral homes and concentrate them in functionally complex, culturally pluralistic and socially heterogeneous urban realities.

The division of labor develops enormously with respect to the past in a plurality of occupational roles and differentiated professions that require specific capabilities, skills and training. Agricultural work, completely predominant in traditional societies, declines with the rise of work in industry and the service sector, involving an ever-widening range of professional roles that require a continual evolution of knowledge and skills. The modalities of female participation in the market change as well. The percentage of women in the workforce tends first to decrease with the decline in the agricultural trade and the growth of industry, then to increase with the evolution of urban lifestyles and the growth of the service sector. The status of women in general changes profoundly due to increasing access for women to education and the independent work roles, and the decline in patriarchal authority and religious traditionalism.

Growing social differentiation is also expressed in the plurality of lifestyles and patterns of consumption, choices and options in the market and in the political arena. The individual, free from the bonds of obligatory membership to a certain rank or a certain community, sees both his means of choice and the associated responsibilities increase.

For Durkheim, the rise in population and social density and, for Simmel, the generalized use of money (fostering distant impersonal relations) and the development of large cities (reducing the social control of communities over the actions of individuals) are the principal processes that promote such transformations of societal life, shaping a variety of diverse forms in various contexts.

Both Durkheim and Simmel seem to be well aware of the inconsistency of the process. While modern society offers greater resources to society and greater freedom and means of self-fulfillment, it also produces anomie and loneliness and poses a crucial problem to the foundations of solidarity in a tendentially individualistic environment.

The social differentiation and personal freedom that are characteristic of modernity vary noticeably in form and degree according to the type of economic organization, political regime and ideological climate. In fact, due to the interdependence among various aspects of modernization, certain economic regimes (centrally planned), political structures (one-party systems) and ideologies (totalitarian) can drastically reduce the autonomy of individuals as well as the differentiation of roles and institutions.

Political modernization

Even more complex is the task of defining the common characteristics of political modernization, since here the variety of arrangements in different countries is greater and one must avoid a simplistic equation of political modernization and democratization, in light of the historical experiences of 'partial modernization' in totalitarian political regimes such as the Stalinist Soviet Union and Nazi Germany and in authoritarian political regimes such as contemporary East Asia.

While the classic modernization of Western countries is characterized by the parallel development, although often conflictual, of liberalization and democratization, the essential elements of both these processes are missing in both communist and fascist states: the real right of citizens to choose through periodic free elections, the progressive establishment of civil rights and liberties, the separation of legislative power, executive power and judiciary power in the modern rule of law, the organization of the structure of representative politics, and the foundation of due process of the law in the administration of justice.

This leads some writers to equate the experience of the communist states of the USSR and Eastern European countries with 'fake modernity' (Sztompka, 1992), due to the mixture of elements of modernity imposed in an authoritarian fashion, pre-modern vestiges and a series of symbolic imitations of institutional modernity. The most obvious examples of such imitations are constitutions that in reality answer to neither the citizen nor to the forms of democracy and elections with a closed list of candidates presented by a single party that controls the state (the 'other' parties being of no importance with no ability to compete for power).

The relationship between modernization and democratization is controversial and not univocal. However, one can gather that in an ever-increasing number of countries at the end of the millennium, the modernization process is accompanied by a substantial increase in the number of democratic regimes. The number of democracies over the total number of states results in a rise in the past 15 years in every region of the world, a figure that continues to be higher in the most developed and modern regions.

Keeping in mind the non-democratic experiences, we define political modernization as those processes of transforming institutions and political relations that are common to extremely diverse political systems. These processes include: (1) the formation of the modern nation-state, with the associated growth of state apparatuses and increase in the government's ability to direct public affairs, control social tensions and pursue political strategies for 'national interests'; (2) the rise in the degree of differentiation and integration of institutions that take part in the political sphere; and (3) the development of equality (that can be merely economic) among citizens.

The formation process of the modern state grows through the disintegration of the political and feudal social order and the establishment of royal absolutism. This implies the centralization of power and the unification and pacification of a territory via the 'monopoly of legitimate violence' (according to Weber's formulation). The modern state exercises a legitimate sovereignty over a population and a territory and holds a military, fiscal and administrative monopoly, expropriating the warriors from their means of war and public functionaries from their means of administration.

With the liberal revolutions in England in the late 1600s and France and the United States in the late 1700s, the absolute state is transformed into a democratic state. As Gellner (1995) observes, with some simplification, human societies have usually maintained order by the use of coercion and superstition.

The culture of modernity

The economic, social and political transformations both influence and are influenced by transformations in the cultural sphere, that is, by all those changes in conceptions of the world, man and society, and in the values and norms that orient individual and collective behavior, that depict a real 'culture of modernity'. Weber's idea of modernization as occidental rationalization, empirically grounded in his comparative sociology of religion and in his political sociology, was very influential. The values of rationalism, individualism/subjectivity and utilitarianism have a central place in this culture. They orient the behavior of institutions, groups and individuals and are internalized in the formation process of the personality. These values are expressed definitively in the constitutional principles of the French and American Revolutions: liberty, equality, the pursuit of happiness, tempered by the principles of fraternity and solidarity (Martinelli et al., 1989).

Rationalism has ancient roots in Western culture, especially in the marriage between Judeo-Christian monotheistic religions (which marked the separation of religion from magic, postulating the transcendence of divinity) and Greek philosophic and Roman juridical culture (which laid the foundation for the worldly concept of society and the state). European rationalism has manifested itself in a variety of different forms, from Romanesque architecture to Renaissance painting, from the philosophy of Descartes to the music of Bach, from the democratic man of the Enlightenment to the *homo oeconomicus* of capitalism. It can be defined *lato sensu* as the capacity of the human mind to know, control and transform nature (according to a conception of the world as an environment that can be molded to the fulfilling of human needs and wants) and as the confidence of human beings in rationally pursuing their own ends and, in the last analysis, in being the masters of their own destiny.

In its confidence in the power of reason to control and transform nature, rationalism is the breeding ground of scientific and geographical discoveries and technological and entrepreneurial innovations; it is related to the perception of an absence of limits (as we said before), to that particular 'restlessness' of the European people, as portrayed in paradigmatic figures of the European literature from Ulysses to Goethe's Faust, and exemplified in many events of European history, from the transcontinental sea voyages to colonial adventures, to the 'spirit of the frontier' which is a distinctive trait of the American variant of the European culture.

At the same time, reason is conceived of as a system of shared rules which made social coexistence possible. Kant does not write the apology of reason, but enquires into its limits. The rational mind is strong only if it is conscious of its own limits, does not pretend to know the truth, opens the way to an endless search. In this sense reason is by definition anti-totalitarian and directly related to individual freedom. But it is only with the advent of modern society that rationality becomes a dominant value. The idea becomes popular that reason is the only sovereign to which every human being can agree to submit. Under the doctrine of natural law all human beings are equal because each has been endowed with reason. In the Enlightenment, reason enables men to be liberated from error, from superstition and submission to the traditional powers of the Church and the aristocracy, to be masters of their own destiny, to pursue individual and collective happiness (as the American Declaration of Independence recites).

Reason, and no longer revealed religion, is the instrument for the search of truth and the foundation of the individual's freedom of choice. Liberty and equality become universal rights, as the constitutions of revolutionary France decree. Rationalization is connected to secularization, seen as 'the disenchantment of the world', the emancipation of civil society and scientific knowledge from religious control, and the privatization of faith. The process of rationalization is at the center of Weber's analysis. For Weber, the specificity of Western history resides in the pervasiveness and intensity of the rationalization process that concerned all principal aspects of societal life, from economic activity to values, from political structures to science, from family relations to artistic expression.

Rationalism also means the quest for knowledge. The quest for knowledge has been a distinctive European trait since ancient times, but it is with modernity that it acquires a new impulse because it is freed from the subordination of knowledge to a given religious truth or to a single political end. The incessant quest for knowledge is the product of the critical mind, which has its roots in the Greek philosophical ethos and develops with the Enlightenment's permanent critique of our historical era. The development of science is linked together with the driving force of capitalism and the massive development of technology, both related in their turn to the belief in continuous progress. European modernity is the age of 'Prometheus unbound', which corresponds to the absence of ethical and religious limits to the technical dominion of nature. Capitalism is a mode of production based on technical instrumentality and on the maximization of economic rationality for successful competition in the market.

Individualism/subjectivity also has ancient roots in Western culture, in antiquity, in the Renaissance, and in the Christian tradition of personal redemption. Individualism has found many different expressions in the time and space of Europe – from Evangelic subjectivity to the individualism of the free citizens in the late medieval independent republics, from the individual economic actor in the market to the individual rights of the free citizen in modern liberal democracies, and to the reflexive subjectivity of contemporary citizens. Individualism, like rationalism, has developed in the cultural heritage of European history, but has fully emerged only with the advent of modernity; it is only with the advent of modern society that free choice and the individual right of self-realization become fundamental values. Not that modern society lacks limits to the freedom of individual choice (actually severe inequalities exist in the opportunities for success available to people belonging to different classes, genders, ethnicities, states and regions of the world). But the idea is established that an individual is free to choose his own destiny and is responsible for his own choices in front of his conscience, without bowing to the will of a *pater familias*, a church or an absolute monarch.

As Durkheim explains, since society has historically come before the individual, individualism is a late product of the evolution of social life. In pre-modern societies the value and position of each individual, with the exception of a few big and powerful ones, reflect the value and social position of the group of which one is a member: one's family, rank, caste, clan, tribe, lineage or religious group. Social status is generally acquired at birth and does not change throughout life. In other words, social mobility – the passage from one social group to another – is limited. In modern societies, on the contrary, individual life chances are more open both within the new economic organization of the market economy and the new political order of the democratic nation-state. As Baker (1994) argues, individualism was not simply a symptom of the dissolution of the social whole, it was also a necessary condition for the 'discovery of society' in the new language of sociology. Not until the ideological primacy of individual interests was postulated could constraints upon these interests be discovered in the life of an autonomous social order subject to its own laws. As Polanyi, Gauchet and Baker among others have pointed out, the rise of individualism was not only a symptom of the dissolution of the primacy of the community in its traditional religious meaning but was also a necessary condition for the discovery of society in strictly secular terms. Not until the ideological primacy of individual interests and passions was postulated could constraints upon those interests be discovered in the operation of an autonomous social and political order subject to its own laws.

Individualism is at the root of the principles of liberty and equality which were affirmed by *ius naturalismus* (which holds that all human beings are equal insofar as they are endowed with reason) and by English political thought, and by the French and German philosophy of the Enlightenment, and were recognized in the prerogatives of the English Parliament after the Glorious Revolution of 1688–89 and solemnly proclaimed in the American Constitution of 1776 and in the *Déclaration des droits de l'homme et du citoyen* of 1789. These principles affirm the inviolable individual rights to life, freedom and the full accomplishment of his/her potentialities. Liberty expresses itself both as negative freedom, i.e. as protection of human rights from the abuses of power, and as positive freedom, i.e. as the citizen's right to participate in the formation of the common will. Equality was first of all defined as equality of the rights and duties of citizenship and citizens' equality before the law, but it soon became equality of opportunities and life chances as well, thus opening the way to the conceptions of progressive liberalism, social democracy and welfare policies which became integral parts of the political culture of Europe in the twentieth century. To be modern means striving to realize both principles of equality and freedom; the struggle over the balance between equality and freedom is a leitmotif in the history of modern political thought.

Individualism and subjectivity are of course not identical. There is a tendency to use the former term among scholars who prefer positive accounts of modernity (the societal) – where the individualistic understanding of the self is put alongside the growth of scientific consciousness, the development of a secular outlook, the doctrine of progress, the contractualist understanding of society as basic characters of modernity; whereas the latter concept is preferred by the supporters of the alternative view of modernity (the cultural) – which is critical of the middle-class pragmatic calculation, the soul-less pursuit of money, and lack of moral passion and is, on the contrary, concerned with the care of the self, spontaneous expression, and authentic experience. In fact, political and economic individualism and aesthetic and moral subjectivity are dimensions of the same principle and this principle is dialectically related to the principle of rationality. They are not the roots of two alternative types of modernity (the supportive and the critical, the societal and the cultural), but are elements of the same cultural and institutional syndrome. The world of the capitalist entrepreneur is a world of incessant change and deadening routine which provides the proper context for the aesthetics of the self as well. Imagination and reason are not enemies, but rather allies in the work of the scientist, as well as in that of the artist. Both wish to explore and experience everything, without limits.

The dialectic relationship between the principle of rationality (with its institutional forms such as market-driven industrial economies, bureaucratically administered states, functionally organized metropolitan cities) and the principle of subjectivity/individualism manifests itself also in the double matrix of change and routine in which the modern self lives:

Each of those unforgettable figures of modernity – Marx's 'revolutionary', Baudelaire's 'dandy', Nietzsche's 'superman', Weber's 'social scientist', Simmel's 'stranger', Musil's 'man without qualities', and Benjamin's 'flâneur' – is caught and carried in the intoxicating rush of an epochal change and yet finds itself fixed and formulated by a disciplinary system of social roles and functions. (Gaunkar, 2001: 3)

The list (to which I would add Schumpeter's 'entrepreneur') is strictly European, a further proof that the culture of modernity is linked to the European identity (including the peoples of the 'Europe outside Europe'), although is by no means confined to the West (Martinelli, 2004).

Utilitarianism as the rational pursuit of one's own interest is closely related to both rationalism and individualism – or, better, to a specific version of them. We have already mentioned the right of all human beings to pursue their own happiness. The concept of utility permeates economic behavior, production, distribution, and the exchange and consumption of goods and services. In Smith and Bentham – and in John Stuart Mills's refinement of the concept – there is also the idea that the pursuit of individual interests can at the same time serve the common good, insofar as the utility of the individual was a part of the public utility in which the individual shared. The value of utilitarianism has implications for the democracy of a modern industrial society: on the one hand, democracy is the form of governance of a society freed from absolute power and tradition, in which individuals have unlimited desires and are dedicated to the maximization of private satisfaction; on the other, a democracy based on the utility principle implies the creation of institutions and the enforcement of laws and policies aimed at the achievement of the greatest happiness for the greatest number – the only scientifically defensible criterion for assessing the public good according to Bentham and John Stuart Mill.

The rationalistic, individualistic and utilitarian values of the culture of modernization express the constant effort to control nature to satisfy human needs, as well as to increase the freedom of choice and well-being of the largest number of individuals. But they raise the problem of society's 'self-defense' – first of all in ecological terms – as Polanyi anticipated and contemporary environmental thinking further developed.

Core values and new institutional formations

The values of rationalism and individualism/subjectivity as both opposing and complementary principles characterize European history from Greek philosophy and Roman law to the Judean and Christian religious traditions, but they crystallize into a specific cultural and institutional setting with the advent of modernity. They express the tension between individual liberty and social organization. As core cultural roots, they contribute to the development of the specific modern attitude which consists in the absence of limits (Cerutti and Rudolph, 2001b: 134).

Rationalism, individualism/subjectivity, utilitarianism, the incessant quest for knowledge, innovation and discovery, the constitution of the self as an autonomous subject, the refusal of limits, the principles of liberty and equality of rights and opportunities, represent the core elements of a modern identity, nurtured in

European historical heritage, first of all, in the legacy of Christianity and of the Greek-Roman antiquity, but fully developed in the civilization of modernity which crystallized first in Western Europe and then expanded to other parts of Europe, to the Americas and throughout the world, giving rise to continuously changing cultural and institutional patterns which constituted different responses to the challenges and possibilities inherent in the core characteristics of the distinct civilization premises of modernity:

> These cultural values and attitudes fostered and were fostered by a relatively open and autonomous social structure characterized by a multiplicity of centres, a high degree of permeation of the peripheries by the centres and of impingement of the peripheries on the centres, a relatively small degree of overlapping of the boundaries of class, ethnic, religious and political entities and their continuous restructuring, a comparatively high degree of autonomy of groups and strata and their access to the centres of society, ...a multiplicity of cultural, economic and professional elites, a relatively high degree of social mobility, a legal system relatively independent from politics and religion, highly autonomous cities. (Eisenstadt, 1987)

These values and attitudes are identifiable in different forms and to different degrees in the other great civilizations, but it is in modern Europe that they crystallized in a distinct cultural programme and combined with the development of a set of new institutional formations: the university and the research academy, the capitalist market and firm, the nation-state and the democratic polity.

The modern university and research academy stem from a particular approach to the knowledge of physical and human reality capable of transforming nature for the fulfilment of human wants. The depth of Indian and Chinese religion and philosophy, the richness of Muslim scientific and religious thought, the advanced astronomic knowledge of Mesopotamia and pre-Colombian America are a few examples of the fact that Western knowledge is not exceptional. What is distinctive and specific in western culture is a greater capacity to unite abstract theory and empirical research and, even more important, to link together scientific discovery, invention and technological innovation under the constant pressure of either war or commercial competition, as well as a greater ability to design institutions particularly suited to the formation and diffusion of knowledge – from the Italian and French medieval universities to the seventeenth-century British scientific academies, from the nineteenth-century German research universities to the great American research laboratories of the present. European modernity was not simply a package of technological and organizational developments; it was intimately linked to a political revolution, and to an equally important transformation of the nature of scholarly and scientific practices and institutions (Wittrock, 2000). Europe has invented and perfected an understanding of science, which has become a global example and role model. The main characteristics of this understanding of science, as it has developed since the Renaissance, are, as Rudolph argues, the recognition of mathematics as the measure of exactness in science, the unity of freedom of scientific enquiry and scientific criticism, and the dependence of empirical knowledge on conceptual reflection (Cerutti and Rudolph, 2001).

Market-driven industrial capitalism is also closely linked to the culture of modernity. The governing principle of capitalism is the constant search for the rational maximization of individual utility in order to successfully compete on the market. The efficient combination of the factors of production in the industrial firm and the exchange of goods and services in the self-regulating market slowly expanding all over the world are the two basic institutions of capitalist development. The Industrial Revolution of the eighteenth century (a very powerful process of innovation, capital accumulation and market expansion) developed thanks to agricultural and long-distance trade surpluses and the availability of iron and coal, but was first and foremost related to the specific link with the scientific and technological revolutions of modernity. Trades and markets had flourished in the early empires and in many non-European parts of the world as well, but the particular combination of the Industrial Revolution with a self-regulating market was a European specificity which gave capitalist growth an unprecedented strength and dynamic.

The third institutional formation – the nation-state – is more controversially related to the culture of modernity than either scientific curiosity, technical domination of nature or capitalist market and industry. The nation-state is the institutional embodiment of political authority in modern society, an impersonal and sovereign political entity with supreme jurisdiction over a clearly delimited territory and population, claiming a monopoly of coercive power, and enjoying legitimacy as a result of its citizens' support. It is a particular institution which is the result of the encounter between a sovereign, autonomous, centralized political organization, and a community (real and imagined at the same time) based on ties of blood, language, shared tradition, and collective memory. Since the late Middle Ages, Europe, at least in its Western part, came to be increasingly made up of societies of peasants, lords recognizing the authority of a king, city merchants and artisans, united by a commonality of blood, language and religious beliefs (Mendras, 1997). The nation-state, characterized by the unity of a people, a territory and a distinctive culture, slowly took shape in opposition to the multi-ethnic empires and to the supra-national church and developed historically through the growth of a civil bureaucracy, an army and diplomacy, and through the formation of a nation as an imagined community (Anderson, 1991), resulting from the action of nationalist elites in the modernization process (Gellner, 1983) and capable of evoking primordial ethno-symbolic roots (Smith, 1991). It is a typical European construction, which has been exported to the other parts of the world.

The relation of the nation-state to the culture of individualism and rationalism is ambivalent and complex. One of the two components, the nation, has long been rooted in primordial ties, making appeal to emotions, and emphasizing collective goals. The other component, the state, is a rationally organized construction which grows through the development of law, an efficient bureaucracy and an effective army and diplomatic service.

The degree of congruence with the values of individualism and rationalism increases with the advent of representative democracy that democratizes the nation-state. Representative democracy, i.e. a political system made up of elected officials who represent the interest and opinions of citizens in a context characterized by the rule of law, which is based on the consensus of citizens and is developed in order to protect their basic rights, is the fourth element of European identity. The Greek *polis*, the Roman Republic and the free cities of medieval

Italy and Germany, are all antecedents of this European specificity. The various forms of parliaments, majority rule in government and the protection of minority rights, free and periodical elections, the separation of powers, the free press, are all institutional innovations which were born and developed in the culture of Europe and of that 'Europe outside Europe' which is the United States of America (the 'first new nation' constructed by European immigrants) in the course of the three major democratic revolutions, the English, the French and the American. Today, the nation-state is undergoing the double pressure of the growing global interconnectedness of social relations from above and of the reaffirmation of regional and local identities and claims of autonomy from below. But it is still the basic political organization and the key actor in international relations, as well as a more or less successful export of European culture all over the world, judging from the growing number of independent states.

The characteristic values of the *culture of modernity* interact with diverse cultural legacies and with the ideological premises of the elites and the collective movements that guide the various experiences of modernization. This applies to the historical experience of Western democracies and even more to events in communist regimes and other non-European countries. I mention only some differences and provide a few examples.

The Soviet proletariat revolution appears to be a continuation and a completion of the French bourgeois revolution, making equality the fundamental value. Faith in scientific-technical progress is accepted even more ingenuously than in Western democracies (as the famous motto 'Communism equals Soviet Power plus the Electrification of the Country' shows). On the other hand, individual liberty is limited in all of its aspects, from freedom of choice in the market to protection of civil and political rights, and individualism is considered a negative value.

An analogous ambivalence, even though different by nature, occurs in Japanese modernization. Alongside the importation of Western science and technology and the acceptance of democratic representative institutions (imposed after its defeat in the Second World War), there was the capacity to convert traditional values, such as community spirit and deference to authority, into conditions that facilitated modernization. But that happened only after having begun a modernization process from above that sought to unite economic growth and social modernization with political authoritarianism and a nationalist-imperialist ideology.

Different perspectives on the contradictory character of modernization

Modernization (which we have outlined in its principal economic, social, political and cultural aspects) is a contradictory and problematic phenomenon. It involves radical processes of change, generally traumatic, that stir up contradictions, tensions and conflicts of unusual intensity. Thus, the Industrial Revolution implicates both the systematic exploitation of workers and the alienation of labor (Marx) as well as the subservience of nature to the imperatives of the self-regulating market and the 'satanic mills' that grind men into masses (Polanyi). The democratic political revolution must fight for a long time, not only against supporters of the traditional order but also against the degeneration of democracy into democratic despotism (de Tocqueville). The bureaucratic rationalization of large public and private organizations reduces spaces for individual autonomy and threatens the functioning of representative democracy (Weber).

The conceptualizations of the transition to European modernity formulated in the seminal works of social science decisively oppose each other in the priority accorded to this or that sphere in determining or conditioning the development of the others. They differ, in other words, by their choice of the 'engine of change'. While materialistic interpretations place social relations of production at the center of the analysis, idealistic interpretations assign priority instead to values and social norms. They both share, however, the fundamental perspective that it is evolutionary and dichotomous. They agree in the conception of modernity as progress and radical difference compared with the past, as epochal transformation and as the most evolved stage of man's course through history.

One can say that sociology was born and develops as a science of modernity, as an attempt at comprehending modern society, a society that has lost every external foundation (God, providence, nature) and that must interpret itself in a self-conscious effort, trying to understand the causes and the sense of becoming (evolutionary perspective) and the distinctive characteristics of modern society compared with traditional society (dichotomous perspective).

For the most notable exponents of the sociology of the 1800s – such as Saint-Simon, Comte and Spencer, who were influenced by biological theory – modern society constitutes the most complex phase of social evolution. The societies that best adapt to their environments grow and, as they increase in size, develop a division of labor, differentiating themselves functionally and diversifying themselves structurally, or rather dividing themselves into ever more interdependent parts that unfurl into ever more diversified roles.

If social evolution as part of the general evolution of living organisms explains the causes of modern society, the dichotomous or dual models explain its specific characteristics with regard to the pre-modern societies that historically preceded them. Maine contrasts the laws that regulate the rights and reciprocal duties deriving from *status* (or social positions that individuals possess beyond their will) against the laws that regulate relations deriving from *contract* (or the accord between individuals that freely contract reciprocal obligations). Durkheim contrasts the *mechanical solidarity* of pre-modern societies (in which the various social units are similar to one another and all are equally subordinate to the only superior unit: the individual is subject to the patriarchal family, the family to the clan, the clan to the tribe, etc.) against the *organic solidarity* of modern societies (manifested instead where a complex division of labor exists and social solidarity is built on difference not equality). Tönnies contrasts *Gemeinschaft* (a traditional community in which relations are characterized by intimacy, the communion of memories, languages and habits, the sharing of experiences) with *Gesellschaft* (a modern society and form of association in which, on the other hand, relations are sectorial, detached, tendentially competitive and often hostile, built on contract).

These diverse exponents of classic sociology agree that the formation of modern society is an unstoppable process, but they evaluate it in very different ways. Next to Maine's optimistic vision and to Durkheim's also optimistic but more problematic view, which interpret modernity as emancipating the individual from the bonds of tradition, lies the pessimistic vision of Tönnies for whom modernity instead represents a loss of the authentic values of community solidarity.

Even the two greatest theorists of modern capitalism, Marx and Weber, share the conception of modernity I have outlined, even if not integrally identifying themselves in that way. In fact Marx's theory, while viewing bourgeois society as built on the capitalist mode of production as radically different from the one that had preceded it and as the most evolved form of the historical process, does not share the gradual character of the evolutionary perspective, which does not distinguish between characteristics of biological evolution and those of social evolution (the latter actually proceeds through revolutions).

Weber, while contrasting modern *Gesellschaft* against traditional *Gemeinschaft*, already belongs to a historic era and a cultural climate in which the certainties about the 'magnificent and progressive fortunes' of humanity have been abandoned. Weber is not at all convinced of the inevitability of progress and is, on the contrary, very preoccupied with the fate of democracy and liberty in a society dominated by large public and private bureaucracies. The Weberian analysis of capitalism, on the one hand, constitutes one of the most organic expressions of the particular rationalist culture of modernity and, on the other, refers to interpretations that underline the intrinsically ambivalent and contradictory nature of the modern condition, such as those by Nietzsche and Simmel.

The most radical version of the critique of modern society is found in Nietzsche's idea that every form of totality disintegrates into a conglomerate of single disconnected components, in an incessant flux, an *eternal return*.

A most interesting sociological formulation is that of Simmel, for whom the experience of the present in modern society appears differentiated, discontinuous and fragmented (Frisby, 1986). Modern social organization is characterized by the centrality of the circulation of merchandise and individuals, exchange and consumption; by the parallel increase in social differentiation (as an effect of the functional specialization of social relations) and cultural homogenization (as an effect of the leveling action of money as universal equivalent of all values); and by the transformation of a culture of ideas into a culture of things and objects. This appears in an especially obvious way in two typical contexts of modernity – large metropolises and the mature monetary economy – in which man experiments in extreme form with the process by which the products of his own spirit become autonomous and reified.

Modernization as a tendentially global process with multiple outcomes

While the complex configuration of interdependent characteristics that I have schematically outlined connotes, above all, modernization as the first transition to modernity (European and Western), it can be retraced with significant variations in the experience of other 'late-comer' countries (at first, mostly European and then non-Western).

Different national situations do not show the same configurations, sequences or outcomes. In certain cases only a few of these characteristics are present, in other cases some aspects appear before others, in still others, all these characteristics co-exist but with different accentuations and intensities. Furthermore in different historical experiences there are 'functional equivalents' of some of the requisites considered essential. All these differences (as well as exciting conflicts of varied natures) set up diverse pathways to modernity that are traversed by different countries, and give rise to a set of multiple modernities, due to their differing genetic codes, the influences exercised by different configurations of international economic and political relations and by the timing and modality of impact with more developed countries.

The relevant variables to explain the problems of the modernization process of a given country are both endogenous such as, for example, class relations in modern society and the degree of centralization of power, as well as exogenous such as, for example, the nature of the international system (whether dominated by a great power like the Concert of Europe of the nineteenth century, bipolar in nature as in the decades after the Second World War, or multi-polar as it is now).

Given the interdependence of the world system, modernization first of all affects European and North American society and then gradually the rest of the world, transforming and modifying the local realities, amidst much resistance and acute conflicts.

As a result, one could articulate a second meaning of the modernization concept. This pertains to the combination of processes through which underdeveloped or developing societies, i.e. the various peripheries of the world, try to reduce or wipe out the gap that separates them from developed countries (the central areas of Europe, North America and Japan) in terms of economic growth, competitiveness in the global market and the social well-being of its people. At first glance and in certain aspects, this second modernization process seems to be similar to the first modernization of today's developed countries in that it presents features of Europeanization and Westernization. This helps to explain the widespread ambivalence of the political and intellectual elites of non-European countries towards a model of society and social development that is not autochthonous and that conflicts with deep traits of their culture and their indigenous social relations.

In reality, modernization in this second meaning does not consist of the mere diffusion of Western techniques, values, institutions and social relations, but also in the interaction between dissimilar social and cultural structures. A plurality of diverse routes and models of society and political systems are triggered by this complex interaction of external influences and internal dynamics, economic processes and social structures, political institutions and cultural attitudes, giving rise to multiple modernities. The process of modernization, by now consolidated in the countries that started first, extends itself on an ever more global scale, creating links and opportunities for the latecomers. But the idea of a homogeneous Western modernity spreading – for the most part imperfectly – to the rest of the world must be replaced by a more complex and messy picture of mixed and entangled modernities (Randeria, 1999). And there are not only multiple and partially alternative modernities at the level of the nation-state (Indian or Chinese modernity) or in terms of cultural tradition (Confucian or Islamic modernity), but also uneven outcomes within a society, for 'modernity as social experience varies in the understandings and practices of different groups of people' (Randeria, 2002).

The process of modernization, from its very beginning in Europe, has been characterized by a high degree of variability in institutional forms and conceptual constructions. It has provided reference points that have become globally relevant and that have served as structuring principles, constraints and opportunities for different societies on a world-wide scale. But, in different societies and within them, relevant processes of interaction and intermixture have taken place, giving rise to uneven outcomes and complex trajectories.

At the beginning of the twenty-first century, modernization does not mean a single process leading to a new unified civilization, but a variety of different experiences facing similar problems and a common global condition. In the controversy between, on the one hand, the supporters of the view that liberal democracy plus market economy represents the sole legitimate model of modern social organization and, on the other, the supporters of the view that no common elements can be identified in the process of modernization and that no global condition can be applied to individuals living in different cultural settings, I take an intermediate stand: a basic set of technological, economic, and political institutions, originating in Western Europe (which I have summarized earlier in this chapter) have become diffuse across the globe, and have made modern or modernizing societies more similar to each other. These processes of diffusion and adaptation, however, do not mean that well-entrenched cultural differences between societies are about to disappear. In their core identities, societies like China, India, Japan, Russia, Brazil remain characterized by the form they acquired during earlier periods of cultural crystallization, and pave the way for multiple modernities. But they all share a common global condition and strive to continuously reinterpret, transform and adapt their institutional structures and value systems in order to take account of the challenges posed by the common global condition. In this sense, as I will argue at length in the last chapter, modernization is a tendentially global process, which at the same time gives way to multiple modernities. 'The trends of globalization show nothing so clearly as the continual reinterpretation of the cultural program of modernity; the construction of multiple modernities; attempts by various groups and movements to re-appropriate and redefine the discourse of modernity in their own terms' (Wittrock, 2000: 24).

In the current scientific debate, the two meanings of the concept of modernization that we have illustrated appear to be inverted in historical sequence, in the sense that the 'theory of modernization' is applied first to the study of developing countries in the 1950s and 1960s of this century and is only resumed afterwards, mostly under the label of the transition to modernity, when analyzing the formation process of developed Western societies. This occurred, first of all, because the attention of researchers, mostly American social scientists, turned to non-European countries in the context of the ideological and political competition between the two super-powers. As I argued in the Introduction, with the US hegemony in the two decades after the Second World War, the economic, social and political development of 'Third World' countries was viewed from the perspective of progressive westernization (actually Americanization) that would in the end lead to a homogeneous system of modern industrial societies. Only afterwards were the critiques directed towards the theory of modernization which considered the experience of Western countries as a univocal pattern for modern society's formation process in underdeveloped countries (or, according to more or less euphemistic definitions, latecomers, or developing, or transitional countries), inducing them to re-examine and reinterpret the same development and modernization routes of Western countries. In this reappraisal, a variety of different approaches can be identified from the early contributions by Bendix and Barrington Moore to the more recent theorists of radical and reflexive modernity such as Giddens, Habermas, Touraine and Beck.

After having outlined in this first chapter the basic structural and cultural characteristics of the formation process of modern Western societies, our analysis will consequently be expanded. This will be based not on the historical sequence of development (first, Western countries and then the so-called Third World countries), but on a reconstruction of the theoretical debate: starting from the 'classic theory of modernization' elaborated in the years after the Second World War, the critiques directed to it will be discussed, which stimulated both new interpretations of developing countries as well as new analyses of the formation processes of Western societies and, finally, the complex relationship between globalization and modernity.

2

The Classic Theory of Modernization

Modernization of traditional Third World societies

Evolutionism and structural-functionalism

The classic theory of modernization (or the first wave of modernization theories) was developed in the United States in the post-war period to study problems of underdeveloped countries and propose strategies for economic growth and political stability. The theory was influenced by two fundamental historical processes: decolonization, and the confrontation between the two superpowers, the United States and the Soviet Union.

The end of the European colonial empires (the English, French, Dutch, Belgian, Spanish, Portuguese, and Italian) brought on the rise of dozens of new nation-states, some with ancient and consolidated cultures and with well-defined geographic frontiers, others with artificial unity and precarious borders. Considering only the countries that have more than 500,000 inhabitants in 1990, the number of independent states – 22 in 1800 and 56 in 1900 – rose from 76 in 1945 to 157 in 1994 (Jaggers and Gurr, 1996). According to other estimates (that do not impose a minimum limit on the population and that also include countries with limited autonomy such as French Polynesia, the Virgin Islands and Greenland), the number even rises to 189, according to the World Bank (1997) and to 191 by Freedom House estimates (1996). All these countries must face complex problems of economic growth, social transformation and political legitimization.

In the post-1945 period the United States and the Soviet Union both sought to draw within their spheres of influence the newly-independent states of Asia and Africa with economic aid, technical assistance and political propaganda. Even the United Nations and other international organizations launched aid programs for development and technological assistance.

Such an international context created a favorable terrain for studies and research on the requirements and models for development and for consultancy work on the policies of governments of emerging countries, so much so that there was a widespread conviction that the process of industrialization must be brought about by suitable public policies and commensurate international aid.

Economists were the first and the most active of the social scientists, but American sociologists and political scientists followed afterwards with the conviction that economic interpretations should be integrated with analysis of the cultural and institutional factors influencing the processes and outcomes of economic development policies. The sociological and political studies were generally located within the fundamental paradigms of evolutionism and structural-functionalism, clearly apparent from the very frequent use of concepts such as adaptation, stage of development, structural differentiation, integration, gradual and continual change, and so forth.

Evolutionism was very much embedded in the social science tradition, from the classic sociological formulations of Comte, Spencer and Durkheim to the anthropological ones of Morgan and Kroeber, and the concept of evolution was present, often implicitly, in most modernization studies. Prevailing, in fact, was the idea of a path to modernization that unfolds according to a predetermined sequence of stages, characterized by increasing complexity and adaptability to the external environment.

The structural-functionalism of Parsons, on the other hand, established in the 1950s and 1960s the dominant paradigm in sociology and extended its influence also into other social sciences, particularly in the systemic approach of political science and in psychological studies of the personality. Parsons took on the role of intermediary between classic sociological thought and contemporary theory of social systems, especially through his original and unilateral revisiting of the work of Weber, Marshall, Durkheim and Pareto in *The Structure of Social Action*, published in 1937. Concepts employed in many studies on modernization made reference to the theoretical Parsonian system, in particular to the analysis of social relations and cultural attitudes that characterize traditional societies and that hinder economic development.

Criteria for the analysis of modernization

The rather vast literature on modernization can be organized according to several fundamental criteria concerning:

1. the unit of analysis, which may relate to different levels of social reality (national, supranational, regional and local);
2. the fundamental characteristics of the types of societies that begin to modernize (in particular, the presence of structural and cultural preconditions and obstacles, constraints and opportunities, to the agency of individual and collective actors);
3. the factors, mechanisms and processes that explain the transformation from one type of social entity into another or the transition from one phase to another (which can be endogenous or exogenous; relating to different aspects of the social reality; adopting unicausal, multicausal or conditional models of explanation);
4. the form, sequence and direction that the process of change assumes (whether unidirectional or multidirectional, gradual and continuous or by breaks and sudden leaps, or marked in two or more phases and critical thresholds);
5. the intentional and foreseen or the unintentional and unforeseen character of the modernization process, and the quantity and characteristics of the various actors (with their objectives, resources, strategies, values);
6. the duration, consequences and outcomes of the process (whether open or closed, a radical morphogenetic transformation or a more or less modified reproduction of existing arrangements).

Unit of analysis

The nation-state is used as a unit of analysis in these studies. Not only political science studies (including those with a clear behaviorialist imprint, such as those of Apter (1965), little concerned with analyzing state organization), but also sociological studies analyzing transformations of social structure and socio-psychological ones that focus on the particular type of modern personality (Inkeles and Smith, 1974), choose nation-states (or more precisely the territories and populations within well-defined borders controlled by nation-states) as a fundamental point of reference. Even if the choice presents methodological difficulties in the cases in which the social cohesion of a nation does not coincide with a definite state entity (Tilly, 1975) – such as post-colonial countries that reflect artificial borders drawn by the colonial powers – it is a methodological choice justified by the centrality of the state in the modern social reality.

History shows, in fact, that the nation-state was both the cause and consequence of modernization. As I will discuss in the final chapter, even in the present day, when its power is threatened both from below (by the growing autonomy of sub-national levels of government and the strengthening of regional and local identities) as well as from above (by processes of economic, financial, social and cultural globalization), the nation-state remains a fundamental actor in economic, social and political relations. Globalization erodes nation-states' sovereignty, but not to the point of preventing governments from being proactive agents of development and modernization.

On the other hand, what can be criticized is the tendency of many modernization studies to think of nation-states as *natural* and *closed* systems and not, instead, as *artificial* and *open* systems that are historically mutable with potentially fragile geographic as well as cultural borders.

Traditional society and modern society as opposing models

The phenomenon of modernization is generally described and interpreted with reference to a list of interdependent analytical, cultural and structural features that characterize *traditional* societies and *modern* societies and that interpret the modernization process as the transition from the former type of society to the latter. As we will argue in Chapter 3, the traditional/modern dichotomy is an oversimplified and somehow misleading conceptualization; but given its pervasive influence in the classic theory of modernization we have structured to some extent the first chapter of this book in a similar way.

In some cases, these analytical characteristics are ordered according to their relevance as requirements or determinants of modernization, until a single factor as the principal independent variable, i.e. the engine of development, is selected. Thus, for instance, Levy (1966) identifies the key factor as the use of machines and inanimate sources of energy, Wellisz (Weiner, 1966) the opportunity for investment, Huntington (1968) the institutionalization of organizations and political procedures, Deutsch (1961) social mobilization, McClelland (1961) the achievement syndrome and so on.

In many studies, the identification of the fundamental analytical characteristics of modernization (more or less organized in order of explicative relevance) and the determination of their reciprocal relations lead to the construction of ideal types. These synthetic concepts – constructed by connecting several extracted essential elements and chosen from the multiplicity of empirical phenomena – essentially fall into two categories. The first category contains *ideal types of social systems* or *characteristic personalities*, which contrast the modern society or personality (generally defined on the basis of Western experiences) against the traditional society or personality (Hoselitz, Levy, Inkeles, Lerner). Or, in some other versions, they contrast industrial society against agrarian society, with the associated personality and culture types.

The second category contains *ideal types of processes* that identify, on the basis of concrete historical experiences, a determinate list of critical stages or phases of the process of modernization or political development and the institutional and cultural requisites that permit one phase to proceed to the next (Rostow, 1960; Black, 1966; Organski, 1965; Almond and Coleman, 1960; Pye, 1965; Rokkan, 1970).

Some writers, such as Lerner (1958), Deutsch (1961), Black (1966), Zapf and Flora (1973), Flora (1975) Krupp (1977) have ventured to empirically measure various societies along the traditional–modern continuum, or in one of the various phases of the process, through appropriate indicators. These indicators include economic growth (gross national product, per capita income, industrialization rate, investment rate, spending on science and technology); social change (demographic growth rate, literacy levels, percentage of population living in cities, degree of diffusion of mass media); and political development (electoral participation, bureaucracy size, number of members in associations and political parties). Comparative studies of this kind illustrate the course of these variables in the modernization process in selected countries and groups of countries in order to analyze the impact of their historical heritage and of their geopolitical position on the timing and sequence of the process.

Contrasting the two ideal types of society – traditional and modern – is not only an exercise in comparative description but is aimed at explaining which mechanisms can foster or hinder the process of change, or which can act as constraints or opportunities for action. The central issue, in other words, is the identification of ideological, institutional, organizational and motivational requirements for modernization (W.E. Moore, 1963).

The classic example of this method of investigation is that of Hoselitz (1960). He starts from the assumption that, unlike the Western experience in which sociocultural variables created the premises for development, the economic development of underdeveloped countries is hindered not only and not so much by lack of economic resources or unavailability of adequate technologies, but by social resistance and traditional cultural orientations that hamper the establishment of social relations and types of personalities that are supportive of development. He concentrates therefore on the cultural orientations that define role expectations in economic and social relations, using for this purpose the five dichotomous pattern variables that Parsons elaborated based on Shils' reconceptualization of the Weberian ideal types: Affectivity–Affective neutrality, Self-orientation-Collectivity-orientation, Universalism–Particularism, Ascription–Achievement, and Specificity–Diffuseness (Parsons and Shils, 1951: 77).

According to this model, modern societies are more likely to present situations in which interlocutors are evaluated not on the basis of natural features or hereditary characteristics beyond their control (such as gender, age, race, membership of an ethnic or religious group), but on the basis of acquired qualities, abilities and performance. In other words, they judge others not based on who they are, but what they do, their achievements, merit-based qualities (*Ascription–Achievement*).

In addition, the accentuated division of labor typical of modern societies implies that functionally specific relationships (such as those of buyer and seller in a market) in which only certain aspects of an individual's personality and behavior are involved, are more common than functionally diffuse relationships, in which the expected performance potentially involves the whole life of the person (*Specificity–Diffuseness*).

The culture of modernity is also revealed in the control of emotions and affectivity. This mainly concerns public life, where a higher degree of control over one's emotions, feelings and impulses is expected. The expression of affectivity tends to be confined to private life where more intimate and personal relationships unfold. The differentiation between the private and the public sphere and the associated degrees of control over emotions are instead absent or very less pronounced in traditional societies (*Affectivity–Affective neutrality*).

Also more prevalent in modern societies are contexts in which individuals are valued based on characteristics they share with others, as opposed to contexts in which they are valued as specific human beings. In modern bureaucracies, for example, officials must interact with the users of public services as equal holders of the rights of citizenship, and in modern commercial organizations vendors have to treat clients as interchangeable subjects, each endowed with the same rights of all consumers (*Universalism–Particularism*).

Finally, modern societies unlike traditional ones, clearly distinguish between contexts and relations in which individuals are expected to pursue their individual interests and those in which they perform a collective responsibility, as in the doctor–patient relationship (*Self-orientation–Collectivity-orientation*).

This combination of different attitudes contrasts the modern pattern with the traditional pattern. Some theorists have, in this regard, opportunely distinguished between *tradition* and *traditionalism*. Tradition refers to the beliefs and practices that are inherited from previous generations and that can be adopted and reinterpreted in the process of modernization. Traditionalism, on the other hand, is a cultural attitude that views tradition as essentially static and considers inherited beliefs and practices from the past to be immutable (Weiner, 1966).

Sociological studies on the transformation of social roles and the differentiation of structures have been integrated from socio-psychological studies on the *modal personality* of modernization. Theorists such as Lerner (1958), Bellah (1985), and Inkeles and Smith (1974) concentrate on personality types characteristic of the two societies, attempting to define real behavioral syndromes.

The most relevant study of this type on the social and cultural aspects of development was produced by the Harvard Project. In this comparative study of six developing countries (Argentina, Chile, India, Israel, Nigeria and Pakistan), Inkeles and his collaborators (Inkeles and Smith, 1974) outlined an analytical model of the modern personality, identifying the following most salient traits:

1. The availability of innovation and opportunities for change and new experiences, taking various potential forms: from the adoption of a new agricultural fertilizer or a new pharmaceutical product, to the utilization of a new mode of transport, to the approval of a new form of marriage ceremony or a new type of schooling.
2. Belief in one's own ability, alone or in collaboration with others, to control the threats of nature and the problems of society.
3. The emphasis placed on the present and the future rather than the past.
4. The ability to anticipate and organize future activities in order to realize public and private objectives.
5. Belief in the regularity and predictability of social life, laws and economic and market-based rules, permitting evaluation of the consequences of action.
6. A strong belief in the value of education.
7. Respect for the dignity of other human beings, including those in socially inferior positions.
8. A readiness to accept, and in fact to positively evaluate, differences in opinion, together with the capacity to form one's own judgements on many issues of public nature.
9. The conviction that the distribution of rewards should not be based on arbitrary criteria but on shared rules that consider ability and contributions made (distributive justice).

As we can see, these are values that echo the values of modern democracy (recognition of the dignity of all human beings, secular tolerance of differing opinions, distributive justice) and the values of modern capitalism (organizational rationality, faith in one's own abilities, openness to change, future orientation) in a strongly optimistic version. An ideal model, a must, for the modern personality is delineated and corresponds more to the desirable plan of modern society than to the contradictory nature of modern reality.

The mechanisms and processes of modernization

Closely connected with the identification of cultural orientations and role expectations typical of the traditional society and the modern personality is the analysis of the mechanisms of modernization, the processes through which a modern social structure, culture and personality are formed. This analysis may differ according to which type of variable is given priority (technological, economic, social, political or cultural).

The rich tradition of thought attributing a central role to technological innovations and transformations in productive processes (bringing together scholars of such diverse orientations as Marx, Schumpeter, Usher, Ogburn) has a strong presence in the theory of modernization of traditional societies. By way of an example, let us illustrate Levy's interpretation, one of the most exhaustive, as well as one of the most unjustly neglected.

According to Levy (1966), who originally applied the structural-functionalist paradigm, the 'universal solvent of modernization' is the use of machines and inanimate sources of energy whose productive superiority is clearly imposed on members of any traditional society that comes into contact with a modernized society, stimulating their interest in improving their own material conditions. Levy's argument is interesting because he recognizes (much more than most studies on modernization) the importance of interrelations between societies at different levels of development, as well as the intentionality of actors in latecomer societies in applying more advanced techniques and methods, endeavoring to control the consequences on social order and stability. In this way Levy implicitly recalls Ogburn's contribution, one of the most penetrating analyses of the effects of technological change, which we will examine later.

Economic interpretations, for the most part, place emphasis on the institutional context of incentives and opportunities for innovation and productive investment and the removal of associated obstacles (Leibenstein, 1957; Kindleberger, 1958; Agarwala and Singh, 1958; Higgins, 1959; Meier, 1970; Rosenstein et al., in Weiner, 1966). We will only touch on these lightly since they do not fall within the specific scope of this study.

The principal obstacles to eliminate are: forms of land ownership (such as large landed estates) that prevent farmers from taking advantage of increases in production; impediments to free circulation of factors of production between sectors, businesses and geographic areas; tariff and customs barriers that block the formation of a vast domestic market and slow down trade flows from one region of a country to another; bureaucratic fetters and constraints that slow investments; the absence or scarcity of public policies that favor investment; and low levels of education that do not permit the formation of a work force with specialized skills. For example, Wharton shows how many empirical studies prove that reduced risks and higher and more stable prices for agricultural products – by virtue of reforms in productive techniques and land ownership systems – are the most effective tools in modernizing agriculture, including the cultural attitudes of agricultural workers.

These interpretations are based on the assumption that every society contains a sufficient number of individuals who orient their behavior on principles of utilitarian rationality, and are therefore able to be mobilized for investment and economic growth by the appropriate incentives. In this framework, Hirschman (1965) maintains (in light of the theory of cognitive dissonance) that when there is a discrepancy between behaviors and values, it is often the latter that adapts to the former; or, in the presence of new behaviors stimulated by a proportionate opportunity structure, it is the traditional values that adapt to the new demands of action.

Social theorists such as Smelser (1968) and Eisenstadt (1966) draw on a classic strain of sociology, in particular, Durkheim's celebrated study of the division of labor. They interpret modernization by looking at complementary processes of structural differentiation and integration (and conflict which was also added afterwards). Structural differentiation (which can be defined as a process through which a role or social organization differentiates into two or more roles or organizations that are structurally and functionally distinct but that, taken together, are equivalent to the original unit) is the principal explicative variable of the transition from traditional society to modern society.

Smelser (1968) offers three typical examples of structural differentiation. In the transition process from household production to the factory, the division of labor increases and economic activity, which previously took place within the family circle, shifts towards corporations. When a system of formal education is established, the educational functions previously carried out by the family or the church are localized within a more specialized unit, the school. The modern political party has a more complex structure than that of tribal groups and tends to be less influenced by kinship ties or competition for religious leadership.

The ever more complex structural differentiation (or the division of labor), on the one hand, increases general productivity of the system and, on the other, sparks conflicts and creates complex problems of social integration. Continuing with the first example by Smelser, we can argue that the advent of the capitalist enterprise causes conflicts to emerge between capitalists and wageworkers and a series of institutions spring up (a system of legal regulations, a labor market, labor unions and entrepreneurial associations) that regulate their relations with different modalities and variable success.

Differentiation involves new activities, rewards, sanctions, role expectations that conflict with traditional modes of social agency and require new integration mechanisms. This process, as Eisenstadt (1961) points out, proceeds in an irregular fashion. For example, colonial powers often revolutionize economic and political relations and educational institutions, but at the same time encourage and impose the preservation of traditional family, religious and class relations. The fundamental problem of colonial societies begins with the unrealistic expectation that the indigenous population will perform new economic and administrative roles, while refusing the rewards and motivational bases inherent in these contexts.

The process of modernization is intrinsically discontinuous not only during but also after decolonization. It creates anxiety, hostility, and anomie because it generates a discordance between life experience and the normative context that regulates it. The more rapid the pace of change, the more serious the discontinuity and the greater are the possibilities for conflict and anomie, and much more complex, therefore, the quest for integration.

Parsons (1966, 1971), having provided many of the analytical tools to scholars of modernization, revised in a neoevolutionary viewpoint his analytic model of the four functional requirements of action systems (adaptation, goal attainment, integration, and pattern maintenance) that set up the four specialized subsystems that respond to such problems at the social system level (the economy, the polity, the societal community and the maintenance of institutionalized cultural patterns). In such a manner, he identifies the fundamental mechanisms that explain the evolution of society in four stages – primitive, late-primitive, intermediate and modern society.

Parsons explains evolution from the primitive stage to historically more complex stages in light of functional differentiation between the four types of structures: politico-military, economic, juridical and cultural (or rather based on four fundamental components: force, economy, law and culture). On this basis, he seeks to establish a typology of early political systems: patrimonial kingdoms, the first administrative and religious empires, confederations of city-states and the most important 'seed-bed' societies such as Israel and Greece.

Socio-cultural evolution, according to Parsons, proceeds like an organic evolution, by variation and differentiation, from simple forms to gradually more complex forms, the general ability to adapt to the environment increasing not in a unilinear way but through a large variety of forms and types in every evolutionary stage. The four fundamental mechanisms that, operating in conjunction, open the passage from primordial societies to more evolved ones are:

1. Structural differentiation, which we have previously defined.
2. Adaptive amelioration, i.e. the availability of the greatest number of resources to liberate social units from several previous constraints, as was the case with the productivity increase in modern industry.
3. Inclusion, or the integration of new elements (structures, roles, values, norms) in society, while preserving a harmonious functioning (as with certain migratory processes).
4. The generalization of values, i.e. the formulation of normative standards sufficiently universal to integrate and legitimize the new elements.

In compliance with such a scheme, modern society is defined by the following: (1) complete differentiation of the four subsystems of the social system (economic adaptation, political goal attainment, social integration, and cultural pattern maintenance); (2) the dominant role of the economy (or mass production, bureaucratic organization of businesses and the generalization of the market and currency); (3) the development of a legal system as principal mechanism of social coordination and control; and (4) an open social structure founded on the principle of achievement and indirectly influenced by the development of education; and by the extension of complex impersonal networks of social relations. Parsons's model, which as we will see, was criticized as ethnocentric, illustrates well the evolutionary and structural-functionalist assumptions of many sociological studies of the classic theory of modernization.

Attitudes in favor of entrepreneurship and geographic, social and psychic mobility

There is a second kind of mechanism which pertains – not to the formation of an economic and social structure and the introduction of technology supportive of modernization – but to the formation of the modal personality that seems most fit for the purpose. Among these, those believed to have particular importance are: (1) attitudes related to the propensity for entrepreneurship and the agencies of primary socialization (the family) and secondary socialization (schools, mass media) that can stimulate them (McClelland, 1961; Hagen, 1962); and (2) processes of geographic, social and psychic mobility (Lerner, 1958).

McClelland (1961) hypothesizes that economic development is aided by the presence of a personality characterized by a strong 'need for achievement'. Based on a comparative analysis of vast empirical material relating to 21 developed and undeveloped countries, McClelland correlates indicators of economic growth with indicators of the need for achievement (including stories and fables of popular literature, scholastic books for elementary schools, and imaginative works). He concludes that children from Western industrial societies interiorize symbols in the course of their childhood and adolescence that encourage such a need, much more than their peers do in underdeveloped countries. In the latter countries, there are fewer potential entrepreneurs also because among the young people more motivated towards achievement the tendency is to embark upon careers other than those having to do with entrepreneurial activity. McClelland's interpretation contains clear normative implications: governments interested in economic growth should eliminate traditional obstacles and stimulate entrepreneurial motivation.

Hagen (1962) presents a more refined version of the nexus between socialization and entrepreneurial personality, combining a psychoanalytic interpretation of the parent–child relationship with a sociological interpretation of group deviance. According to Hagen, entrepreneurs tend to come from social groups that uphold values unaccepted by or otherwise not adequately appreciated by other groups that they respect and from whom they would like to receive respect. This causes a loss of social status, which in turn causes a break in parental authority with considerable consequences for the formation of the child's personality. If favorable conditions exist (such as the presence of a protective mother) such a situation, instead of producing feelings of anxiety, anger and resignation, can stimulate the development of an autonomous personality, trusting in his or her own abilities.

The main weakness in McClelland's theory is the unsatisfying measurement of the need for achievement, while Hagen's theory can be criticized for the scarcity of historical cases examined. Nonetheless, the accent on the nexus between social marginality, entrepreneurship and modernization points out an important aspect of the phenomenon.

In another view, the idea of mobility as mechanism for modernization is argued by Lerner (1958). He distinguishes three types of mobility – geographic, social and psychic – between which a sequence of relations develops. The modernization process begins, according to Lerner, when people obtain the possibility of moving around geographically. The principal form of such mobility is urbanization (but we can add international migrations). This physical mobility is often the vehicle for and is accompanied by social mobility, involving changes in status (such as the transition from farmer to wageworker), stimulating literacy and creating a public for the diffusion of mass media.

As a result of physical and social mobility and the role of education and mass media, people also acquire psychic mobility, or the capacity to imagine themselves in situations, roles and places different than traditional ones, and to identify with others through an empathetic process. The propensity and the desire to participate in all sectors of societal life also follow, making up one of the main elements of contrast between traditional and modern society (Finkle and Gable, 1966).

Social mobilization and political participation

Lerner's contribution adds a third type of mechanism of modernization to the analysis, one that occupies a central position in political studies: social mobilization and political participation in new states. The concept of social mobilization is rooted in the first experience of a people's army in the French Revolution of 1793 and in the complete German mobilization in the First World War, whose social effects were theorized by writers like Jünger in the 1930 essay *Die totale Mobilmachung* in the volume *Krieg und Krieger*.

Mannheim gave it an articulate interpretation with the concept of 'fundamental democratization', which describes the uprooting of a large number of people from their old environments, breaking with their old habits and old ties and their insertion into new forms of commitment, of association and of organization; or, in rather different terms, the distancing from a life in which isolation, traditionalism and political apathy prevail in order to move towards the complexity of modern life and mass politics.

Deutsch (1961) developed the concept of social mobilization as a basic change from old to new ways of life and the process through which relevant clusters of old social, economic and psychological ties are eroded or broken up and people become open to new patterns of behavior and socialization. This new kind of social commitment assumes different forms that tend to be connected to each other through reciprocally reinforcing effects. Deutsch seeks to quantify this ensemble of interconnected processes through several statistical indicators that measure typical processes of modernization, such as the general process of change. Such indicators deal with per capita income, the transition from agriculture to industry and the service sector, urbanization, demographic change (population growth and variations in consistency of different age groups), literacy, exposure to mass media, the transition from traditional and localist culture to modern and cosmopolitan culture, and increases in political participation.

For each one of these dimensions, Deutsch tries to identify *critical thresholds*. The crossing of these thresholds (whether singly or several combined) produces substantial changes both in social needs and behaviors and in political demands and participation in politics. Thus, for example, a notable increase in the literacy rate in the population of people above 15 years of age – let us say from 10 to 60 percent – does not seem significantly correlated to the birth rate. Whereas when the threshold reaches 80 percent, in fact important changes take place. None of the countries studied with a literacy rate above 80 percent have a birth rate higher than 3 percent. Another, more recent example made by Huntington (1997) deals with several Islamic countries such as contemporary Algeria. Huntington points out that when the percentage of young people between the ages of 15 and 24 passes the critical threshold of 20 percent of the population, radical political movements, serious social conflicts and political instability develop.

The implications of increased social participation for political development is shown also in the conflict that opposes the old elites against the new elites who demand better bureaucratic efficiency and governmental and institutional effectiveness.

As we have previously seen, individuals – uprooted from their traditional work environments and residences and removed from their physical and intellectual isolation – sense drastic changes in their needs in their new urban industrial context. They need government services for work (against risks of cyclical or seasonal unemployment), for housing (against high rental costs and interest on loans), for transportation, for medical assistance, for social security against sickness and old age, for their children's and their own education, for anti-inflation precautions and measures for boosting employment. It is a matter of partly completely new needs and partly traditional needs that take on new and often dramatic connotations due to the transition under way.

It is unlikely that these needs can be satisfied by traditional leaders (maharajas, sheiks or chieftains) or the governmental institutions inherited from a pre-industrial and pre-modern era. They require, actually, an increase in the capacity of government, in particular in economic and social policies, a quantitative and qualitative growth in public administration, a change in the political elite, in its methods of recruitment, its functions and its language.

In contemporary developing countries it is unlikely that the ineffective traditional authority will be replaced by liberal democratic institutions, as occurred with the first modernization in many Western countries in the nineteenth century. Among the uprooted and disoriented masses (created by modernization processes) the idea is not very widespread that the best government is a government of rules, procedures and guarantees of rights and individual initiatives. An attempt to move directly from traditional government to some kind of authoritarian political system (with a single party system, limited pluralism and state control) is much more likely, with the risks of reproducing the inefficiencies of the military bureaucratic regimes or the communist regimes and of raising contradictions in their relations with the world market, which only grow as the globalization process intensifies.

The form of modernization: phases and critical thresholds

The form of modernization illustrates the number and sequence of the phases, the likely directionality of the process, and its character (whether gradual and continuous or characterized by breaks and erratic leaps). A large part of the literature on the subject tends to attribute a directional character to modernization, a cumulative sequence made up of phases or stages, every stage incorporating elements of the previous stage that, in turn, become prerequisites for passing to the next stage. Complementary to and partially contrasted with this prevalent orientation is the concept of critical thresholds, which problematize the analysis, identifying specific problems that must be overcome in order for the process to continue and also implying therefore the possibility of a stasis or an inversion of the trend.

The study of fundamental phases in the course of modernization – the problems and critical thresholds that must be surpassed in order to proceed to the successive phase – is also a part of the evolutionary perspective. Indeed, the dichotomous model translates smoothly into a sequence of stages (traditional, transitional, modern). The study of phases or critical thresholds of modernization (which is commonly of interest to economic historians and scholars of political development) is, therefore, a complementary strategy to that of sociologists who outline contrasting models of traditional and modern societies and analyze the factors and mechanisms that determine the transition from one model to another (transformation processes of roles and social structures, cultural orientations, types of characteristic personalities).

One contribution on the border between the two research strategies we have illustrated is that of Apter (1965), one of the most committed scholars in the study of modernization. He depicts a three-stage succession: (1) the decline of traditionalism; (2) the passage to industrialization; and (3) the advent of modernization, which he analyzes as a succession of phases along the traditional–modern continuum. There are three basic dimensions of the analysis: (1) the normative dimension that defines the values that orient action; (2) the structural dimension that establishes limits within which actors must make their choices; and (3) the behavioral dimension that reviews the choices made and the underlying motivations. Apter proposes a typology of four political systems (mobilization systems, reconciliation systems, bureaucratic systems and theocratic systems) which are situated inside the traditional–modern continuum. At the extremes of the continuum are two models of society traceable in the course of history: the sacred collectivity model based on his conception that society has to be changed and that the good of society is different and superior than the good of single individuals; and the secular libertarian model that accepts society as it is and is oriented towards gradual changes through processes of spontaneous adaptation. The four different types of political systems also appear to be, according to Apter, more or less functional with respect to the demands of the various stages of the modernization process.

The interpretations of Rostow, Black and Organski (which we will look at now) and those of Almond, Pye and Rokkan (which we will illustrate in the following section) offer a more precise formulation of the phases of the process and the configuration of political development as a series of critical thresholds, in which the passage to the next phase implies having successfully overcome the problems of the previous critical threshold (analogous to Piaget's and Erikson's theories of child personality development).

The best-known theory of the classic period of the theory of modernization is that of Rostow, author of the very popular book *The Stages of Economic Growth* (1960). He identifies five stages: (1) the traditional society; (2) the preconditions for take-off; (3) the take-off; (4) the drive to maturity; and (5) the age of high mass-consumption. The *traditional society* is founded on a pre-Newtonian technology and on a non-scientific attitude with regard to nature. As a result, productivity is not able to increase beyond a certain limit. A large amount of resources are dedicated to agricultural production. Political power is decentralized. Culture is dominated by fatalism. In the *preconditions for take-off* stage, a society begins to utilize products of modern science, whether they emerge from autonomous innovations or, more often, by introduction from the outside. This introduction generally occurs with an impact and a traumatic intrusion of exogenous influences, through a military invasion or economic and cultural contacts, which produces shock and defensive reactions in the traditional society. Nevertheless, the idea of economic progress as a desirable goal takes root in this phase. Institutions for the mobilization of capital such as banks spring up and investment grows, especially in transportation, communications and the extraction of raw materials. And the process of building a nation-state expands through the unification of manifold local units under one government. *The take-off* takes place when the acceleration of techno-logical innovation is joined by the assertion of new economic and political elites, advocates of economic progress and reactive nationalism, capable of accomplish-ing effective public policies for the transformation of agriculture, the mining of raw materials, and the creation of infrastructures. The rate of saving and invest-ment rises to 10 percent or more of the national income and industrial expansion creates higher profits that are mostly reinvested in production. In the next stage – *the drive to maturity* – modern technological sectors spread throughout the entire economy. As much as 20 percent of the national income is invested and the growth in production surpasses the increase in population. The country finds its position within the international economy. Real maturity, which is reached, according to Rostow, about 60 years after take-off, is defined by a country's technological and entrepreneurial capacity to produce everything that it chooses to produce. Finally, when the growth of disposable income creates mass demand for goods other than the essentials that were previously considered luxury items but have by now become normal expenditures (such as automobiles, televisions and suburban homes), the country reaches the *age of high mass-consumption.*

Rostow is aware of the differences between the original European experiences and those of Third World countries. The delay of the latter presents both advan-tages and disadvantages. Among the advantages are the availability of new, already-tested technologies and international loans at subsidized rates for investment. Among the disadvantages are several imbalances between demographic growth (particularly high by virtue of progresses in modern medicine) and employment opportunities, and between the consumerist aspirations of the urbanized masses and the increase in production and disposable income. These imbalances fuel frus-tration and political strife in the population. This situation places leaders of emerg-ing countries, at the threshold of economic take-off, in front of a choice between democratic nationalism and communist nationalism. The communist solution is considered, however, a 'disease of the transition' by Rostow, destined to be aban-doned when the path to maturity brings demands for prosperity and freedom, which are not compatible with the institutions of communist power.

The sequence proposed by Black (1966) is similar to that of Rostow. The four critical issues that characterize the four modernization phases and that every country must face, although with different modalities, are: (1) the *challenge of modernity* phase, in which a society, given its cognitive resources and traditional institutions, must confront modern ideas and institutions and indigenous support-ers of modernity; (2) the *consolidation of modernizing leadership* phase, in which, through a revolutionary struggle that can often go on for generations, power passes from traditional leaders to innovative leaders; (3) the *economic and social transformation* phase which shifts a predominantly agrarian and rural society into a predominantly industrial and urban one; and (4) the *integration of society* phase, in which the previous transformation produces a fundamental reorganiza-tion of the entire society's structure. Even though his typology is not very origi-nal, Black stands out from constructors of uniform models like Rostow in his attention to the diverse routes developing countries may adopt. The adoption of one of the seven identified courses depends on the way in which the specific critical problems of the four phases are faced, which is in turn influenced by a crucial variable: the *geo-political position* of the territory in question. By virtue of this heightened sensitivity to the non-univocity of modernization paths and the relevance of exogenous variables, Black proves to be much less vulnerable to the main criticisms directed at the classic theory of modernization.

In an analogous effort, Organski (1965) concentrates on the *role of the state*. In particular, he focuses on the fundamental function it must perform in the passage from one stage of political development to the next as well as on the various models of government that have historically faced the challenges of economic modernization. In the first phase – *primitive unification* – the basic function of government is to take actual political and administrative control over the population, laying down the foundations for a domestic market. In the second phase – *industrialization* – the state and the new social class in power must support the accumulation of capital, even if it entails high social costs connected with the migration from country to city, in addition to limiting wages and consumption. In the third stage – *welfare state policy* – the main task of the government is to alleviate the social costs of industrialization imposed on the masses by implementing welfare policies aimed at guaranteeing economic prosperity, spreading a higher standard of living and helping the poor. The change in government strategy comes about to respond to the collective action of mass political movements (parties and unions), whose growth is aided by the success of the industrialization process and often involves, in democratic regimes, the establishment of a different electoral coalition. The final stage – *abundance policy* – is the most indefinite in Organski's scheme, also because it deals with trends happening at the time the book was written (the 1960s). It presents analogies with Rostow's maturity stage but with a more problematical and less optimistic tone. The central point, which is not unprophetic, is that the most important function of the state, guided by a narrow circle of elite planners, is to manage contradictions such as mass unemployment and the concentration of economic and political power.

Of all the phases in his analysis, Organski dedicates the most attention to the start of industrialization and states' problems with reference to the three historically realized models of government: (1) bourgeois (in Western democracies); (2) Stalinist (in the USSR); and (3) fascist (in Italy, Spain, Argentina). Faced with the common problem of stimulating the accumulation of capital, each political strategy was quite different. Bourgeois democracies gave free rein to private initiative and employed the state apparatus to suppress union demands and keep salaries low. The Stalinist regime was characterized by its use of coercion in recruiting the industrial workforce through compulsory transfers of farmers to factories and by its extremely rapid pace of accumulation. Whereas, in the fascist regime (defined also as synchronic) a coalition took place between the two dominant elites (agrarian and industrial), each guaranteed complete freedom in their own economic and social field.

According to Organski, the situation of emerging countries, eager to industrialize, seems more in favor of the 'Stalinist short-cut' or the fascist 'synchronic compromise' than the mass bourgeois democracy. However, especially in the case of fascism, the social and political transformations of industrialization make way for political changes in the democratic sense through the growth of the collective action of mass political movements.

The crises of political development

The idea of a limited number of crises, challenges and problems that modernizing countries must face is even more explicit in the strain of political science's studies on *political development* (especially Almond and Pye and collaborators and Rokkan's review). Whereas Rostow's sequence of stages concerns economic growth first of all, Black and Organski's periodizations place both industrialization and political leadership and the role of the state at the center of attention (along with challenges and inherent contradictions), recording a variety of possible routes (even if only generally dealing with the historical experiences of already-industrialized countries). In Almond and Pye's work, however, the analysis of political development becomes the dominant theme. Studies of political development are complementary and often not easily distinguishable from sociological studies of modernization. The relationship between modernization and political development is not, in fact, completely clear because different writers use both terms with sometimes dissimilar and sometimes analogous meanings. In Pye's clarifing effort (1966), for example, the concept of political development presents a whole range of different meanings. It can be synonymous with political modernization, it can coincide with *tout court* modernization in that it is a multidimensional process of change throughout an entire society, it can connote mass mobilization and participation (which, however, as we have seen before, involves in turn a series of connected modernization processes), or it might have to do with intrinsically more political problems such as the struggle for power, the construction of democracy, administrative and juridical development. For Apter (1968), instead, modernization concerns the diffusion and use of industrial-type roles in non-industrial environments, which require an exceptionally well-organized political system capable of maintaining control over the transition process.

The most satisfying definitions are those concerning the specific political dimension inside a more general process of modernization. A formulation of this type was made by the Committee on Comparative Politics of the American Social Science Research Council (founded in 1953 and directed first by Almond and then, in 1965, by Pye). Here political development is defined in relation to: (1) the diffusion of attitudes supportive of equality (demand for citizenship rights, growth of mass participation); (2) the capacity of the political system to govern the commonwealth, respond to demands of the people, control conflicts; and (3) differentiation, specialization and integration of roles and political organizations (Pye and Verba, 1965).

Similar, but different in that it pertains to relations between political growth and modernization, is Huntington's definition (1965) which views political development as a growing institutionalization of political organizations and procedures, a process that in turn involves the four dimensions of adaptability, complexity, autonomy and coherence. As one can see, it is an approach that utilizes categories of the evolutionary perspective (adaptation, complexity) very similar to sociological contributions to the differentiation–integration scheme.

The most systematic formulation of the crises and challenges of political development came from the research and seminars of the Committee on Comparative Politics and Rokkan's formulation. The Committee developed a paradigm of six 'crises of development' (Binder et al., 1971): identity, legitimation, penetration, participation, integration and distribution. The two crises of penetration and integration are, in a previous version (Almond and Powell, 1966), summed up in the problem of state construction, while the other two crises of identity and legitimation are summed up in the problem of nation construction.

On the other hand, of the six crises Rokkan borrowed only those four that are associated in the paradigm with more concrete 'institutional solutions' (Rokkan et al., 1971; Rokkan, 1975): (1) initial state building, when political, economic, and cultural unification at the elite level takes place and institutions are developed for the extraction of resources for common defense, for the maintenance of internal order, and the adjudication of disputes; (2) building a national identity, through the creation of conscript armies, compulsory schools, mass media, and channels for direct contact between the central elite and parochial populations of the peripheries; (3) equalization of rights of participation, or the establishment of political citizenship, through the establishment of privileges of opposition, extension of the electorate, formation of organized parties, bringing subject masses into active participation; and (4) redistribution of resources/benefits, or the establishment of social citizenship, through the growth of public welfare services, development of nation-wide policies for the equalization of economic conditions through transfers and progressive taxation.

The sequence of these crises, challenges, or critical thresholds varies profoundly from one historical case to another. The closer they appear, the higher the tension and the more intense the conflict. In the new state formations that emerge from colonial dependence these crises tend to build up, or even overlap each other, rendering these societies more fragile, conflictual and vulnerable to failure of the whole process.

The sequence which seems more suitable in analyzing the difficult path of developing countries seems the following: the most important and first crisis (logically although not necessarily chronologically) is the *crisis of identity*. Citizens of a new state need to recognize the national territory as their own country and the other members of society as their compatriots; they must feel that their personal identity is in some way defined by the collective belonging to their country. In most new states, the growth of a sense of national identity is contrasted with traditional sources of identity – tribes, castes, ethnic, religious and linguistic groups. The institutions especially engaged in promoting national identity are schools and mass media, which perform a socialization function. Also playing an important role are rites and collective myths, symbols such as flags and anthems, certain types of expressive leadership, the spread of literary works that celebrate national heritage and struggles for independence. Like revolutionary processes in general, these struggles in particular are manifested in collective states of euphoria and enthusiasm in which, as Durkheim pointed out, the leading principles take on a sacred meaning and become objects of a sort of revolutionary cult, and the individual tends to lose his or her own personal identity in acquiring a collective and more broad identity that transcends the former (Martinelli et al., 1989).

Closely tied to the identity crisis is the *crisis of legitimation*. It is a matter of reaching an accord on the source of legitimation of authority and on the responsibilities of government, expressed in a constitutional pact. The problem can be seen in a series of issues – from the relationship between politics and religion (as in, for example, Islamic countries) and between politics and ideology (as in, for example, communist countries), to relations between central and local authorities, to the role of the army and the bureaucracy in the life of the nation, to the degree of break/continuity with the colonial past. In many new states a series of difficulties exists in instilling loyalty and trust in the political institutions of the nation and ensuring respect for the laws. This not only applies to new states, as Banfield's well-known study (1958) on a southern community in Italy in the 1950s shows, for example, where inhabitants operate in a situation of *amoral familism* in which family interests and values are not only considered to be of utmost importance but also more wide-ranging compared with those of society. In this situation, family obligations (according to the famous Italian expression *'tengo famiglia'* 'I have a family') justify any kind of behavior, even illegal, and are accompanied by the rejection of civil duties and distrust of the state.

Problems of public administration are at the root of the third crisis, which is defined as the *crisis of penetration* to illustrate the efforts of government to operate deep in the social fabric by making its policies effective. The government of a society in transition to modernity is much more demanding than that of a traditional society. To attain its objectives of accelerated economic growth, the development of an infrastructure, civil order, territorial defense, it has to create an administration capable of mobilizing the necessary human and financial resources. This problem is connected to the previous in the sense that, in order to achieve effectiveness in its policies, the government must strengthen national identity and establish a relationship of trust with its people – all the people (including the inhabitants of the most remote villages) – and must provide motivations and justifications to citizens in order to assure that they are committed to the ongoing changes.

On the other hand, if the action of the governors is particularly effective in exciting expectations of change among the governed, these expectations can translate into demands for greater control and participation, triggering the fourth crisis, the *crisis of participation*. This appears when the emergence of new needs and the gathering of new interests create pressure for the entry of new participants in the political process; that is, when the volume and intensity of requests to take part in the decision-making process grow at a rapid pace. The crisis can have diverse outcomes. It could evolve towards democratization through the extension of suffrage, recognition of the rights of the opposition and the formation of a system of parties and representative special-interest organizations. Or it could be manipulated and even stimulated by a totalitarian regime that wants to supply itself with mass support. Or it could also give rise to feelings of anomie when widespread demands for participation are not satisfied by an authoritarian regime.

The fifth crisis, the crisis *of integration*, has to do with the problem of organizing the entire political system as a system of relationships between government, bureaucrats, interest groups and citizens, and defining rules for a just distribution of administrative tasks, benefits and resources among all the culturally – and politically – identifiable sectors of the national community. It can be said that this crisis is overcome when the performance of the political system (measured by the capacity to implement effective policies and the efficiency of the public administration) reaches satisfactory levels. In many traditional and transitional societies such performance is, instead, rather low due to inadequate processing of interest group demands and the tendency of government to try to respond to all simultaneously.

Finally, the *crisis of distribution* concerns a transfer of resources (which we could define as solidarity) from the richest areas and groups to poorer ones through progressive taxation, redistribution of income, creation of social services and a system of social security. This usually arises from a rapid increase in the intensity and volume of social demands for well-being.

It is worth pointing out how the distribution crisis concerns, on the one hand, the competition between different ideological models of helping underprivileged groups (direct state intervention, creation of business opportunities through market liberalization, growth of voluntary associations, development of the service sector); and, on the other, the conflict between the need for economic accumulation and the need for political consensus. Such conflict was manifested with different intensities in Western democracies in the 1970s and it was interpreted variously – as a fiscal crisis of the state (O'Connor, 1973), a crisis of state legitimation (Habermas, 1973; Offe, 1984), or as a crisis of overloaded government (Crozier et al., 1975).

The implicit assumption (which becomes at times an explicit theory) of political development as a sequence of crises and challenges is that, when rates and sequences of modernization do not proceed gradually, they prejudice the chances of success of the entire process. We prefer to make this interpretation explicit through the notion of critical thresholds.

The contradictions between the various aspects of modernization, or the critical thresholds of social development

The analysis of critical thresholds of political development we have illustrated is closely connected to the analysis of inconsistencies and contradictions among various aspects of modernization; a problem that was examined in general by comparing the experiences of post-colonial countries with those of Western countries.

In many cases it turned out that an extremely rapid change of pace impeded the formation of a modern and legitimate political system, a strong and centralized state before industrialization, and the associated social phenomena (urbanization, demographic growth, schooling, revolution of expectations of wide-ranging social groups). In cases of anti-colonial struggles for independence, in fact, intense political and social mass mobilizations occurred. After independence, they voiced growing demands to the political power-holders, who were, however, incapable of satisfying them due either to the weakness of the economic structure or to the cultural deficiencies or the absence of institutional mechanisms for governing political demand.

The situation is rendered more serious by large increases in population, especially among young people who cannot find employment and are politically restless. The imbalance between population growth and resources impedes the formation of levels of saving and investment necessary for sustained economic growth and for mechanisms of self-sustainable growth; and it accentuates the frustration of the masses who perceive a serious discrepancy between what they want and what they can obtain (Desai, 1966).

As Lerner (1968) observes, the *revolution of expectations* proceeds more quickly than economic growth and political development. The needs of the mass rapidly transform into the demands of the masses. They are needs that have been largely unsatisfied for centuries, since for hundreds of years these populations have known poverty, famines and inadequate resources. But with the process of modernization a change of mentality takes place. What was fatalistically accepted in the past is no longer accepted. In fact, economic growth – even when it is insufficient to trigger a process of sustainable growth – shows people that it is possible to improve their standard of living and that resources do exist for satisfying needs. In addition, those cases where independence was obtained by a fight for freedom demonstrate that it is possible to act collectively to modify an unpleasant situation. Finally, at work are both the *multiplier* mechanism of mass media, which amplifies needs, as well as the *demonstration effect* of developed societies' lifestyles and patterns of consumption which, at first imitated by the elites, tend to spread into ever more broad levels of the population.

Phenomena of demographic growth, growing expectations and mass mobilization inconsistent with economic growth processes and socio-political development, occur, in fact, even in Western countries' experiences of modernization. Even with a better-organized political system and institutions better equipped to manage the tensions of industrialization and social mobilization (Deutsch, 1961), such inconsistencies create deep contradictions and bitter social conflicts for a long time. But the more rapid rates of change and the compression of time and space in the current global economy render such contradictions even more dramatic and palpable than in the past.

Whether referring to the experience of Western countries or to that of Third World countries, we can therefore identify contradictions and levels of incoherence between the different dimensions of the modernization process that create social imbalances of varied nature. By analogy to the theory of crises of political development, I have drafted a theory of the critical thresholds of social development and the main public policies aimed at coping with them (Martinelli, 1987). More than in the case of political development, social crises often overlap one another without a rigid temporal sequence; but in general the inability to completely or partially resolve one of the crises compromises the possibility of overcoming contiguous ones.

The first critical threshold is the crisis of *demographic control*, or the relationship between demographic growth and the increase in resources produced. The population rises, especially among young people, by virtue of the drastic reduction in infant mortality due to the application of modern medicine and the propensity of farming families to continue to produce a numerous offspring, a typical example of the persistence of traditional cultural attitudes during modernization processes. Even when the transformed medical health conditions, the transformed demands of work in the countryside and the introduction of pension plans would allow a change in mentality, farming families continue to have high fertility rates, convinced of the need to bring many children into the world in order to guarantee the survival of a sufficient number to provide an adjuvant workforce for machine-less agricultural activity, and to provide a sort of insurance for old age. Such a crisis can be considered overcome when the demographic tree loses the typical pyramid formation, due to a drastic reduction in fertility rates and the number of children per couple (which generally occurs due to processes of agricultural transformation and literacy, industrialization and urbanization) and the connected transformation of the position of women in family and society. Along with the lengthening of average life span, the decline in fertility produces a progressive reduction in the youth population and a corresponding increase in the adult and elderly age brackets.

In defining the modalities and rates of crossing this critical threshold (as with the subsequent ones), an important role is played by the governance of the processes, or the combination of adopted public policies – in this case especially those regarding health, mass education, and agrarian reform, and related changes in social practices and cultural attitudes of the people.

The second critical threshold is the crisis of *urbanization*, i.e. the relationship between urban growth and occupational opportunities in large metropolitan areas (and today, in particular, the megalopolises of the Third World). Again, it is a matter of shifts in population, but this time it has to do with migratory movements, not natural ones. It could be considered a threshold following that of the imbalance between demographic increase and economic growth because it originates in part from the phenomena of overpopulation of the countryside characteristic of the first threshold. The percentage of urban population grew greatly in every region of the world and has risen to over 50 percent not only in developed countries but also in modernizing countries such as Brazil, China and Turkey, and it is over 50 percent for the whole world at the down of the third millenium, while residents in cities of more than 100,000 inhabitants have come to be over 37 percent in countries such as Mexico and Columbia, over 27 percent in Egypt and over 20 percent in countries such as Nigeria and Senegal.

For at least some of these countries, one could speak about *overurbanization* being dysfunctional to development, seeking to determine the critical threshold beyond which a process becomes dysfunctional, or creating more problems that it helps to resolve. This critical threshold is crossed whenever a migratory movement, driven by the perception of an intolerable discrepancy between departing conditions in the country and arriving conditions in the urban reality, assumes unmanageable proportions and rates. Objective conditions of misery *push* migration, acting together with the enticements that *pull* towards real or presumed better living conditions. The problem is that work opportunities in the arrival realities are often insufficient to integrate a surplus workforce lacking in necessary skills. An underclass is thus created, made up of diverse marginal groups that survive with very precarious jobs, forms of semi-begging and illicit activities of petty crime (when they do not become members of organized crime). Dysfunctional over-urbanization is not inevitable and can be controlled. Governments seek to deal with this problem by adopting public policies directed at modernizing agriculture and, more in general, stimulating economic growth through appropriate fiscal and infrastructural incentives. The most effective measures for overcoming this critical threshold, which, however, meet opposition from established interests, are effective *agrarian reform* that eliminates large landed estates and absentee ownership and *urbanization of the countryside*, or the extension to the rural areas of transportation, social services, consumer opportunities and the 'commodity' of modern city life. If such measures are not taken, social problems and migration abroad escalate, which for many is the only possible individual strategy for changing things, at the risk of robbing the nation of many of its most enterprising citizens.

The third critical crisis (or in other words, a third problem of consistency among the various dimensions of modernization that tend to proceed at different rates) is the threshold of *class conflict*. It can assume different forms and intensities but tends to manifest with the greatest intensity at the industrial take-off. At this point, the contractual power of workers in the labor market and the importance of their wages increases with the amplification of domestic demand, and the gap worsens between expectations and actual conditions for many members of the lower classes. The crisis can be said to be overcome when social integration of the working class (and the subordinate classes in general) is achieved through generalized lifestyles and consumption patterns, which symbolize a citizenship status, and the generalization of common values and norms of interclass nature. According to a well-known trend in sociological thought that runs from Weber to T.H. Marshall, in Western societies a sort of *social pact* or class compromise between the working class and the bourgeois state takes place: working-class loyalty towards institutions of liberal democracy and refusal of violence as tool of political struggle in exchange for progressive extension of citizenship rights (first legal rights, then enlargement of suffrage and union rights, and finally social rights to welfare, health and education). The public policies involved in class compromise are labor policies and social policies, in addition to interventions aimed at peaceful regulation of labor conflicts and distributive controversies.

Among social policies, the development of education occupies a particular place of importance. The fourth critical crisis of social development is the threshold of *mass education*, which consists of very rapid growth in school-attendance rates, more rapid than the increase in demand for specialized skills in the job market. The thrust to expand education comes both from families who see education as a vehicle for social mobility, as well as from governments that count on literacy to strengthen national identity and the development of human capital to increase productivity and economic competitiveness. However, such educational development can prove to be imbalanced with respect to the requirements of the productive system, giving rise to unsatisfied expectations and widespread frustrations among educated young people who are either unemployed or underemployed and who often become especially inclined to mass protest and political radicalism. This critical threshold, which often overlaps with the previous one, can be dealt with both by interventions aimed at making the labor market more flexible, as well as by professional training and labor policies that fall within the general policies of the *welfare state*.

The fifth critical threshold after the establishment of a welfare state (which in turn is a tool for integrating the working class and, therefore, surpassing the previous threshold) is the *state fiscal crisis*. This substantially coincides with the distribution crisis we illustrated in the theory of crises of political development. It is triggered by the conflict between the demands of economic accumulation and the demands of political consensus; a conflict that was widely manifested with varying intensity in Western democracies of the 1970s. In representative democracies, founded on competition for consensus among parties, the state must, on the one hand, appear as a neutral force with respect to the principal class interests if it wants to obtain a mass consensus and, on the other, it must make decisions that are compatible with the needs of the capitalist economy and consistent with entrepreneurial interests. To assure conditions of accumulation as well as political order, the state must assume ever more broad responsibility, from necessary infrastructure to entrepreneurial activity and from investment incentives to welfare policies, expanding bureaucratic complexity and public spending. Therefore, what takes places is what Habermas (1973) and Offe (1984) define as the *crisis of legitimation and administrative rationality of the state* and O'Connor (1973) and the group behind the review *Kapitalistate* the *fiscal crisis of the state*. Resolution to this crisis is sought through a model of economic growth that is the product of the interaction between private initiative and public regulation, according to which *welfare* is the result of an institutional mix, varying from one country to the next, of four institutions: (1) markets that produce goods and private services; (2) bureaucracies that produce public services; (3) associations that produce collective goods; and (4) families who produce personal services (Chiesi and Martinelli, 1989).

The sixth critical threshold, that overlaps in part with the preceding ones, has to do with the transformation of the *role* and *position of women*. The decline in fertility, the crisis of the family model centered on patriarchal authority, the growing participation of women in formal education and the labor market – all contribute to a gradual recognition of the civil and political rights of women and a profound transformation of cultural attitudes and social relations, which are expressed in the extension of suffrage and in changing family rights and norms of parity between the genders, as well as in family and labor laws. The role of women in modernization processes, whether as individual subjects or in collective liberation movements, is a theme that has not yet been adequately analyzed (Blake, 1976) and that merits much more attention than it has received so far. It is in fact very probable that in the next few years in many developing countries women will be the protagonists of processes of innovation and change, opposing religious fundamentalism and power held by traditional authorities.

The seventh critical threshold concerns, at last, the *environmental issue*, or the emergence of an increasingly acute contradiction between technical-industrial growth and conservation of the environment. The problems of such a threshold tend to be handled with policies aimed at ensuring conditions for an ecologically-compatible economic development. This constitutes one of the biggest points of contention between countries that are in different phases of the modernization process. The environmental conditions in the majority of developing countries (industrial pollution, chaotic traffic, unsafe working conditions, substandard hygienic conditions, health risks) are much worse than in developed countries. And yet, since industrialization is the primary objective to attain at any cost, sensitivity to environmental damage is scant while suspicious hostility is strong towards developed countries that request ecologically virtuous behavior without substantially helping to bear the costs and without changing their ways of life that imply high levels of consumption of natural resources.

In the passage through the various critical thresholds that we have illustrated, *collective movements* of various natures form that are among the main actors of the modernization process (farmers, workers and unionists, feminists, students, environmentalists, activists for peace, for civil rights and political liberties). These movements stimulate, in turn, individual strategies as well as institutional responses, in the two-fold sense of shared forms of conflict regulation and implementation of effective public policies, of economic growth and welfare, according to what I define as the *cycle of growth and modernization* (Martinelli et al., 1999). Such a cycle is formed by vast and intense processes of economic growth with related social changes that create conditions for emerging contradictions, conflicts and collective movements of demands and protests. These in turn generate a variety of institutional responses, i.e. changes in political institutions and culture and in government policies (land reforms, welfare policies, non-violent modes of conflict resolution) and collective and individual strategies to respond to such contradictions. Institutional responses seldom corresponded to the manifest goals of the collective movements, but, insofar as they changed the general context and the specific situation where collective action develops, they brought about a new configuration of social relations, a modification of social conflicts, and new power relations among political actors, in short, a new social order. The relationship between processes of economic modernization and social and individual mobilization and the efficacy of institutional and individual strategies in the market and the political arena are in this regard of primary importance.

Overcoming the critical thresholds seems to be more or less difficult in various contexts and various historical epochs. But, in general, modernization problems and crises in latecomer non-Western countries trying to catch up appear, with the passing of time, to be more complex than those of the first modernized countries. In the prevalent version of the classic theory of modernization (and in particular for Lerner, 1958, and Deutsch, 1961) the problems mostly concern the inability to develop the institutional and cultural requisites that have characterized the Western experience. Subsequently, a more pessimistic version develops (as, for example, in Eisenstadt, 1966, and Desai, 1966), which points out substantial differences between the modernization of Western countries and that of ex-colonial countries.

Focusing on the phases and critical thresholds of modernization raises another important question concerning the forces and the actors of innovation and change, along with their strategies, resources and ideological conceptions.

The actors of modernization

Every process of modernization requires innovation. Identification of innovators, the obstacles they have to overcome and the characteristics of the innovation process are therefore of primary importance. The difficulties of innovation and the strength of the traditional mentality are well illustrated by Machiavelli in *The Prince*:

> The innovator has for enemies all those who have done well under the old conditions, and lukewarm defenders in those who may do well under the new. This coolness arises partly from fear of the opponents, who have the laws on their side, and partly from the incredulity of men, who do not readily believe in new things until they have had a long experience of them. (1975)

To overcome obstacles, both an appropriate context supportive of innovation as well as individual and collective actors capable of achieving it are required, that is, both the right soil and the right seeds.

At the end of the last section, I mentioned collective movements as actors of modernization. Here I concentrate instead on the role of *modernizing elites*. I have already spoken of *entrepreneurs as innovators* who act based on motivations of achievement, referring to Hagen and McClelland, and have discussed the mechanisms and processes that promote modernization. But entrepreneurs are only one type of modernizing elite.

Also taking on particular importance are *national political leaders*, often heads of revolutionary parties who are legitimized by the fight for independence and use symbols to overcome difficulties of transition and internal differences, and *administrative elites*, sometimes formed during the colonial period and generally bearers of a technocratic mentality (Dube, 1966; Riggs, 1964). When these two types of elites take the form of pragmatic technocrats and custodians of ideology and revolutionary purity, they often enter into conflict with each other. Emblematic of this was the opposition in Chinese communist society between the *reds* and the *experts* (Schurmann, 1966), who took their power from various sources of legitimation, the former by the Marxist-Leninist ideology and the thought of Mao Tse Tung and the latter by the organizational efficacy vividly expressed by Deng Xiaoping ('it does not matter what color the cat is, as long as he catches mice').

Two other primary actors in modernization processes are the military and intellectuals. The *military* bases its power on the control of essential resources of technological nature (weapons and weapon systems, first of all) and organizational nature, such as military discipline, hierarchies and systems of rewards and punishments (Pye, 1966; Rustow, 1967; Huntington, 1968).

Intellectuals produce and spread technical-scientific knowledge essential to economic growth and social development and ideological conceptions that orient and legitimate the political actions of groups that compete for power. Often intellectuals find themselves having to conduct difficult mediations between defending indigenous cultural legacy and assimilating foreign political and economic theories from more developed countries (Shils, 1960).

The scholar who has dedicated most attention to analyzing the role of elites and ideological conceptions was Eisenstadt (1966, 1992a). In the synthesis of his long-term studies published by Haferkamp and Smelser (1992), which I liberally rework to make it more consistent with my theory of the cycle of development and modernization illustrated previously, Eisenstadt notes that every institutional system forms through a combination of three fundamental elements. The first element is the prevailing social division of labor, or the level of distribution of resources among the various social groups. The second element is made up of elites or institutional entrepreneurs who compete to mobilize such resources and articulate the interests of principal social groups generated by the division of labor. And the third element is the nature of the conceptions of reality or ideologies that shape the actions of these elites and that are derived from the principal codes and cultural orientations of the society.

The most important elites are political ones, engaged in the regulation of power, those intellectuals oriented toward the construction of meaning, and those who organize the solidarity of the main social groups and who are engaged in the building of trust. Through the cooperation between these elites, a hegemonic rule – in Gramsci's sense – can be exerted over the whole of the population (Martinelli, 1968). These elites are constantly in alliance or in conflict with each other, control access to the largest institutional markets and the conversion of principal resources (economic, informational, etc.), and shape the major chacteristics of the various collectivities, institutions and organizations that make up the social system. In such a way, they exercise social control and ensure innovation through complex cycles of protest, conflict and change. Conflict is inevitable not only due to the number of competing actors, but also because these actors represent different cultural orientations and behavioral codes. And from conflict constantly emerge demands for change and social integration.

The outcomes and consequences of the transition to modernity

Recognizing the outcomes of modernization is affected in general by an inadequate ability to distinguish between intentional outcomes that correspond to actors' strategies of action – the results of their interaction – and the unintentional effects and the unintended consequences of action. The strategies of actors unfold within a combination of structural constraints (in particular, the characteristics of the pre-modern society and its position in the international division of labor) and cultural constraints (ideologies, mentalities, specific subcultures), which also include the strategies of other actors. The results of interaction also comprise the unintended and unintentional consequences of action.

The complexity of the outcomes is generally overlooked by most studies in the classic approach to modernization, which is limited to verifying the convergence of different country-systems towards univocal models of industrial economy and modern society. An accurate analysis of the outcomes and consequences of modernization cannot therefore emerge from the classic theory alone but must also draw on subsequent critical approaches. Thus, it concerns not only this section but the entire book and in particular the chapters that follow.

The prevalent attitude in the first versions of the theory of modernization was optimistically centered on the inevitability of the development of so-called traditional countries with mechanisms and processes analogous to those already tested by Western societies. The most explicit formulations of this attitude are Rostow's theory of the stages of development (which we have already illustrated) and the *theory of convergence* elaborated by Kerr, Dunlop, F. Harrison, H. Harrison and Myers (1960), a group of American scholars who, departing from an analysis of the labor market, approached a comparative analysis of models of industrialization.

According to these scholars, industrial societies (which at present already differ much less among themselves than they differ from non-industrial societies) are destined to become ever more similar by virtue of the intrinsic logic of industrialism and the constraints erected by technology. Whatever structural processes and institutional mechanisms that were followed to arrive at industrialization (free market, planned economy, mixed models), industrial societies will try to adopt the most effective productive technology, which in turn will influence social relations not only in the economic sphere of labor and consumption, but also in the political sphere and in various aspects of the culture. Societies will proceed, therefore, gradually in the direction of modernity – towards the specialization of professional roles, occupational mobility, development of education, growth of large hierarchical and bureaucratic organizations whether private or public, pluralism of interests, reduction and regulation of conflict, attenuation of all-absorbing ideologies, development of materialistic values, orientation towards work and individual success.

In the late 1950s when Kerr and his collaborators were writing, they noticed how this institutional convergence in different politico-ideological systems manifested itself in the reduction of the market in the West and in a parallel reduction of state control of the economy in communist countries. The theory of convergence assumes that technology has its own immanent logic of growth composed of inventions and innovations and that a single technology at a time can assure the best results in terms of productivity. This theory fits, therefore, into the rich vein of technological determinism, framed within a concept of universalized trends in the world economy. Industrial society is a world society, because the science and technology on which it is based speaks a universal language.

The idea of the standardizing and universalizing effect of industrial economy is shared by many other scholars, like Huntington (1968) and Goldthorpe (1971), the latter pointing out that with its progress the range of institutional structures and compatible value systems necessarily decreases until asymptotically approaching the pure 'industrial form'.

As we will see in the following chapters, these predictions of the tendential universalizing of the industrial economy were either disproved in the name of specificity of different historical experiences or were interpreted in the sense of a universalization of the capitalist rule over dependent societies. Instead a more balanced conception was approached in the most recent studies on developing countries and in the debate on late-modern society and the processes of globalization. On the one hand, this conception strives to delineate and interpret the various routes toward and through modernity within a general process of growing economic and cultural interdependency of societies and peoples. On the other, it considers the generalization of the industrial market economy as a source of both constraints and opportunities for developing countries. These countries are, in fact, at the same time limited in their choices by the international division of labor and distribution of power as well as aided by several advantages of 'latecomers' and they find in their indigenous cultures obstacles as well as resources for making the leap towards the status of more developed countries.

3

Critiques of the Classic Theory of Modernization and Alternative Approaches

The classic theory of modernization – even though more interested in constructing ideal types and identifying abstract mechanisms of change than in working out comparative studies on actual processes of modernization – formulates, like every theory, a series of empirically verifiable hypotheses and predictions and suggests in a more or less explicit way suitable strategies for overcoming underdevelopment.

The empirical tests of its predictions of rapid development were limited or at least contradictory. Notwithstanding the fact that the gross national product of the so-called Third World grew in the third quarter of the twentieth century to an annual average of 3.4 percent, which is higher than the average rate of Western economies, the optimistic predictions of these studies did not come true on a consistent basis. Economic growth did not necessarily bring modernization (in its broadest definition of generalized social transformation); and the increase in gross national product often was not accompanied by significant improvements in the standard of living, levels of education, health conditions of the masses, diffusion of modern technologies, or the strengthening of political institutions. The obstacles to modernization (resistance of vested interests and traditional attitudes, disrupting effects of imported models, phenomena of internal colonialism) turned out to be stronger than predicted. This stimulated a series of criticisms and contributed to the development of a second wave of theories of modernization that refutes the ideal-type approach and the evolutionary perspective implicitly or explicitly present in most studies in the classic theory.

There are reasons of both a methodological and an ideological nature at the root of the critiques and the temporary decline of the concept of modernization in the scientific debate. Starting from the late 1960s, close criticisms are formulated by writers of diverse cultural orientations – from Bendix, whose 1967 study, 'Tradition and modernity reconsidered' can be taken as the starting point of the critical revision, to Gusfield (1967), from theorists of the *dependencia* such as Frank (1967a, 1967b) and Cardoso and Faletto (1969) to those of the world-system (Wallerstein, 1974–89), from Goldthorpe (1971) to Boudon (1984), to whom we owe the best-argued methodological critique of the theories of social change.

The principal critical targets are as follows:

1. The construction of dichotomous models that rigidly contrast *traditional* and *modern* as coherent systemic combinations of interdependent elements.
2. The identification of a standard and uniform model of development (which can be traced back to an ensemble of *evolutionary universals* such as industrialization and urbanization) impoverishing and reducing the variety and

complexity of the routes and the many-sidedness of social change in different historical situations.

3. The emphasis on endogenous variables of change (and, in particular, processes of institutional and cultural differentiation as motors of social transformation), ignoring the interdependent and dependent relations between countries at different levels of development within a world-system (where the more appropriate distinction would not be between advanced and backward countries, but among countries and regions of the world involved in different ways and measures in a condition of global modernity).

4. The accentuation of the role of systemic forces of change with respect to the strategies of individual and collective actors.

These epistemological criticisms are often also joined by the ideological critique that the classic theory of modernization does the following: (1) considers modernization and Westernization as identical; (2) asserts the inevitability of the Western model of development of the capitalist market economy and the convergence of developing countries towards this model; and (3) deducts from the historical experience of Western democracies in political struggle with the Soviet Union a rigid scheme of economic and political development for Third World countries, and in doing so, completely ignores alternative strategies, based on autochthonous characteristics of the concerned countries or taken from experiences other than Western modernization (first, communist planned economies and, then, after the collapse of the Soviet Union, the mix of authoritarian regime and market economy).

Critique of the traditional–modern dichotomy

A first type of criticism deals with the conceptualization of traditional society and modern society as contrasting models. As Bendix points out (1967), modernization becomes a 'Procrustean bed' where very different historical experiences are placed, whereas both modern Western countries and developing countries have followed and still do follow partially different paths. The insufficient empirical foundation of these studies encourages an undervaluing of the internal diversity of traditional societies, which are deductively described in order to contrast them with the traits of modern societies, which are flattened in the same way onto a univocal model.

In a similar vein, critics such as Gusfield (1967) and Tipps (1973) point out how the static nature, the lack of differentiation between the various spheres of social life, the importance of the sacred, and other characteristics of the ideal type of traditional society, can vary profoundly from one historical society to another and were exaggerated and standardized in the dichotomous model. Some critics, like Wolf (1982), even assert that, in identifying tradition with static nature and the lack of development, one denies societies defined as traditional their own history.

It should be pointed out, moreover, that already by the beginning of the twentieth century very few 'traditional' societies were left. Besides a few groups in the Amazon, New Guinea, Borneo and limited areas of Africa, inhabitants of undeveloped countries had already experienced prolonged and traumatic contacts with the modernized, industrialized and politically dominant Western world (Chirot, 1977). The characteristics that define so-called 'traditional' societies are not therefore to be considered intrinsic, but as resulting from interaction with the West.

The same argument is valid for the distinctive traits of the 'modern society'. Here also the routes to and through modernity are profoundly diverse in different contexts. Here also one often notices a mingling of 'traditional' and 'modern' elements. For example, the family business, characterized by little structural differentiation between family life and economic activity, persists in many modern contexts, among them contemporary Italian society.

As recent studies show, family, ethnic and religious ties contribute to the development of those intangible but essential elements of commercial relations – trust, cooperation and other ingredients of social capital (Hamilton and Biggart, 1988; Hamilton and Kao, 1991; Granovetter, 1992). A typical example in this regard is the precious gems market in which forms of ethnic solidarity and trust between actors can be a prerequisite for efficiency and competitiveness.

Also criticized is the idea of the strict interdependence among the constituent elements of the two ideal types. Certain aspects of modernization can, in fact, proceed faster than others or even remain completely isolated, provoking conflicts and contradictions, as is the case when consumption growth precedes the production of new goods and services, or when the demand for participation is not accompanied by a democratization of political institutions.

In that way, often unwittingly, the same criticisms are revived that had been made by sociologists like Ogburn and anthropologists like Malinowski about Radcliffe Brown's classic functionalist theory of the functional interconnectedness of institutions and the linearity and unilinearity of change. Ogburn (1922) criticizes classic evolutionary theory as empirically unproven by either historical studies or ethnographic studies, replacing it with his *theory of cultural lag*. Starting from the assumption of the systematic interdependence of social institutions, Ogburn stresses the uneven pace of their transformations and points out, in particular, that changes in material culture (technology and economic organization) always precede changes in adaptive culture (family, religion, art, laws and customs), and that this chronic delay creates a series of social problems and poses the risk of social confusion.

Malinowski (1945) asserts, in turn, that colonial societies are not integrated wholes, but rather the result of many contrasting and conflicting cultural elements. The 'three columns' on which such cultures rest are: the colonial culture with its institutions and interests; the repository of living indigenous beliefs, customs and traditions; and the processes of contact and change in which members of the two cultures conflict, cooperate and make compromises. He thus criticized diffusionist theories such as Kroeber's (1923), according to which the vast majority of cultural elements of a people are learned by other peoples.

Furthermore, neither the constraints nor the potential advantages of 'latecomer' societies are considered in the 'traditional–modern' dichotomous perspective. A particularly vivid illustration of such advantages is offered by Dore's comparative study (1973) on the organization of English and Japanese factories, showing how the latter, having more advanced technologies at its disposal, could 'skip' many phases of the traditional productive process, avoiding the connected social problems.

Critique of the evolutionary perspective

The second type of critique, closely connected to the first, addresses the evolutionary perspective of the theory of modernization. Such a perspective is criticized, first of all, because it views modernization as a unilinear and irreversible process that tends to go through the same fixed phases already crossed by modern societies. Ignored therefore are the breaks (Eisenstadt, 1966), the standstills (Riggs, 1964), the uneven character – discontinuous and extremely disturbed – of change in developing societies (Smelser, 1968), and the political decadence (Huntington, 1965).

From this critique of the reversibility of processes, Huntington infers the need to distinguish between modernization and political development. He applies the first term to processes of industrialization, urbanization, growth of literacy and national product, which he considers generally irreversible. He reserves the second term for the process of institutionalization of organizations and political procedures, which can in fact give way to stagnation, regression, or instability.

As well as ignoring standstills, breaks and trend inversions, many modernization studies undervalue conflict in favor of integration and revolutionary change in favor of gradual evolution (even though from their theoretical apparatus one can find interesting ideas for interpreting conflict as well as revolutionary outcomes). Ignoring revolutionary outcomes seems even more incorrect in that these studies take Western experience – marked by three revolutions (the English revolution in the late 1600s and the French and American revolutions in the late 1700s) – as the model of modernization for developing countries (Tilly, 1973).

The analysis of modernization cannot omit the study of revolution, not only because it would correct its anti-conflictual myopia, but because the principal concepts employed in the theory of revolution – collective action and mobilization of resources (Tilly, 1978), political violence and related deprivation (Gurr, 1970), lack of synchronization between values and social environment (Johnson, 1966), class contradictions and political conflict (Skocpol, 1979) – can also be usefully employed in the theory of modernization in general, not only in that specific variant of the modernizing revolution (a subject of interpretation treated by Barrington Moore, that we will discuss later).

The evolutionary perspective can be criticized, moreover, because it considers modernization a process in some way complete, instead of open and continuous – as contemporary events of Western societies show – where examples abound of incomplete, or better, uneven modernization, such as in contemporary Italian society (Martinelli et al., 1999).

Many studies that adopt the evolutionary perspective can be criticized, finally, because they tend to conceive of modernization as a univocal process of structural differentiation and adaptation to a given environmental situation. They do not recognize the multilinear character of evolution, which derives from the high variability in cultural and institutional responses of different societies to similar stimuli, risks and opportunities (those generally connected to technology and the formation of a world economy). They believe that all societies converge toward a single model, whereas the results can be very different. Such model being that of Western societies, these studies are guilty of ethnocentrism in as much as they intend the 'exemplary' experience to be that of Western societies, disregarding multiple and partially alternative modernities, as we will discuss in the final chapter.

The multilinear character of the evolution of human society had already been argued convincingly in the 1950s by the anthropologist Steward, in the two-fold sense of diverse pathways of various societies and differences in the evolution of various aspects of societal life (cultural, economic, political, artistic, legal, etc.). But this formulation was acknowledged only by some evolutionary studies, such as those by Parsons, Smelser, Eisenstadt.

Critique of modernization as mere internal dynamic and critique of the positive role of external influences

The third kind of critique, in addition to those directed at the traditional–modern dichotomy and unilinear and irreversible evolutionism, focuses on the fact that the classic theory of modernization neglects and under-evaluates the international dimension. When it is considered, it evaluates relations with the outside in a unilaterally positive way. They are seen only as stimuli and opportunities, and not also as constraints and obstacles to modernization.

This last target of criticism presupposes the first two. If in fact, as in the evolutionary perspective, modernization is conceived of as society's growing capacity for adaptation – through the creation of differentiated social roles and structures with respect to the physical and social environment – relations with the outside are interpreted as opportunities for forces and actors of endogenous change. And when the ideal types of traditional society and modern society are contrasted, one generally attributes an implicit positive value to the model of modernity drawn from Western experience.

Conceiving of modernization as an internal dynamic of a nation that occurs by imitating the process that took place in a more advanced country ignores the basic fact that international relations (in both their economic dimension of international flows of goods, persons and capital, as well as in their political dimension of competition and conflict among states) have, from the beginning, characterized the process of modernization, first, in Europe and then in the rest of the world.

The most radical version of this type of critique was formulated by Wallerstein (1991). In his recent criticism of misleading concepts inherited from the social sciences of the nineteenth century from which we need to be liberated, the principal target is the concept of development. Going back to the arguments of his previous critique of the concept of modernization, Wallerstein (1976) holds that such a concept is inadequate for essentially two reasons: first, because it refers to endogenous changes and to the gradual unfolding of immanent potentialities; and, second, because it sets the nation-state as the unit of analysis, viewing every society as an isolated entity, sovereign, in a certain degree autonomous, evolving according to its specific tendencies. Wallerstein believes, on the contrary, that the fundamental factors of social change are international factors and global influences; that the impulses for change come from contacts both peaceful and violent, and from the competition and conflict between various peoples; that the configurations different societies take on are mainly the products of global processes, and responses to the dynamics of the world system. Finally, the concept of development can be criticized since it is closely linked to the concept of progress with its fallacious claims of the unidirectionality of change and of constant improvement.

Other critiques: an evaluation of their reliability

The other principal critiques are of an epistemological and ideological nature. The first have to do with the excessive weight placed on the role of systemic forces of change compared to the subjects' strategies of actions; and the widespread tendency among those who do take strategies of action into consideration to focus on the strategies of collective actors while disregarding the strategies of individual actors (Sztompka, 1993; Martinelli et al., 1999). Also criticized is the pretense of constructing general interpretive models of broad applicability on a limited empirical base and limited comparative investigations, a pretense often joined by the preference for system analysis instead of agency study. Finally, the ideological character of most studies of that period is criticized. The theory of modernization was, in fact, a model in a double sense: on the one hand, it was a theoretical simplification of empirical reality as any model of scientific inquiry; on the other, it portrayed a desired course of action and provided a criterion for judging individual and collective behavior actors and government policies.

Some of the critiques addressed to the classic theory of modernization are unilateral, tend to inappropriately generalize the defects of the roughest and most naïve versions, and do not recognize that this theory offers a rich collection of hypotheses and interpretations that can be opportunely utilized in the study of modernization processes currently taking place in emerging countries. Other critiques suffer from the same defects they reproach. Nonetheless, they are often successful in clarifying the fundamental assumptions of the classic theory, disproving its methodological shortcomings, and denouncing its excessive ambitions. The value of these studies, in fact, lies more in the ability to illuminate limited but crucial issues of the modernization process, than in the ability to create a general theory.

The critiques of the theory of modernization that we have briefly illustrated involve partial or radical changes in perspective. They shift from a linear vision of development to a much more problematic and composite vision; from a systematic approach to a comparative historical approach; from an endogenous conception of development to a conception of international conditionings; from the almost exclusive focus on emerging countries to the comparison between Western countries' experiences of modernization with those of the Third World. Alongside highly ideologized and unilateral interpretations, we also find analyses methodologically more attentive, less ethnocentric and more aware of the plurality of routes to modernity and through modernity than the classic theory of modernization.

The need to distinguish themselves from such theory induces most of the scholars of these new research perspectives to ignore, or even reject, the concept of modernization, replacing it with others such as development, under-development, dependence, nation-state building, and so on. Their inclusion in a book on critical analyses of modernization is, nevertheless, completely legitimate (beyond the contingent lexical preferences) by virtue of the comprehensive meaning that we have attributed to this concept.

The new research perspectives, which originate from the principal critiques we have illustrated, are: the historical sociology of modernization and the comparative-historical analysis of political development, which study the plurality of the formation processes of modern societies and nation-states and which are rooted in a tradition of critical continuity with the classic theory of modernization; and the neo-Marxist approaches of *dependencia* and the world-system which represent, instead, a more radical alternative, studying the dialectic between development and underdevelopment.

In parallel, an internal revision matures of the theory of modernization from writers such as Eisenstadt, Smelser, and Tiryakian (Haferkamp and Smelser, 1992), who acknowledge several contributions to the alternative theories and who, especially Eisenstadt, make an effort to link the macro-level of structural characteristics to the micro-level of strategies of actors, in particular, the modernizing elites (as we stated at the end of Chapter 2). Later on, these efforts join with the contributions of non-Western scholars and develop in the direction of the multiple modernities approach that I will discuss in the final chapter.

The historical sociology of modernization: Reinhard Bendix

We will discuss separately, for purposes of expositive clarity, the historical sociology of modernization and political science's studies of political development, even though the distinction between scholars such as Bendix or Rokkan is arbitrary, since they have in common not only a subject but also a method and a large part of the conceptual apparatus of their research. Both the sociological as well as the political science's approach share, in fact, the attempt to formulate models of general significance, paying, however, great attention to diverse real historical experiences. They seek, therefore, to avoid the opposing errors of repeatability of the more advanced country model (which negates specificity) and the impermeability of single historical experiences (which impedes generalization).

The most interesting contributions of the historical sociology of modernization are those of Reinhard Bendix and Barrington Moore. Proposing to reconcile the attention to a country's historical peculiarities with that of the general movement of history, Bendix strongly argues for the historical specificity of the various experiences of modernization. Western modernization – embodying the success of large-scale industry, scientific culture and a centralized state apparatus and the eclipse of sacred and personal authority – is a historically specific process that deeply contrasts with the experiences of developing countries.

Even within Western modernization, though, a plurality of routes – or multiple modernities – exist due to the diversity of the politico-institutional arrangements and cultural patterns. These arrangements exercise a fundamental influence both on the level of backwardness (and therefore on the start of the process of modernization of various societies), and on the ways of governing the resulting contradictions and conflicts.

The influence of the various politico-institutional arrangements in the process of modernization is broached by Bendix (1978) in his work, *Kings or People: Power and the Mandate to Rule*. He examines from a Weberian perspective the emergence of the *people's mandate* from traditional political structures founded on monarchic and aristocratic authority and the construction of the nation-state as the new basic unit of economic and political life in five historical contexts – England, France, Prussia/Germany, Japan and Russia, with more sketchy references to China and the Islamic world.

Bendix defines modernization 'as a breakdown of the ideal-typical traditional order: authority loses its sanctity, monarchy declines, hierarchical social order is disrupted. Secular authority, rule in the name of the people, and an egalitarian ethos are typical attributes of modern society' (1978: 11). Within this general and ambitious analysis of the evolution of patterns of authority in processes of nation-state building and of modernization, two more specific contributions prove to be particularly interesting: the study of the role taken by the intellectual elites and the analysis of the relationship between central authority and local autonomies. As to the first, Bendix argues that it is the condition of backwardness that stimulates profound transformations in a country. The condition of backwardness is, in fact, a threat to the survival of the country and brings about an intolerable sense of inferiority. The sense of danger and inferiority stimulates an intellectual response from the emerging new elites who are sociologically well differentiated from the rest of the population. These elites introduce innovations into the national culture, assimilating foreign ideas and models. But at the same time, they are induced by the external threat to rediscover the most authentic values of the indigenous tradition and therefore strengthen the national sentiment.

Backwardness is overcome by the birth or the consolidation of the nation-state through modernization (understood as total or partial destruction of sacred, personalized and hierarchical authority and as economic and scientific-technical development) and through the establishment of a people's mandate ideology, required by the modernizing intellectual elites to defeat traditional authority. This process occurs within the more general process of establishing a capitalist bourgeois society, characterized by the commercialization of land, labor and capital and the diffusion of culture (growth of a reading public and the advent of intellectual professions that no longer depend on the protection of the powerful).

The other key argument in Bendix's analysis is the balance of power between central and local authorities, which in turn influences the possibility of establishing a constitutional representative democracy. The roots of this balance between center and periphery can be found in the relationship that is set up between monarchy and aristocracy in pre-industrial societies. Where centralism prevails, tendencies toward despotic government are evident, while, where local centrifugal forces prevail, the tendency is toward anarchy. If the aristocracy does not have (or loses) its bases for autonomous power, the establishment of a despotic government is facilitated, which blocks the formation of an autonomous civil society with respect to the state and brings about a situation of economic backwardness.

England and Russia illustrate two opposite cases. In Russia, the despotism of the czars encounters no religious limits (given the reduced authority of the Orthodox Church) and follows a policy of territorial uprooting of the aristocracy, transforming it into a 'service class' active in the army and the bureaucracy that integrally depends on the goodwill of the czar. In England, however, the insular configuration of the territory makes early formation of a nation-state possible without the need to abolish institutions of feudal origin created to protect the local autonomies. The relationship between an aristocracy rooted on its own estates and a monarchy proved to be, therefore, much more balanced and the same state bureaucracy was retained, aiding constitutionalism as well as capitalist development.

In a previous work, *Nation-Building and Citizenship* (1964), Bendix also analyzed the politico-institutional responses to social contradictions and political conflicts (in particular, the workers' protest) that are intrinsic to the process of modernization. The social conditions generated by industrialization and the commodification of the labor force entail a crisis in the fundamental mechanisms of social integration, such as the Church, the patriarchal family and the local community, as well as the uprooting of urbanized peasants. These conditions fuel the protest and push the workers to demand equal political rights (union and party representation, the vote, political associationism) as tools to defend their interests. In situations in which, as in England, the demand for citizenship rights by the working class is gradually granted by a democratic and 'open' political system, thanks to the particular politico-institutional tradition, the working class becomes integrated in the democratic system which is in turn reinforced. Where, however, the demand for citizenship rights is severely limited or even denied, as in Germany and Russia, the workers' movement is radicalized in a revolutionary sense, impeding the formation of a democratic set-up, as in 1917 Russia, or contributing to its fall, as in the Weimar Republic in 1930s' Germany.

The historical sociology of modernization: Barrington Moore

Barrington Moore's (1966) study *Social Origins of Dictatorship and Democracy*, complementary to Bendix's research, places relations between social classes before and during modernization at the center of the analysis. By reviewing the origins of capitalist democracy in England, France and the United States and the three Asian experiences of modernization in China, Japan and India, Moore extracts elements for a theoretical model that outlines three routes toward the modern world: (1) the democratic route; (2) revolution from above; (3) and a peasant revolution. In his comparative analysis, every country has its own specificity, but the key variables of the process are the same.

In the first route, the *democratic route*, Moore identifies the principal preconditions of a bourgeois revolution resulting in industrialization and political democracy.

He sees the development of a democracy 'as a long and certainly incomplete struggle to do three closely related things: 1) to check arbitrary rulers, 2) to replace arbitrary rules with just and rational ones, and 3) to obtain a share for the underlying population in the making of the rules' (1968: 414). The first prerequisite is a balance of power between monarchy and aristocracy which prevents either an overly strong monarchy tending toward absolutism or an overly independent aristocracy (powerful enough to obstruct a revolutionary break with the past and to prevent peasants mobilizing in defense of the traditional order). In this balanced situation those notions were developed – the immunity of certain groups from the power of the sovereign, the right of resistance to an authority deemed unjust, and the liberally undersigned pact between sovereign and vassal – that form a firm basis for the formation of democratic institutions. Actually speaking of balance of power between monarchy and aristocracy seems appropriate to the English case only; in France, a two-stage process took place, first with royal absolutism destroying the independent power of feudal lords, and creating the centralized state political-administrative organization and, second, with the bourgeois revolution destroying the absolute power of the king and the building the democratic nation.

The second fundamental precondition is the commercialization of agriculture by either a portion of the landed aristocracy or of the peasantry. In this regard Moore outlines two different experiences: in England (in which the aristocracy devotes itself to commercial agriculture, on the one hand, acquiring bourgeois values and attitudes and, on the other hand, transmitting some of its aristocratic outlook to the commercial and industrial classes), and in France (in which the nobility leaves *de facto* possession of the land to the peasants only to find its power extremely scaled down by the revolution). He contrasts these experiences with the historical events of Eastern Europe (where, instead, the great landowners remain powerful and reduce peasants again to serfdom within vast landed estates, preventing them from being integrated into a market economy). The breaking of the power of an independent landowning class is the outcome of a revolutionary rupture, which can take quite different forms as in the English revolution of the seventeenth century, the American War of Independence and the French Revolution of the eighteenth century. Finally, the democratic route to modernization is further aided by the competition and antagonism between the industrial and commercial bourgeoisie and the landed aristocracy that hampers a 'marriage between steel and rye', i.e. a bourgeois-aristocratic coalition capable of standing up to the peasants' and workers' demands for political representation.

In the second route, *revolution from above*, industrialization is started and sustained by the state that protects nascent industry from international competition by protectionist policies and defends the interests of large land-owning exporters. The bourgeoisie is weaker than in the first route, while resistance to modernization by the landed aristocracy is stronger. In top-down modernization, forces favoring the installment and consolidation of democracy are weaker and, in fact, social conditions favoring fascist-type authoritarian regimes appear. These regimes are founded on coalitions between landowners, land-owning peasants and a weak bourgeoisie and are supported by the monarchy and connected military and bureaucratic systems. Regimes such as those of Germany and Japan tried to solve a problem that was inherently insoluble, to modernize without changing their social structures, through the development of militarism which united the upper classes, but also led both countries – and the entire world – to the great tragedy of the Second World War.

Moore's portrait of the second route to modernity is similar to Gerschenkron's (1968) thesis, claiming a correlation between the economic backwardness of 'latecomer' countries (such as Germany and Italy) and the use of institutional development factors different from those of the first industrialization – factors such as the state (with its administrative and coercive apparatus), the investment bank, and related technocratic ideologies.

In the third route, the path of the *peasant revolution*, societies that depend on a centralized authority and an agrarian bureaucracy for extracting the surplus are most vulnerable to peasant rebellions. The most important reasons for peasant revolutions have been the absence of a commercial revolution in agriculture led by the landed upper classes and the concomitant survival of peasant social institutions into the modern era when they are subject to new stresses and strains (1968). A centralized and despotic power transforms the aristocracy into a subordinate bureaucracy and hinders the growth of the urban bourgeoisie and its participation in the process of capitalist industrialization and modernization, in either the democratic form of the first route or in the fascist form typical of the second route. In this situation, the mass of peasants who live the contradictions caused by the disintegration of traditional society (as a consequence of wars, struggles for power over the centralist despotism and failed attempts at top-down modernization) support the revolutionary effort of narrow intellectual circles, joining forces with nuclei of the rising working class. In countries such as the Soviet Union and China, the process of modernization is then begun and consolidated by post-revolutionary communist regimes.

Historical sociology is also certainly not immune to criticism (which also applies to the theory of political development we will discuss shortly). In the first place, the construction of typologies, phase sequences and critical thresholds is often deeply influenced by single historical experiences that become generalized in theoretical models. This is not always the case; for instance, Moore's interpretation of the Indian case as a mix of the various routes to modernity is proof of the lack of correspondence among the various ideal types of modernization and single historical cases. But it often happens.

Furthermore, these studies tend to select aspects from single countries' historical experiences that appear consistent with the hypothesis of the theoretical frame, neglecting or ignoring completely the other aspects. For example, the relationship between royal absolutism and modernization is more complex than Bendix seems to recognize: it is exactly the alliance between absolute monarch and the rising bourgeoisie that in fact allows, in France, the defeat of the landowning nobility.

On a more general note, Bendix's study can be criticized for the close identification of nation-building processes with the establishment of a people's mandate and modernization, which at times do not coincide at all. Regarding the link between modernization and the people's mandate, it should be noted that not all that is traditional can be traced back to royal authority and not all that is modern can be identified with the people's mandate. Regarding the nexus between nation-building and modernization, it should be pointed out that in many historical situations the first process considerably preceded the second. At times Bendix gives the impression of reconstructing *a posteriori* a universality and a sequence into industrial societies' modernization process that have not proved true in several historical cases. And the importance Moore attributes to the role of large land-owners in establishing one of the three modernization routes seems excessive. In spite of the specific criticisms directed at these studies, they represent a fundamental step forward in the construction of historically-based theories of the various forms of modernization.

The comparative analysis of European political development: Stein Rokkan

Rokkan's interpretation of modern European society's formation is very similar to the contributions of Bendix and Moore. Rokkan's contribution is, however, more difficult to summarize because it is scattered in a vast number of essays and it has been reformulated several times (1969, 1970, 1975; Flora, 1999). A partial formulation of this theory is found in Rokkan's version of the critical thresholds of political development, which I have already illustrated in the preceding chapter.

Rokkan does not construct a general theory of political development applicable to a multiplicity of different empirical cases far-flung in space and time, but rather a *family of models for the comparative history of Europe*. In Weber's footsteps, and like Bendix and Barrington Moore, his interpretative models, typologies and multidimensional variables do not purport to formulate valid universal patterns, but they are instruments for examining unique historical configurations, for appreciating uniformity and differences. However, unlike Bendix and Moore, he limits his analysis to an ensemble of countries belonging to the same geographical area, that is to the historical experience of European countries, an experience he considers unique and unrepeatable.

Through a highly experimental methodological attitude that combines and works out diverse theoretical contributions in an original manner, Rokkan examines (based on a vast amount of data) the principal differences and uniformities in European countries' transition from absolutism to mass democracy, reconstructs the fundamental structural breaks from which originated contemporary political configurations (particularly party systems), and builds in such a way *a geo-political map of Europe*.

Rokkan's model seeks to fuse together Parsons's paradigm of functional differentiation and Hirschman's classification scheme of decision systems. As we saw, Parsons explains the evolution from primordial communities to those historically more complex in the light of functional differentiation among four types of structures – politico-military, cultural, juridical and economic – or rather based on four fundamental components: force, culture, law and economy. On this foundation,

Parsons tries to establish a typology of the first political systems: patrimonial kingdoms, the first administrative and religious empires, confederations of city-states and the most important 'seed-bed' societies such as Israel and Greece. This model is also connected to the distinction between center and periphery and Hirschman's (1970) theory of *exit, voice* and *loyalty*, as alternatives of individual and collective action.

Reinterpreting Parsons's model, Rokkan seeks to respond to questions concerning the internal dynamics of political systems, i.e. what are the characteristics of primordial communities situated in subject peripheral areas, and in what ways are they connected to the differentiated central communities (via the military-fiscal apparatus, through a communion of juridical traditions, by means of networks of cities or religious and linguistic affinities)? What are, instead, the characteristics of centers, what are the modalities of control over domestic resources and those beyond territorial borders, what are the dominant alliances? And reinterpreting Hirschman's theory, what are the principal problems of state formation and nation-building, complementary to the previous, such as the construction of borders, the development of national loyalties, and the conflict between forces that tend to stabilize borders (principles, bureaucracies, national languages) and forces that tend to transcend them (universal religions, commercial trade, international erudite languages like Latin)?

These highly abstract models are then employed in a historical-empirical analysis of the formation of centers and the incorporation of the peripheries in the political development of Western Europe. To such an end, it is necessary, according to Rokkan, to start from six 'givens': first, the heritage of the Roman Empire (in particular, the supremacy of the emperor, the systematization of legal rules in Roman law, the idea of citizenship); second, the role of the Catholic Church as an organization that transcends ethnic and territorial borders and facilitates the communication of elites; third, the Germanic kingdoms and traditions of legislative/judicial assemblies of free heads of families; fourth, the extraordinary revival of trade between the Orient, the Mediterranean and the North Sea after the defeat of the Moslems and the consequent growth of a network of independent cities all over Western Europe from Italy to Flanders and the Baltic; fifth, the development and consolidation of feudal and manorial agrarian structures and the resulting concentration of landed property in important areas of the West; sixth and finally, the emergence of literatures in vernacular languages and the gradual decline of Latin as the dominant medium of cross-ethnic communication, particularly after the invention of printing. On this foundation, Rokkan outlines his conceptual geo-political map of Europe and his sequence of phases of development that are meant to explain the strikingly different configurations of various European countries during the crucial state-formation and nation-building period from around the eleventh to the eighteenth century.

The map is based on two dimensions: a north–south dimension that is mostly cultural-religious and ethnic-linguistic and that is important in nation-building; and an east–west dimension that is mainly economic and significant for state formation. More precisely, the first axis measures the geo-political distance northward from Rome, 'the fountainhead of the old Empire, the focus of Western

Christendom after the Schism of 1054, and the symbolic center for the effort of legal unification through the revival of Roman Law' (Rokkan, in Flora, 1999: 150). Nation-building is more difficult the closer the proximity to Rome, because resistance is greater from the Catholic Church to cultural and national identities and resistance is greater from elites to the establishment of national languages (through Latin) and national legal systems (through Roman law).

The second axis – east–west – is defined instead based on the geopolitical distance westwards or eastwards from the central belt of trade route cities (with their commercial and monetary function) from Northern Italy to the areas once controlled by the Hanseatic League. Between the sixteenth and the eighteenth centuries there was a continuous strengthening of single dominant centers within territories to the west (London, Paris, Madrid) and the east (Vienna, Munich, Berlin, Stockholm) of the medieval trade-route belt, which controlled larger peripheries and could build great military-administrative strength. The greater the distance, the greater the dominance of the capital city and its role in state formation and nation-building.

The decisive thrust towards this formation thus occurred first in the outer regions of the old Roman Empire in territories with a dominant urban center and only much later in the internal zones, while for centuries cities in the middle zone, from the Mediterranean to the North Sea and the Baltic were strong enough to thwart any attempt to establish borders of a unified military administration. Hence the 'great paradox of European development', namely, that the strongest and most durable systems emerged at the periphery of the old Empire, whereas the heartlands, and the Italian and German territories remained fragmented and dispersed until the nineteenth century. The typical sequence in peripheral nation-states was as follows: gradual expansion of an ethnic center, rapid imperial expansion, interior consolidation of a more homogeneous territory. While in the West, however, the capital fostered – as a center propelling commerce and the monetary economy – the development of the bourgeoisie who become a precious ally to the sovereign in state formation, in the East, the extension and the much greater power of large landed estates forced the monarchs, in their territorial consolidation effort, to ally themselves with the landed aristocracy who exploited servile work. The vertical section, including Italian and German states and cities, had a delayed state development, even more delayed in Catholic areas.

The geo-political map of Europe aims to explain the strikingly different routes taken by various European countries in the historical moment in which, starting from the late eighteenth century, the double revolution – industrial and politico-national – launched large waves of political mobilization, culminating in mass democracies.

Rokkan also compares the fundamental differences between Western European and post-colonial countries, applying the four 'master variables' of the conceptual map of Europe drawn from the uniqueness of the European experience two of these are cultural variables (independence/dependence of the Church and distinctiveness/unification of a territorial language), and two are economic variables (independence/dependence of the city network and level of concentration of the rural economy), and reworking the sequence of critical thresholds of political development (which we illustrated in the second chapter) before and after the start of mass democratization.

In comparing the unique and unrepeatable experience of state formation and nation-building in European countries with that of non-Western post-colonial countries, a fundamental difference emerges: most political systems of Latin America, Asia and Africa had to face a large number of challenges and crises of nation-state building in a very short time. Contrary to the oldest Western European countries nation-states that were built slowly and where the challenges of modernization got out of phase with each other, most countries which became sovereign states after the collapse of colonial empires had to face at the same time problems of cultural identity, political participation, and economic inequality. Unlike Western nation-states, post-colonial countries did not therefore have the chance to resolve some difficult problems in state formation and nation building before having to face the difficult trial of mass politics and social cohesion.

As is even recognized by harsh critics of generalizing models of modernization such as Tilly, we owe to Rokkan the most promising and interesting proposals in comparative studies of political development. His creative imagination in building theoretical models and interpretive categories makes him one of the most stimulating social scientists of the contemporary period. However, Rokkan's theory, centered on the continuity and long time periods of the various routes to modernization, is not able to interpret as convincingly the discontinuities and the breaks, in particular, those represented by the 'Thirty Years War' of the twentieth century, i.e. the period from 1914 to 1945, when totalitarian regimes were established, the big economic crisis began, and the two world conflicts broke out.

The theory of *dependencia*

If historical sociology and comparative studies of political development have made innovations in the theory of modernization by reclaiming the variety and complexity of actual routes, then it was studies of the economics of development and the neo-Marxist *dependencia* and world-system approaches that brought back the international perspective, which had been at the center of theories of imperialism in the first two decades of the 1900s. Already in 1950, when the evolutionary and functionalist theory of modernization was dawning, economists gathered around Prebish of the Economic Commission on Latin America (ECLA) of the UN Department of Social and Economic Affairs (Prebish, 1950) pointed out that the underdevelopment of Latin America was not primarily imputable to internal factors, but to the fact that these countries were an integral part of the world economy, organized into a core and a periphery. Once the relevance of the international dimension was established, these scholars criticized, however, the prevalent theory of international exchange outlined within a neo-classical paradigm.

Neo-classical economic theory argues that the terms of trade are favorable to peripheral countries in so far as the growing use of technology in central countries reduces prices of industrial products, compared to agricultural products and raw materials exported by developing countries. In reality, the opposite occurs, by virtue of the action of both oligopolistic enterprises and unions in industrialized countries in maintaining artificially high prices on industrial products. In peripheral countries, the manufactured goods market expands, moreover, at a more elevated rate than the foodstuffs market and than the amount of income required by the more affluent classes to purchase expensive imported goods. For the ECLA economists, the problem is rooted in the conflict between domestic capitalism and international capitalism. This can be successfully handled by a strong state role and an *imports substitution* strategy, by way of imposing elevated duties on imported goods that can be locally produced (Furtado, 1970). In the same period, Baran (1957) – revisiting and reviving the theories of imperialism by Hobson, Lenin, Bucharin and Luxemburg – asserts that the underdevelopment of a large part of the world is dialectically linked to the development of capitalist countries and, in the final analysis, is caused by it. Far from fostering economic growth, the entrance of underdeveloped countries in the world market fuels, as a consequence, their own underdevelopment.

The theory of *dependencia* – exposed by sociologists like Cardoso and Faletto (1971) and Frank (1967a, 1967b), economists such as Dos Santos (1970), or political scientists like O'Donnell (1972) – develops the internationalist perspective concentrating on the modality of the process of incomplete accumulation of capital in dependent countries. Lacking independent technologies and therefore being forced to import them from abroad, dependent capitalism is crippled because it lacks a fully developed capital goods sector. Local capital is not able to complete its cycle of accumulation, expansion and self-realization, because it depends on a dynamic complement outside itself. In other words, it must enter the circuit of international capitalism in a subordinate position.

The negative consequences for the possibility of autonomous development as well as for democratic institutions in dependent countries are represented, first of all, by an *échange inégal* (Emmanuel, 1969; Amin, 1976) between the prices of raw materials and agricultural products exported by dependent countries and the prices of industrial goods imported from the metropolises. Second, governments and national ventures of dependent countries become more and more indebted to foreign banks. Third, dependent capitalism is particularly vulnerable to the cyclical phases of the international economic system. Furthermore, the indigenous productive system progressively breaks up and the conflict between a weak national bourgeoisie and capitalist sectors connected to international capital (particularly the commercial bourgeoisie and big land owners) intensifies. Finally, the dominant classes of dependent countries frequently resort to authoritarian political solutions, often with the help of core countries who are committed to maintaining the status quo.

If, on the one hand, these interpretations have the merit of highlighting international conditions ignored by many modernization theorists, on the other, in most cases they make the opposite mistake of making underdevelopment exclusively dependent upon exogenous constraints and seeing only as negative the outside influence of developed countries (defined as neo-colonial and neo-imperialist), to the point of predicting the impossibility of economic development of such countries. Therefore, they are not able to explain the recent, impetuous economic growth of countries like the four 'Asian Tigers', contemporary China's vast processes of industrialization, modernization and opening up to the market economy, and the economic and social transformations of several Latin American countries.

In reality, some dependency theorists such as Cardoso (1980) offer more balanced and complex analyses of the interaction between endogenous factors and exogenous conditionings of underdevelopment. Even though underlining the common subordination to the global dynamic of capitalism, they do show the ability to detect specificities and differences among various dependent countries. They do so not only in light of the time periods and sequences of dependent countries' incorporation into the international economy and of how they are differently equipped with natural resources, but also in light of conflicts between groups with national interests and groups connected to foreign capital, various conflicting ideologies, diverse institutional arrangements and different governmental strategies.

The world-system theory

The most ambitious attempt to place the analysis of underdevelopment within the general framework of the world economy is the *world-system theory* of Wallerstein (1974–89, 1979) and his collaborators. This interpretation is premised on Marxist thought and that of the Marxist theorists of imperialism, on the one hand, and the historical studies of Braudel on the Mediterranean as an integrated economic-political system, on the other.

The key concept of Wallerstein's theory is that of a *world-system*, understood as an entity capable of developing itself independently of both external events as well as social processes and relations occurring within the societies or states that make it up. The self-sufficiency of such an entity is attributed to the extended division of labor that is achieved among the component units. The world-system and the multiplicity of its societies and cultures are considered all together by their members as phenomenological constituents of the world. Wallerstein identifies three types of world-systems. The third type – *world socialism* (in which both capitalism as well as nation-states are replaced by a single economic system that integrates a multiplicity of cultures) – remains a utopian construct. The other two types, the *world empire* and the *world economy*, correspond instead to different actual historical stages, together with the initial historical phase of mini-systems of relatively small dimensions that are culturally univocal and based on a self-sufficient division of labor (first, hunting and gathering, and then sedentary agriculture).

In the type of *world empire* corresponding to historical experiences such as those of ancient Egypt, ancient China, the Roman Empire, Mogul India, feudal Russia, and the Ottoman empire, a multiplicity of socio-cultural elements are incorporated into a broader entity through wars of conquest and unification under the dominion of a single government. Such empires are founded on agriculture and ensure economic coordination by means of politico-military dominion, a centralized administration and rigid methods of conscription and taxation. The principal causes of their decline and fall are administrative difficulties with territories so vast as to generate bureaucratic hypertrophy.

The second type of world-system is the *world economy* in which a multiplicity of politico-cultural entities (nation-states) is integrated by a common economy. This type of world-system emerges at the end of the fifteenth century and the beginning of the sixteenth century, with the rise of capitalism as dominant economic system. The market progressively replaces the state as fundamental institution of regulation and coordination. The European world economy that is established in these centuries 'was not an empire yet it was as spacious as a grand empire and shared some features with it. But it was different, and new. It was a kind of social system the world has not really known before and is the distinctive feature of the modern world-system' (1974: 15). It was an economic but not a political entity, unlike empires, city–states and nation-states, but it included within itself empires, city–states and nation-states:

> It is a 'world' system, not because it encompasses the whole world, but because it is larger than any juridically-defined political unit. And it is a 'world-*economy*' because the basic linkage between the parts of the system is economic, although this was reinforced to some extent by cultural links and eventually by political arrangements and even confederal structures. (1974: 15)

Similar to classic theories of imperialism and unlike some interpretations of dependency such as those of Frank (1967a, 1967b) and Amin (1976), Wallerstein considers states as central actors in the world-system theory, but mostly insofar as they are competitive units in the world market. They carry out essential functions, such as guaranteeing a favorable context for economic activity and free enterprise and seeking the most advantageous terms of trade, first of all through the control of workers' demands.

The fundamental mechanism of the functioning of a capitalist system is the world market in which the owners of the factors of production (whether individuals, corporations or states) compete to maximize profits. It is exactly this competition among sovereign nation-states that maintains the world economy. If, in fact, there were a single political entity, competition would end and the capitalist system would collapse. One can observe that, also thanks to such competition, the capitalist economy has shown an extraordinary potential for duration and growth through complex cycles of expansion and decline. In fact, before the modern era, world economies were highly unstable structures, which tended either to consolidate into empires or to collapse. 'It is the peculiarity of the modern world-system that a world-economy has survived for 500 years and yet has not come to be transformed into a world empire – a peculiarity that is the secret of its strength' (Wallerstein, 1974: 348).

The structure of the world economy is based on an international division of labor that differentiates various countries, hierarchizing them into a *core*, a *periphery* and a *semi-periphery*. The core, originally made up of a small group of European countries strongly committed to international trade, spread out after the Industrial Revolution to include all industrialized countries. They are rich countries, with capital-intensive industrial and service sector production, low percentages of people employed in agriculture, and strong state institutions integrated in a national culture. They progressively have absorbed peripheral and semi-peripheral areas. Inside the core, one country may perform a hegemonic role (like Great Britain in the nineteenth century or the United States after the Second World War) or there could be a more balanced and cooperative situation (as in the present co-leadership among the United States, Japan and the European Union).

Historically, the role of the *periphery* was that of providing raw materials and agricultural products not processed by the center. They were forced by central countries to enter the capitalist world system, but they remained at the margins, both in terms of power and in terms of shared benefits. In peripheral countries, the profits derived from production and other financial resources are drained by the center, so that capital accumulation sufficient for modernization is impossible. These countries depend economically on the center, have weak state structures, and cultures 'invaded' from the outside. The late twentieth-century examples include the 'developing' countries of Asia and Africa.

Semi-peripheral societies share characteristics of both the center and the periphery (for example, high industrialization levels as well as vast marginalized social strata), and they occupy intermediate positions in the various dimensions of the center–periphery continuum. For instance, their state structures are only moderately effective; their industrial production tends to be low-tech and single-product. They can be emerging peripheral countries or central ones in decline. Semi-peripheral societies carry out a very important function in that they energize the system (which, even though a substantially stable system, involves ascending and descending mobility of countries and regions of the world) and prevent a conflictual polarization between center and periphery. Contemporary examples include oil-producing countries, the 'young dragon' societies of South-East Asia, South Africa, and some Latin American countries such as Brazil. The semi-peripheries enjoy greater autonomy than peripheral countries, yet they also depend on the center, with whom they are often allied and from whom they ask military protection. Soviet bloc countries have always remained ambiguous in Wallerstein's scheme. But with the fall of the USSR, it seems a dispersion has occurred in all three societal categories (center, periphery and semi-periphery).

Wallerstein's study is a wide-ranging and powerful attempt to interpret the dynamics of the world conceived as a single system; it provides many valuable insights for the analysis of modernization and modernity (although Wallerstein would not accept such terms); it is one of the few paradigms in social sciences which havs not been 'taken by surprise' by the acceleration and deepening of the processes of globalization.

The world-system theory, however, has been criticized, like the dependency theory, on account of its unilateral negative connotation of international influences and due to the excessive emphasis placed on economic aspects and exogenous factors. The institutional mechanisms of integration considered by the world-system are in fact exclusively economic. It is therefore difficult satisfactorily to account for such phenomena as the rise of the nation-state and the Westphalian system of nation-states, and to acknowledge the role played by political power in explaining the origins and spread of capitalism. The distinction between core, periphery and semi-periphery based upon economic criteria does not allow us to understand political or military patterns of power distribution and concentration, which do not exactly correspond to the international economic division of labor. The analysis of the struggles for hegemony among the core countries resembles the studies of the realist school in international relations, but it differs from them because of the importance given to economic rather than political variables.

The main critique, however, is due to the scant attention paid by world-system theory to the social and cultural contexts of interacting countries, both core and peripheral. The absolute priority assigned to external variables entails a certain difficulty in connecting the international division of labor with the class structures of core societies, although it is suggested that the ability of core states to remain at the center depends on their capacity, on the one hand, to maintain capital accumulation in the face of working-class claims for redistribution and, on the other, to 'sell' Western domination as the universalizing process of modernization to the people of subjected countries. The concentration of the analysis on the world-system level leads, in particular, to the neglect of the ways in which various societies react and process imported cultural elements. Although this critique does not apply to all of Wallerstein's writings and to all followers of the world-system approach (e.g. Bornschier, 1980, Chase-Dunn and Hall, 1997, or Arrighi and Silver, 1999), on the whole, the emphasis on the single capitalist world economy does not make room for the existence of multiple modernities within a global world which is economically and culturally interconnected in various ways, but not rigidly hierarchical.

Recent studies on non-European countries: the new political economy and the comparative analysis of cultures

Historical sociology, political development, dependency and world system approaches – in addition to some aspects of the classic study of modernization – have influenced in various ways recent studies on change processes in backward and developing countries which in the past few decades have placed more stress on the growing diversity of national experiences and on plural modernities. In fact, contrasted with countries such as most of those on the African continent that have not made substantial steps forward on the road to overcoming under-development, are countries of east and central Asia and several in Latin America that have recorded high rates of social and economic transformation.

It is clear that recent studies are aware of the results and limitations of preceding theories and have taken into account, in particular, the following:

1. the comparative-historical dimension and the connected recognition of a plurality of routes toward and through modernity (by analyzing state–market relations as well as diverse cultural traditions and forms of civilization);
2. the influence of exogenous variables within the international context in the age of economic globalization, avoiding, however, the conceptual reductionism and ideological unilinearity of the dependency and world-system theories.

The most interesting studies of late are studies belonging to the strain that Evans and Stephans (1994) define as new *political economy*; the comparative analysis of the diversity of cultures (Dore, 1987; Hamilton and Biggart, 1988); and Eisenstadt's studies (1992b) that more directly link up again with the classic theory of modernization.

Central to *political economy* studies is the role of the state in modernization, as was the case with scholars of diverse orientations, like Gerschenkron, Bendix, Rostow, Prebish, and many others. They examine, in particular, the functions performed by the state in starting and sustaining the industrialization process and in guaranteeing competitiveness of the country-system in the international market (Evans et al., 1985; Clapham, 1985; Harris, 1986).

The differences in the results obtained from the various countries (Asian, Latin American and African) are traced back to different efficacies of state intervention and different strategic abilities (Deyo, 1987; Gereffi and Wyman, 1990). Efficacy and strategic ability depend in turn on two fundamental requisites:

1. an administrative structure and an efficient bureaucratic class capable of negotiating with outside interests (using international ties as opportunities rather than as constraints) and controlling indigenous interest groups;
2. a political leadership favorable to economic development, legitimized by the cultural traditions of the country and sufficiently autonomous from the main social classes and interest groups.

From comparative studies of Asian countries (even with different politico-ideological orientations) such as China, South Korea, Taiwan, Singapore, Malaysia, Thailand, Indonesia, one can envisage a model of *East Asian modernization*. This model combines the entrance into the international market and the acceptance of the rules of free trade with state authoritarian structures that seek to maintain state control of key economic sectors and to adopt policies to control the most disruptive social consequences and criticisms of industrialization, such as unchecked demographic growth, over-urbanization, the weakening of deference, increasing cultural pluralism, and so on. If, and how much, the intensification of the modernization process and the integration into the world market are compatible with the preservation of authoritarian political regimes and non-democratic ideologies, forms one of the most interesting theoretical and political questions of the coming years.

An emblematic example of the East Asian modernization model is the case of China, in which the role of the state is quite substantial in pursuing a strategy of progressive liberalization and integration in the world market; a state that tries to conserve the politico-administrative structures and the ideological orientations of the authoritarian political regime and that nevertheless expands, cautiously but progressively, the individual's freedom of choice. The acute problems and the dramatic choices of Chinese modernization are heightened by the very size of the country, the radical state of its political transformation, and the complexity of its society. For this reason, state policies to control the change processes were also implemented with extreme firmness, often bringing about surprising results, yet stirring up bitter controversies and eliciting high social and ecological costs (as in the family planning policy that strongly influenced families to have only one child and the forced transfer of villages and 1,200,000 people so that the large dam could be built on the Yangtze).

The other vein of research on Western modernization of particular interest is the *comparative analysis of cultures*. Its was also born out of the need to interpret the success of modernization in countries like Japan and recently industrialized Asian countries where several characteristics considered 'necessary preconditions' (following the Western experience) were absent. These studies – starting from the classic study by Dore (1973) comparing an English and Japanese factory – concentrate on specific characteristics of Asian civilization (either religious such as Confucianism, Hinduism and Buddhism, or politico-ideological such as nationalism and communism, or social such as local community institutions) to examine the influence they exercise on forms of enterprise and labor organization, authority relations and collaboration, models of legitimation of economic and political power (Hamilton, 1994). The case of India, the other Asian giant, is particularly interesting in this respect, since the interplay between exogenous and domestic factors, democracy and market, local and national identities is extremely complex and it provides a powerful antidote against any kind of one-sidedness and over-simplification in the study of modernity (Chandra, 1981; Beteille, 1991; Mahajan, 1995).

Reviewing this line of studies, one draws three conclusions of particular relevance. The first is that some characteristics of traditional society (such as the importance attributed to the integration of the individual into the group and the robustness of ties of personal, familial and community belonging and their consequent obligations) seem to support development rather than hinder it. Even though involving little social differentiation and hampering the establishment of individual autonomy, these characteristics turned out to be useful resources to modernization, contrary to what many advocates of the traditional–modern dichotomy predicted. The second conclusion is that there are 'multiple modernities', i.e. different routes to modernization, determined both by native social characteristics and specific cultural traditions as well as by the modalities of its encounter with Western modernization and its response to the consequent challenges. The third conclusion is that, contrary to what neo-Marxist approaches argue, international relations can be in a certain measure managed and negotiated by modernizing elites of peripheral countries. In addition, international relations can be used as opportunities for development and redefinition of the country's position in the international division of labor, not simply as constraints that condemn it to a fate of dependency and underdevelopment. We will elaborate on these conclusions in the final chapter.

Shmuel Eisenstadt's critical revision

The accent placed on forms of culture introduces Eisenstadt into the analysis, whom we discuss at the end because he makes the most interesting attempt at critical revision of the classic theory of modernization. For Eisenstadt, 'modernization or modernity is one specific type of civilization that originated in Europe and spread throughout the world, encompassing – especially after the Second World War – almost all of it' (1992a: 423). Not unlike the major religions and great empires of the past, but with more force because its influence is more rapid and more pervasive and because it combines economic, political and ideological aspects, this civilization challenges institutional and symbolic conditions of the societies that become incorporated within it, provoking a large variety of reactions and responses and opening new options and new possibilities. The many modern or modernizing countries that have risen from these responses and new options have significant common characteristics, but also marked differences. Common characteristics and differences are the result of the selective incorporation and transformation of main symbolic requisites and institutional forms, both from the original Western modern culture and from their own culture.

The cultural orientations and the organizational structures of modern Western civilization (rational and secularized culture, efficient and competitive economy, nation-state and pluralistic civil society) are spread by a series of social, political and cultural movements that, unlike revolt movements in the past, showed a strong tendency to combine protest and institutional construction. While, nevertheless, in Western Europe, modernization came about in large part through endogenous causes and through the potential for transformation of several indigenous groups, in the rest of the world the principal causes of the process were responses to the external challenges and stimuli produced by various international systems created by Western modernization.

The type of response and therefore the specific form of modernization vary from one context to the next according to a series of factors:

1. The point of entry of the society in question in the new international systems and the specific institutional aspects that are undermined by this entry; the available options and the continual dynamic begun by these processes.
2. The existing technologies and economic formations in this society.
3. The fundamental cultural preconditions of this society, their conceptions of the world and social order, hierarchy and equality, and the configuration of the principal elites that articulate these conceptions and control their application in social relations.
4. The traditional indigenous responses to situations of change (whether of adaptive, reformist or revolutionary type); the potential for innovation of the different elites and their relationship with the orthodoxies and heterodoxies; and the level of autonomy and social rootedness of religious institutions.

The continual interaction among these factors and processes crystallizes the particular cultural reinterpretations of modernity and indigenous tradition, and develops the various meanings, programs and institutions of modernization and the specific policies of economic development.

As in all cases of historical change, the crucial element in the crystallization of new symbolic and institutional forms is represented by old and new elites, by their relations with the principal social groups, by the visions they advocate, and by relations of coalition they are able to build with both internal and external actors. The analysis of the role of elites (which we discussed at the end of the second chapter) was the constant in Eisenstadt's long-term study of modernization, which in the most recent phase, is increasingly framed in a Weberian-inspired comparative study of civilizations.

Eisenstadt's contribution is also not exempt from criticism. It seems to be quite sensitive to the plurality of routes to and through modernity in relation to the diverse responses to modernization's challenges, yet it sometimes gives the impression of considering modern Western society as univocal, and of neglecting the diversity of industrial societies and forms of capitalism, which implies the existence of 'alternative societies of reference' and 'epicenters of modernity in movement' (Tiryakian, 1985). And it also does not adequately investigate the 'borders' of the various state entities within the international system. However, in his more recent writings Eisenstadt is more aware of modernization as a multiple process from the start. In explaining the idea of 'multiple modernities', he states that '[it] presumes that the best way understand the contemporary world – indeed to explain the history of modernity – is to see it as a story of continual constitution and reconstitution of a multiplicity of cultural programs' (2000: 2). His work demonstrates that the theory of modernization is still alive and vital today.

Synthesis

As we have shown in the previous pages, good arguments exist both in favor and in opposition to the various theories of modernization and their critiques. We will now extract from the different theories examined the six theoretically most significant elements in order to construct a synthetic approach to the study of modernization.

First of all, the notion must be accepted that a single model of modernization (that must be emulated by developing societies) does not exist. Instead, there is a *plurality of different routes to and through modernity*, so that we can more properly speak of *multiple modernities*. The fundamental elements of modern Western society became, with industrialization and globalization, constituent traits of a world civilization. But various societies interpret and metabolize these 'universal' elements in very different forms. This is due not only to the diverse historical legacies existing at the start of the transition to modernity, but also to the interactions and interdependent relationships among groups of countries that belong to different waves of modernization.

In the first instance, it should be pointed out that the formation process of modern society in Western countries is substantially different from the modernization of Third World societies. Different paths to modernization exist even among countries belonging to the same wave or the same region of the world. Western countries themselves manifest different routes, depending on whether they were part of the first modernization like England and France, or the second like Germany and Italy (who also went through totalitarian and authoritarian experiences of modernization); depending on whether it has to do with European countries or 'new worlds' (beginning with the United States) created by European migrations in the two Americas and Australia; depending on the presence or lack of historical experience of communism in countries of what was the Second World, such as communist Russia, the other ex-Soviet republics and Eastern European countries.

The so-called Third World is also profoundly differentiated within itself, among countries that had a colonial past, in which modernization was imported and imposed by colonial forces, and countries threatened by the new Western imperial powers. For the first group of countries, it is necessary to ascertain what were the various modalities of the decolonization process (war of independence, revolutionary struggle, peaceful and consensual transfer of power); what was the level of differentiation among the various activities, the various elites and the various social groups before the start of modernization; whether nuclei of market economy and administration existed with the development of administrative and entrepreneurial skills. For the second group of countries – those threatened by imperial powers of the West – it is best to concentrate on the diverse modalities in which modernizing elites selectively imported economic and political institutions and cultural attitudes from the more developed societies, effecting a top-down modernization (the comparison of Japan and China is enlightening in this regard). These different routes are not only historical trajectories but they can also be considered ideal types that co-exist within a single historical experience (as the case of Russia shows: first, czarist, then, Soviet, and now in transition towards democracy). The result of all these different historical and conceptual ideal types paths are *multiple modernities*.

Second, the modernization process is a *global process* and modernity a *global condition* in a dual sense, in the sense of world-wide, and in the sense of affecting all aspects of social life. In the first sense, modernization progressively concerns the whole world, connecting distant and different states, regions and communities in a web of systematic interdependence and interconnectedness, within a compressed period of time and space (we will develop the relation between modernization and globalization in the next chapter).

In studying real cases of modernization one must, therefore, attribute necessary importance to exogenous variables. The international and global dimension is certainly quite important, but it requires an accurate analysis that analytically defines the exact nature of the type, the quality and the intensity of international and global influences. This information can be drawn from the role performed by a given country or a given region in the international capitalist division of labor, from the nature and magnitude of the import and export of capital, goods and services, from the migrations of the labor force, from the role played in integrated productive processes (as in the case in which a transnational enterprise decentralizes phases of production), from the extension of global networks. Or this analytical information about international influences could be drawn from the position of the nation-state in the world geo-political balance (with consequences regarding border security, adherence to military alliances, the existence of threats of war, etc.), or yet still from cultural influences (scientific and technological knowledge, political ideologies, consumption patterns, modernizing values and attitudes, socio-political doctrines that support this or that type of modernization).

The analysis must then specify how such influences impact on economic and political institutions and indigenous cultures; through what mechanisms they work (the market, mass media, norms and coercive tools, opinion leaders who act as 'gate-keepers' between different cultures); and what reactions they provoke in the local elites, in collective movements and single individuals who act in the political arena, in the market and in other environments of the civil society. Recognizing the importance of interdependences should not, however, cause one to neglect endogenous factors – in particular, the diverse institutional and cultural responses to common influences and challenges. In this regard, Ogburn's classic distinction between material culture (rapidly and easily spread) and immaterial culture (much more tied to various specific contexts and reactive to the first) is still valid.

Fitting into this perspective are the studies following the lead of Karl Polanyi's ideas, which analyze the different institutional varieties of contemporary capitalism, such as those that distinguish between Anglo-Saxon, German and Japanese capitalism (Albert, 1991; Berger and Dore, 1996; Kitschelt et al., 1999) and those that study the various modalities of cultural and institutional embeddedness of actual relations of production (Hollingsworth and Boyer, 1997).

Third, modernization is also a global process in the sense that it involves all aspects of social life. One must avoid an excessive emphasis on only one type of factor, such as economic or cultural. This is linked to the previous point in that some aspects are more rapidly and univocally transferable (technology, the market), while others express specificities of different cultures. It also means avoiding univocal formulas that, for example, extol the role of the state or, on the other hand, the complete adhesion to free trade and private initiative.

These various aspects have different time periods, speeds and sequences, not necessarily synchronized. Dahrendorf (1990) called attention to the dilemma of the three clocks of post-Soviet societies, in which six months can be sufficient to pass a constitutional reform, six years might not be enough to implement economic reforms, while the formation and diffusion of values, attitudes and lifestyles in a modern civil society can take generations.

Fourth, once the fundamental role of exogenous variables within the concept of modernization as global process has been recognized, it is necessary and completely justified to focus on a more limited unit of analysis such as the *nation-state*. Notwithstanding the decline of its importance as an independent actor in the global economy, it continues to be the basic unit of socio-political analysis, the privileged context within which the modernization process is studied. Such a process seems like an obstacle course in which neither the route, nor the duration, nor the outcome is known. And it is in the analysis of this course that the theory of modernization in its most refined and complex versions continues to offer very interesting suggestions.

It is necessary to begin with the recognition of the structural characteristics of the society studied, not by identifying them in a univocal ideal type of 'traditional society' that flattens the specificity and ignores external influences, but by identifying the society's genetic code. Useful in this regard is the method of prerequisites and obstacles to modernization, such as religious beliefs and their relations with economic ethics, the availability of a wage-earning workforce for production, craftsman and commercial skills and utilizable financial resources in industrial production, and a combination of differentiated political institutions that are both effective and legitimate. Even though it is best to avoid the error of defining them in the light of a univocal model of modernization, it is useful to try to determine which aspects of social, cultural and institutional relations of the country may create either favorable conditions or obstacles to this or that type of modernization.

It should be pointed out that aspects of the indigenous tradition of a country (concerning, for example, the formation of a collective identity and trust relations between members of a community) can perform a favorable role in modernization, while, on the other hand, the premature introduction of modern elements (for example, mass education before forming a substantial demand for an intellectual labor force) can give rise to serious problems, standstills and trend inversions. The success of a modernization process depends in large measure on the ability of those who govern the process to select which elements of the indigenous tradition are to be conserved and transformed and which are to be cleared away.

Fifth, it is then a matter of examining the time periods and sequences of modernization processes triggered by endogenous factors as well as international factors, with the contradictions and conflicts that provoke (at various rates of change) the types of crises and attempts at resolution. Here the *critical threshold* method of political development and social modernization proves to be particularly promising, since it makes it possible to deal with fundamental social problems of change and social order, of differentiation and integration, in short, to respond to the basic questions: what holds a society together in the course of processes of profound and traumatic transformation such as those of the transition to modernity? What determines gradual and peaceful change processes or revolutionary breaks? Here again we must adopt a multiple modernities approach, avoiding reifying a single sequence of stages or crises.

Finally, at this point can be inserted the analysis of actors who act with specific resources and cognitive maps and within the structural and cultural constraints that we have specified before. It is a matter of analyzing in particular the role of individual and collective actors who act as *entrepreneurs of modernization* and the actors who instead fight to conserve traditional arrangements, with their strategies, identities and cognitive maps: charismatic leaders, modernizing elites, spontaneous collective movements, but also the daily behaviors of people influenced by the large processes of industrialization, urbanization and social mobility and by the demonstration effect of the prosperity and freedom of developed countries and the consequent expectations.

As we will argue in the final chapter, particular importance is assigned to the study of the *role of the state* and its relations with individual and collective actors, whether indigenous or foreign, by analyzing factors and conditions that affect the efficacy of the state intervention (such as the level of efficiency, honesty and competence of the bureaucracy and its ability to interact with the various stakeholders, and the modernizing strategies of the leadership and the dominant political coalition and their levels of autonomy from sectional interests).

A research issue of equal importance in the study of actors is the analysis of cultural orientations, *ideologies*, and *conceptions of modernization* of the different political, economic and intellectual elites (such as nationalism, free-market ideology, revolutionary Marxism, authoritarian paternalism, technocracy, populism) and their troubled relationship with the prevailing conceptions and ideological climate in what were considered 'model societies'.

The collapse of the Soviet Union and the ideological crisis of Marxism strengthened the option of market economy and, even though in a much less firm way, representative democracy. But this happened in a historical phase in which the conception of a triumphant modernity was soon replaced in the West by a much more disenchanted view – aware not only of the benefits but also the ecological and technological risks of modern society resulting from uncontrolled economic growth. This greater awareness of the mixed blessings of their own modernity in the Western countries combines with the greater awareness of their specificities and particularities in the non-Western societies. This creates objective tensions and conflicts between countries that have just boarded the train of modernization and countries that, having started the journey much earlier, are conscious not only of its advantages but also its risks, but also greater opportunities for cooperation and dialogue on the basis of mutual respect.

Two views of the world after the fall of the USSR – Fukuyama's (1992) 'end of history' and Huntington's (1996) 'clash of civilizations' – although very different and in some ways even opposed in their analyses and predictions, converge on the denial of multiple and continually evolving modernities. Fukuyama proclaims the end of ideological-political conflict, and Huntington portrays conflicting civilizations – first of all, Islam – as unchanging and Western modernity as unique. Both seem to under-write a view of Western modernity as a unique type of civilization which can either reproduce itself in the same way all over the world or clash with all those other 'traditional' cultures that do not want to accept it.

In recent years, however, a renewed debate has developed in the social sciences – and sociology in particular – over the uniqueness of modernity or the existence of multiple modernities, as well as over the real or presumed passing of an era from modernity to something different, and over the costs and benefits of modernity. The next chapter is in fact devoted to the theme of modernity and its future.

4

Modernity and its Future

At the end of the twentieth century, can we still define the societies and cultures in which we live as modern or have we entered into a qualitatively different historical phase? To what extent was the *modern project* achieved and is still to be achieved in the various parts of the world? What are the routes to and through modernization and how many are there? What are the possible future outcomes of modernity? What is the relationship between modernization and globalization?

In this chapter, I will examine these problems with reference to the contemporary sociological debate on the concept of modernity, which has prompted some scholars to consider the present age an expression of *incomplete modernity* or a *radicalization of modernity*, in substantial continuity with the previous phases, and others to consider it radically different and *postmodern*. I will seek in such a way to interpret the current trends of the modernization process in developed countries (which, as has been pointed out many times, is not concluded once and for all), bringing together the implications for the countries that are today living through the transition to modernity, since (as has also been emphasized) both groups of countries are part of a single transformation process in an increasingly interdependent world. The concluding chapter will then specifically analyze the relationship between globalization and modernity.

Revisiting the concept of modernity: postmodern society

In the course of the 1980s, some social scientists became convinced that modern societies and cultures that formed in the last two centuries were taking on a radically different physiognomy that, 'faux de mieux', they define as postmodern. The concept was born almost contemporaneously in the history of North American architecture and in French philosophy.

In the critique of North American architecture, the adjective postmodern defines a new style of never-ending choice that combines many different traditions and shows a firm preference for the popular and vernacular style, symbolized by Las Vegas, with respect to the soul-less high tech functionalism of New York skyscrapers (Jencks, 1977, 1989). According to Jencks:

> The Post-Modern Age is a time of incessant choosing ... no orthodoxy can be accepted without self-consciousness and irony, because all traditions seem to have some validity ... When Everyman becomes a Cosmopolite and Everywoman a Liberated Individual, confusion and anxiety become ruling states of mind and *ersatz* a common form of mass culture. (1989: 7)

Jenks sees this at least partly as a consequence of the information explosion, and the advent of organized knowledge, world communication and cybernetics, and considers it as an irreversible phenomenon that no attempt to impose a fundamentalist religion or a Modernist orthodoxy could stop. Postmodernism is actually both the continuation of Modernism and its transcendence.

In the French philosophy of Lyotard (1988), the concept of the postmodern is, instead, tied to the idea of the end of the *grand narratives* – the great historical-philosophical schemes of progress, of totalizing meta-languages and meta-theories – like Marxism and psychoanalysis, which claim to discover and reveal universal and eternal truths. The abandonment of grand narratives opens the way to the *petits récits* (little narratives); a plurality of power discourses and linguistic games are established, which correspond to the fragmentariness of social relations in the present age.

Postmodernism quickly sparked the interest of numerous sociologists (in addition to several geographers and anthropologists), such as Campbell (1987), Lipovetsky (1987), Bauman (1989, 1992), Baudrillard (1981, 1996), Harvey (1989), Turner (1990), Lash (1990), Featherstone (1991), Jameson (1991), Smart (1992), Crook et al., (1992), Boisvert (1997), and Inglehart (1997). 'Post-modern' signifies a new type of social organization and individual condition and defines, in the most ambitious attempts, a new method of research.

Somewhat distant philosophical roots (generally unrecognized) can be found in Nietzsche's theory and especially in his idea of the deeply chaotic nature of the modern condition and the interpretative impotence of rational thought. Much closer philosophical roots are to be found in Foucault's (1966) study of the archeology of the human sciences, where he criticizes the 'anthropologization' of reality and urges us to analyze not the human subject but rather language, i.e. the discursive practices that construct man. Several classic sociological categories, however, also have great importance, particularly: Weber's ideas on the repressive character of the techno-bureaucratic rationality, which were taken up again and developed by Adorno and Horkheimer (1947) and other sociologists of the Frankfurt School; Durkheim's concept of anomie that denotes situations of rapid and intense social transformation in which laws and moral norms are no longer able to orient and channel individual behaviors; and Simmel's concept of the fragmentary, differentiated and discontinuous character of the experience of the present in modern society.

The closest sociological ideas, however, taken up by advocates of postmodernism are (in addition to McLuhan's theory of mass media's pervasiveness in the global village, 1964 and 1967), those expressed in the 1970s by theorists of the 'end of ideologies' and post-industrialism such as Touraine (1974) and Bell (1974, 1976). The postmodernists take up many of these ideas, radicalizing them and changing their meaning. Where post-industrialists speak about the unending growth of knowledge applied to social progress, postmodernists see an arbitrary variety of interventionist theories evaluated only on the basis of their efficacy. Where the former identify enlightened elites at the apex of an organized society in which the various social groups criticize and legitimize, the latter see an accumulation of decisions, uncontrollable by an amorphous and hyperconformist mass, in a sea of simulation.

In postmodern interpretations, various trends of the economy and contemporary society (such as flexible specialization and post-Fordist labor organization, the computerization and diffusion of mass media in the *global village*, the globalization of the markets and the decline of the nation-state), become compressed and integrated into an image of postmodern society that is contrasted with an image of modern society.

Many advocates of postmodernism expose themselves to the same kind of criticism directed at the classic theory of modernization: they hypothesize two models of society and the human condition, neglecting the manifold internal and intermediate variations, the overlapping, the continuity and the contiguity between the two types, placing the modern/postmodern concept pair where the traditional/modern pair once stood. The principal difference is that, while the first theorists of modernization generally situate their analysis on a macro-sociological level examining the structural and cultural characteristics of society, the postmodernists (by virtue of their rejection of systematic theorizations) tend to start from a micro-sociological level of the condition of the individual and his or her perception of reality.

Other scholars close to postmodernism like Delanty, however, do not pretend to outline modernity and postmodernity as quite opposite ideal types, but, on the contrary, stress the continuity and the close link between modernity and postmodernity. The central argument of Delanty's book is that 'postmodernity is deeply rooted in the culture of modernity, just as modernity itself was rooted in the premodern worldview' (2000: 4). He sees the movement from pre-modernity to modernity to postmodernity as a gradual distantiation of subject from object, first in the transformation of knowledge, then in the transformation of politics/power and then in the transformation of the self. New cultural logics emerge in the spaces that are opened up in these cultural shifts from skepticism in knowledge to radicalization of public discourse in politics to reflexivity in the reconstitution of the self around a new responsibility for history and nature.

The most interesting contributions of postmodern social science regard the new concept of time and space, the fragmentation and the discontinuity of experience, the instability of language, the pluralism of identities, accentuated subjectivity, the eclecticism of choosing and the broadening of the potential for choice. Individual identity, they argue, is not unified but fluid and changeable, is sustained by many sources and assumes different forms. The experience of the present is reduced to a series of pure and unrelated presences in time, often exceptionally vivid thanks to television images and the sensationalism that characterizes all aspects of life. At the same time, the postmodern condition expands the range of possible choices; experiments with a plurality of eclectic lifestyles, languages and modalities of social interaction; offers the greatest opportunities for generational, ethnic and gender groups to develop alternative subcultures that establish their specific public identities. This brings liberal thinkers like Rorty (1989) to stress the connection between liberalism and postmodernism since they share a strong privatism, pragmatism and skepticism about the possibility of universal validity and of foundations.

Some scholars, such as Harvey (1989) and Jameson (1991), frame the interpretation of postmodern society in the analysis of capitalism in the era of globalization. Harvey, to whom we owe well-argued contributions, makes an effort to present postmodernity as a general interpretive category yet links it to the development of capitalism. Global postmodern society is not the result of a gradual evolution, but of sudden accelerations that are associated with periodic crises and restructurings of capitalism. In particular, it was the 1970s' crisis (exemplified by the end of the dollar's gold standard and the oil crisis) that accelerated the processes of financial and productive globalization and the international mobility of labor, ushering in a period of rapid changes, fluctuations and uncertainty. In defining globalization, Harvey emphasizes (as we will see later on) the process of spatial-temporal compression, in which time is organized in order to reduce the constraints of space, and vice versa. The acceleration of transportation and communication is associated with the reduction of the life cycles of products and of fashions in influencing ways of thinking and acting and the meanings that are attributed to them. The geographical complexity of the world is reduced daily to a series of TV images. Gastronomic traditions of the world are stocked in the same huge stores in Berlin and Los Angeles.

In a similar vein, Jameson (1991) asserts the idea that postmodernism is the cultural logic of late capitalism. The main features of late capitalism are the new international division of labor of transnational firms, the vertiginous new dynamic in international banking and stock exchanges, new forms of technological inter-relationships between media and computers, gentrification on a new global scale. Contrary to classic Marxist theory, culture is no longer the reflex and concomitant of economic and social relations; culture has a become a product in its own right, the basic determinant of macro-social reality and of psychological reality. And postmodern culture tends to be commercialized and evaluated based on its ability to give pleasure and make money.

Crook, Pakulski and Waters (1992) attempt to systemize the concept slightly differently from Harvey and Jameson. For them, the principal trends of modern society described by classic social theorists – social differentiation (Durkheim), commodification (Marx) and rationalization (Weber) – are still at work, but it is exactly from their intensification that postmodern society emerges. In expanding themselves, the processes of social differentiation, commodification and rationalization tend to cancel out their own effects, instead of mutually reinforcing each other. And once the apex is reached, each one of them transforms into its opposite. For example, de-differentiation springs from hyper-differentiation, de-rationalization emerges from hyper-rationalization, de-commodification evolves from hyper-commodification.

Even though contending that in the contemporary world an inversion of the differentiation process takes place that permeates the different social spheres and erases borders, descriptions of postmodernity are generally not able to do without traditional divisions and therefore distinguish between changes that happen in the culture, in the productive organization, in the political sphere, in the social structure.

The transformations connected to culture occupy a central position. Lash (1990) and Jameson (1991) claim that, while every phase of modern culture involved a growing level of differentiation and autonomization (which culminated in the self-validation of art in the late 1800s' modernist movement), today it implies the opposite – a generalized process of de-differentiation. The various dimensions of the culture (aesthetic, moral, theoretical) become, in fact, always less autonomous of each other.

Art loses its 'aura', in Benjamin's sense, that is, in the sense of the creative originality of the artist devoted to art for art's sake, who produces unique irreproducible cultural objects that, exactly by virtue of their uniqueness, can be commercialized at a monopolistic price. Distinctions between high culture and popular culture disappear. The cultural sphere is no longer separated from the social sphere and, in particular, culture and commerce fuse together and feed on each other. Moreover, distinctions are progressively eroded between author and reader, actor and public, artist and critic. The distinctions between producers and receivers of messages and meanings become problematic – in fact, according to McLuhan's famous definition, the medium becomes the message.

The electronic world and the new media perform a fundamental role in this process. The electronic scene is not, however, celebrated optimistically like cyberspace and virtual reality are by their enthusiasts. Lash observes that in our real and imaginary daily experience, these two worlds melt together, creating chaos, 'flimsiness' and instability in our experience of reality.

Baudrillard (1981, 1996) paints a catastrophic picture in which the individual is no longer 'an actor or dramaturge' but 'a terminal of multiple networks' in a hyper-real world of *simulacra*, or images that are copies for which the originals have been lost (1983). In this world, the individual experiences the absolute proximity and the total instantaneousness of things; there is no place for intimacy and interiority; everything completely dissolves into the information and the communication. The excess of information and simulated reality offered by the media precludes the response of those that receive it. The only possible reaction is the strategy of silence and passivity, which undermines the code of communication and weakens the effects of the media.

Two other components of the postmodern cultural climate are the rediscovery of localism and the reinvention of tradition. It is argued that, also in reaction to the disorienting influence of the media in the culture of postmodernity, individuals rediscover their territorial identities, regional traditions, and attribute a renewed importance to local roots, without, however, being able to remedy the intrinsic perception of the precariousness and fragmentariness of their own experience. According to Delanty, while modernity was essentially post-traditional in that one of its central driving forces was the critique of tradition by secular rationality, or 'the emancipation of human beings from the prejudices of tradition' (1999: 3), 'postmodernity does not involve the rejection of the past by a triumphant present, but is an expression of the creative appropriation of past and present' (2000: 153).

In the economic sphere, it is consumption, no longer production, that occupies a dominant position. Consumption being the central motor of the postmodern society (not mass consumption but the proliferation of consumption connected to eclectic and ephemeral lifestyles), the demand for goods and services is always more fragmented and requires flexible *ad hoc* responses by corporations, it needs a production system articulated in a large number of series and types (each one with a limited number of copies), a flexible organization of labor, and a versatile and just as flexible and decentralized workforce with limited-contract, part-time and seasonal working terms. The systems of production evolve, therefore, from a Fordist–Taylorist large-scale assembly line organization of industry to a flexible organization that finds the most favorable conditions in small businesses. In postmodern society even science and technology's charter is changed. Scientific rationality's grand design – to control nature, assure the continual progress of knowledge, and guarantee science's autonomy from its social and political implications – breaks down.

Furthermore, postmodernity overturns several spatial movements typical of modernity. The concentration of the population in large cities is contrasted with processes of decentralization and dispersion. Many regions of the developed world, on the one hand, de-industrialize exporting phases of production to developing countries; while, on the other hand, they re-industrialize, creating research-based high-tech production sectors in suburban areas often near large universities.

Metropolitan reality is also modified: cities typical of modern culture like Paris or New York are contrasted with cities typical of postmodern culture like Los Angeles, 'a town whose mystery is precisely that it is nothing more than a network of unreal circulation without end, a town of fabulous proportions, but without a sense of space or dimensions' (according to Baudrillard, 1981) or Las Vegas, described by Eco (1987) as 'a completely new phenomenon in city planning, a "message" city entirely made up of signs, not a city like others, which communicate in order to function, but rather a city that functions in order to communicate'.

The changes in culture, in modes of consumption and production, in science and technology's charter, in the configuration of urban and suburban realities, are also expressed in class and rank structures. The hierarchical social stratification articulated in well-defined classes is replaced by a fluid and fragmented structure of ranks, portions of classes and social groups defined on the basis of criteria different from the traditional socio-economic criteria. The two extremes of the social hierarchy become deformed: on one side, the working class tends to divide into marginalized social groups and groups assimilated into the middle class; on the other, the upper class distinguishes itself less and less from the constellation of the middle ranks, and the economic power of the traditional bourgeoisie is eroded by the political power of the 'professional class'. The cultural criteria of differentiation (lifestyles, consumption patterns) intersect with economic and social criteria (income, wealth, occupational role) and are freed from their structural conditionings.

The position of women changes profoundly and gender inequalities are reduced in schools, job market participation, and political representation. All these changes do not make inequalities disappear, but they do bring about a greater fluidity and instability in the mosaic of social ranks and an intensification of the mobility flows.

In the political sphere, postmodern sociology focuses, on the one hand, on changes in the role of the nation-state, and on the other, on micro-politics and new collective movements. The nation-state is, as we have seen, a typical modern institution that embodies in Weberian fashion organizational rationality. Its transformations and, in particular, the development of regulatory functions in both productive processes and in social reproductive processes via the welfare state, offer an example of hyper-organizational rationality. The crisis of the welfare state and, more broadly, the weakening of the nation-state (challenged by the institutions that grow within it as well as by the globalization process that transcends it), show, however, the limits of organizational rationalization and the trend inversion of this process.

In parallel, when analyzing political agency, macro-politics based on the antagonism between the bourgeoisie and the working class become less important, giving way to the micro-politics of power relations in various social contexts – from the manifold local liberation struggles to the linguistic codes of conflicting actors. Traditional collective movements founded on 'general' national and class identities, progressively lose influence while new movements founded on 'partial' identities connected to ethnicity, gender, age and position in the lifecycle become more important. And the once dominant 'Left–Right' axis of political cleavage based on class and religion is increasingly sharing the stage with a new 'postmodern' political dimension, which opposes such values by demand for a less impersonal and more humane society, respect for the environment, greater people empowerment, more openness to changing gender roles and ethnic diversity to fundamentalist religious and nationalist values (Inglehart, 1997).

A critique of postmodern sociology

In contrast to interpretations like Bauman's (1989) maintaining that postmodernity is an aspect of a fully developed and functioning social system that has taken the place of 'classic' modern capitalist society and that needs to be theorized on its own terms, I think that postmodern interpretations do not seem to portray an essentially different and contrasting type of society.

The description of the characteristics of postmodern society, inferable from the postmodern sociology that we have summarized, does not seem in a significant way to diverge from the interpretations of contemporary society (information age, post-Fordist society, disorganized late capitalism), if it were not for the radical nature of certain propositions. Some scholars explicitly state this correspondence, affirming that postmodernism is the culture of post-industrial society (Lash, 1990) or of late capitalism (Jameson, 1991). But most postmodernists negate it, underlining the newness of the postmodern condition – the experience of day-to-day reality, the perception of space, time and causality – which are radically different from those of modernity. I do not think that this is the case.

The idea of fragmentation and chaos has always been second nature to modernity, just like idea of rationality and organization. As Frisby (1985) points out in his study of Simmel, Kracauer and Benjamin, a fundamental trait of the modern condition is a clear experience of time, space and causality as transitory, fluctuating, fortuitous and arbitrary. Some 130 years before postmodern sociology, Baudelaire wrote in his famous essay of 1863, *The Painter of Modern Life*, that modern society has made a radical rupture with the past; and that modernity as the theatre of the 'transient, the fleeting, and the contingent' is one half of art, the other being the eternal and immutable.

The history of modernism as aesthetic avant-garde movement (which is a part of the culture of modernity but should, therefore, be conceptually distinguished from modernity) has always oscillated from one extreme to the other. It continually strove to discover, as Klee said, 'the essential character of the accidental', but it also always made clear that it had no respect for the past in general, not even for its own modern past.

The idea of the modern already contains counter-modern aspects. As Foucault argues: 'rather than seeking to distinguish the "modern era" from the "pre-modern" or "post-modern", … it would be more useful to try to find out how the attitude of modernity, ever since its formation, has found itself struggling with attitudes of countermodernity' (1997: 309–10). And as Harvey (1989) also recognizes, the cultural traits of what is defined as 'modern' and 'postmodern' can be considered opposite dynamic trends of a unique model of society that characterizes a unique era. It is interesting to note in this regard how the huge Berlin art exhibit of 1997 aspiring to definitively map out the artistic values of the twentieth century was entitled 'Die Epoche der Moderne'. After years of postmodernist criticism – mainly expressed in the philosophy of art, in epistemology, and in the sociology of culture- the art of the 20th century (including the most recent trends) is defined as art of the modern epoch.

What sets apart the most radical advocates of postmodernism from all those who perceive the complexity and the persisting vitality of the concept of modernity is the ambition to unify the distinct images of post-industrial society, post-Fordist society and the global communication society in a single synthetic type in order to rigidly contrast it with an opposite modern society type, negating in such a way the complex and contradictory character of the multiple processes of modernization which have developed in the past 200 years.

Added to this assertion of a radical break with modernity is the ambition to construct a new social epistemology, since all pre-existing foundations of epistemology are considered unreliable and history is considered devoid of any teleology. The new epistemology – never clearly defined – should decree the end of the modern project of the Enlightenment, a project which also aims to develop, in addition to a universal morality and law and an autonomous art that responds to its own internal logic, a rigorous scientific method. According to postmodernists, in fact, the experience of the inadequacy of every political representation of social interests by parliaments and parties is accompanied by the experience of inadequacy of every cognitive representation of human action and social reality by science.

To this rejection of science can be attributed the main defect of postmodern interpretations – the avoidance of any effort to verify their hypotheses and measurements of the size of the phenomena. With a few rare exceptions, scholars of postmodernism do not seem to be concerned with the problem of empirical verification of their hypotheses. They offer instead descriptions of heterogeneous phenomena that they consider illustrative of postmodern social realities. Verification and measurement, like the attempts in themselves to define the postmodern phenomenon and to work out a consistent theoretical model, are in fact considered an expression of the rational scientific method the postmodernists strive to deny.

The result is that, in most cases, one does not go beyond the assembly of heterogeneous traits that are distinctive of postmodern society without leading to systematic and consistent interpretations; that the style is often hyperbolic, richly imaginative and declamatory; that many hypotheses only find partial empirical confirmations, because several of the trends presented as general characteristics of postmodern society are present in very different forms and degrees in the various contexts observed, while other hypotheses are not empirically validated in a significant way at all.

For example, it is a matter of controversy whether the flexible organization of small businesses is the dominant social system of production in postmodern society in so far as it is the most qualified to satisfy the ever more differentiated demand for goods and services in relation to the multiplication of lifestyles and consumption patterns. Doubts are raised because, in the first place, flexible organization also works effectively in big businesses where automated processes, 'just-in-time', flexible hours, etc. are put into practice. Furthermore, flexible organization is accompanied by other still widespread and not necessarily less competitive social systems of production, such as customized production (common in the clothing industry) and diversified quality mass production (characteristic of the contemporary automobile industry) in which the preoccupation with improvement in quality of the product and greater attention to the client's tastes do not involve the abandonment of the Fordist model but are rather the result of its evolution (Hollingsworth and Boyer, 1997).

Even the postmodernists' characterizations of social stratification and the nation-state appear generally stereotypical in contrast to the results of many studies. Empirical research on stratification and social mobility paint a much more articulate and differentiated picture than that offered by the postmodern interpretation. Studies on the formation and implementation of public policies show how nation-states, even though weakened by globalization processes and demands for local autonomy, continue to be fundamental actors in the political arena. As we showed at the end of the previous chapter, the state continues to be a fundamental actor in the transition to modernity processes that are taking place in East Asia. And the examples could multiply.

Nevertheless, if one skips over the most banal 'end of modernity', 'end of labor' and similar versions of postmodernism, and one turns to the best-argued contributions, one realizes that theorists of postmodern culture and society have introduced useful critical elements in the studies on the nature and routes of contemporary societies.

Critical discussion of the basic theories of postmodern sociology is therefore appropriate in a book on modernization because these ideas (even though unconvincing in their depiction of a fracture between modern and postmodern) offer useful elements for re-examining modernization processes in contemporary societies. In fact, the merit of postmodern theory is having called attention to several important processes taking place – especially the generalized influence exercised by new forms of mass media on individual experience and social relations.

However, for critics of the postmodern approach, these processes do not at all imply the 'end of modernity' but continue to be a part of the modernization process, accentuating some of its distinctive traits and signifying at most a new phase that we may define as 'hypermodern' or 'late-modern', 'radical modernity', 'second modernity', or 'incomplete modernity'. For many scholars it does not make sense to speak of postmodernism when the fundamental traits of the society and culture in which we live are still those of modernity.

In the following pages, first, we will briefly discuss the theories of Berman, Habermas, Touraine and Wagner who share, although with different reasoning, the idea that modernity is still an incomplete process. Then we will examine more deeply Giddens's interpretation of radical modernity and Beck's concept of the risk society. Some major differences exist between these theorists and the 'classical' theory of modernization: first, they prefer to talk about modernity rather than modernization, about a common global condition rather than a processual change. Second, in the recent theories cultural variables are at least as important – and often more important – than economic variables in the characterization of modern society. Third, although modernity can be widely used to characterize historical change, recent theories tend to concentrate on the twentieth century as the age of modernity, whereas former modernization theories tended to see the nineteenth century as the crucial breakthrough period.

The focus on the historical experience of the twentieth century – which includes dictatorship and totalitarianism – makes the concept of modernity much more contradictory and ambivalent, and paves the way for the plea for a still unaccomplished fulfillment of the potentialities of the modern project, that is, modernity is still incomplete. Latour goes much further than this thesis of the incompleteness of modernity, claiming that modernity has never begun, there has never been a modern world and no one has ever been modern. Therefore, according to him, to speak of post-modernity is nonsense:

> We no longer have to continue the headlong flight of the post-post-modernists; we are no longer obliged to cling to the avant-garde of the avant-garde; we no longer seek to be cleverer, even more critical, even deeper into the 'era of suspicion'. No, instead, we discover that we have never begun to enter the modern era. Hence the hint of the ludicrous that always accompanies postmodern thinkers, they claim to come after a time that has not even started!' (Latour, 1993: 47)

Incomplete modernity: Marshall Berman, Jürgen Habermas, Alain Touraine and Peter Wagner

Marshall Berman

The argument for the persisting relevance of the modernity concept is contended with particular vigor and lucidity by Marshall Berman in his book on the experience of modernity (1983). According to him, 'to be modern is to find ourselves in an environment that promises adventure, power, joy, growth, transformation of ourselves and the world – and, at the same time, that threatens to destroy everything we have, everything we know, everything we are' (ibid.: 15).

> To be modern is to live a life of paradox and contradiction. It is to be overpowered by the immense bureaucratic organizations that have the power to control and often destroy communities, values, lives; and yet to be undeterred in our determination to face these forces, to fight to change their world and make it our own. It is both revolutionary and conservative: alive to new possibilities for experience and adventure. (1983: 13)

Modernity unites all mankind, but it is a paradoxical unity, a unity of separateness that catapults all of us into a vortex of disintegration and renewal, of contradiction and ambiguity. Therefore, the experience of Western modernization needs to be completely understood – not in order to propose a rigid model to imitate – but to help us understand similar but not identical problems that other populations in the world are facing today.

Berman is particularly critical of the French postmodern ideas of Derrida, Barthes, Lacan, Baudrillard, and their numerous followers, heirs of the dashed hopes of May 1968, who appropriated the whole modernist language of radical breakthrough, wrenched it out of its moral and political context, and transformed it into a purely aesthetic language game.

According to Berman, postmodern criticism is irrelevant because modernity is the 'only reality that we have' and we are actually in the first stages of the modernization process, as many parts of the world are only now beginning to fully feel the effects. Reflecting on the formative process of Western modernity and re-reading the classics – such as Marx and Nietzsche, Dostoevsky and Baudelaire, who knew how to grasp modernity's contradictions, losses and unprecedented potentialities – is therefore necessary in order to interpret the vast changes under way.

Jürgen Habermas

The conviction that modernization is a still-incomplete process, with a great potential to realize, is completely shared by Jürgen Habermas, the most influential critic of postmodern interpretations who passionately defends the legacy of the Enlightenment and the relevance of the modern project as an unfinished project.

Habermas (1985) believes that what we have defined as the classic theory of modernization has transformed the Weberian concept of modernity into an abstraction full of consequences – it is separated from its modern European origins and is outlined in a model of general social processes that disregards its temporal and spatial determinations. This involved the interruption of connections between modernity and the historical context of Western rationalism, impeding the self-comprehension of the modernization process, which appears functionally autonomous, self-sufficient and crystallized. This induced postmodernists to talk about the end of modernity as the end of the capacity of rational comprehension of the processes, as the conclusion of the history of ideas.

Habermas is instead convinced that it is too early to abandon modernity as a cultural project. He recognizes that enlightened rationality involves many risks, beginning with the concept of subjective reason that, seeking to comprehend the totality of reality from the point of view of the individual mind, can lead to a purely instrumental and utilitarian notion of rationality, encouraging an attitude of domination and exploitation of nature and society. But the Enlightenment and two hundred years of philosophy after Kant have already supplied antidotes to these risks.

From this rich legacy of philosophic and sociological thought (especially from Weber's theory of rationalization), Habermas obtains the tools for his 'critique of reason through reason' (according to Adorno's expression) and works out his concept of communicative reason which contrasts with subjective and utilitarian reason. Extremely synthesized, Habermas's theory is that the 'omniscient' individual subject is subordinated to the consensual accord that is reached in the communicative interaction between equal and conscious subjects. The reproduction of social systems requires that, within the common way of life, individual motivations are founded in cultural practices, social solidarities are reproduced in a significant way, and individuals are effectively socialized as subjects well rooted in their own social and cultural environment.

Contemporary society suffers not from an excess but a deficit of rationality, or better a deficit of communicative rationality with respect to an excess of instrumental rationality, which is manifested in the powerful technological and bureaucratic structures of capitalist modernization.

Capitalist modernization not only distorted but also developed the communicative potential of reason. On the one hand, in fact, agency oriented to instrumental or strategic success is based on efficacy criteria, pursues selfish interests through rational calculation, and is connected to the logic of domination and technical manipulation. On the other, communicative agency oriented to understanding is based on the free confrontation between rational subjects as to choices concerning their lives, and collective consensus is reached through discussion and cooperation mechanisms.

It is up to us to realize, via the development of the communicative potential of reason, the un-implemented project of the Enlightenment – that is, the creation of a community of equals aware of their own rights and duties, responsible for their own actions, tolerant and committed to making shared meanings through public discourse and communicative reason.

Alain Touraine

Reason and the individual subject are also central to Alain Touraine's *Critique of Modernity* (1992), which, however, develops such concepts in a different way and comes to different conclusions. The history of modernity is the story of the dual establishment of reason and the subject and the contradiction between instrumental rationalism and subjectivism. Modernity is in a state of crisis because the rationalization process was radicalized to the point of oppressing the individual and provoking the unilateral establishment of his or her subjectivity. On the one hand, instrumental rationality dominates the life of individuals, subordinating every action to the pursuit of efficacy and output. On the other (also in reaction to this oppression), the pursuit of separate and partial identities exasperates subjectivism.

In the contemporary age of *exploded modernity*, the global market's logic of instrumental rationalism is opposed to unlimited multiculturalism. While the logic of the global market compresses and oppresses subjective identities, collective movements and autochthonous cultures, the obsession with identity leads those who oppose globalization (such as religious fundamentalists) to a fanatical demand for diversity as radically oppressive as the one of the global market.

In this framework Touraine develops his critique of the postmodernists (even though he shares some of their characterizations of contemporary reality – from the breaking up of human experience to the prevalence of signs and symbols in the society of mass consumption). What Touraine criticizes is the postmodernist assertion of the absolute predominance of the subject, implying the destruction of the social dimension as a sphere of shared meanings. And also the fact that by rejecting the functional differentiation between domains of social life – culture, economy, politics – the postmodernist position arrives at a kind of cultural totalitarianism. As Castoriadis (1993) reproaches postmodernists with the abandonment of the commitment to critique, which was central to modernity, Touraine accuses them of the negation of the dialectics between rationalization and subjectivation and the key role of active citizenship. As Habermas (explicitly) recognizes, Touraine also (implicitly) recognizes that modernity has yet to fulfill its potentialities, rearranging its two fundamental elements: rationality and subjectivity.

Peter Wagner

Peter Wagner's interpretation (1994) represents a further variation on the theme, although he makes a different pair of concepts central to the analysis – *liberty* and *discipline* – which are connected to rationality and the subject. Wagner agrees with Touraine that the contradictory characteristics of modernity are shown with particular clarity in the current historical phase.

Modern society is essentially ambivalent in as much as it weaves together liberty and discipline in an unprecedented way. On the one hand, the principal discourse of modernity defines the modern condition in light of the principles of liberty and democracy and the institutions that should guarantee them, such as political democracy, market economy and that autonomous pursuit of the truth defined as science. On the other, a critical alternative has always existed that stresses the coercive character of institutions. According to Wagner (1992), these two discourses cannot be separated because the condition of the individual in modernity should be interpreted as a dramatic parallel process of freedom and regulation.

In this view, relations are analyzed between freedom of individual action and ties of community belonging, between actor's strategies and opportunities and structural constraints, and between human lives that unfold in well-localized contexts and the social norms of broad application that regulate them. Postmodernists are wrong in thinking that the individual experience of disjointedness and incoherence corresponds to a disorganized world; on the contrary, it is linked to an extension of organization. It springs from the necessity of individuals to deal with a plurality of abstract systems organized in different ways and at times conflicting with one another, and to integrate them into their personal lives.

Anthony Giddens and radical modernity

Berman, Habermas, Touraine and Wagner believe that the contemporary era is still the modern era. Berman even points out that for many peoples the transition to modernity has just begun; Habermas maintains that the potentialities of the modern project are still only partially realized; Touraine has faith that exploded modernity can rearrange itself into a superior synthesis; Wagner believes that only one type of modernity has ended, organized modernity. All of them reject the idea of the end of modernity.

For other scholars who also reject this thesis, contemporary society can nonetheless be defined as hypermodern in so far as it has radicalized qualifying aspects of modernity – such as the worldwide interdependence of economic and cultural relations and the responsibility of individual choice (according to which man is master of his own destiny, to the point of both achieving extraordinary scientific progress and technical innovations as well as making nuclear self-destruction possible, or shocking biological manipulation via genetic engineering). The most thorough formulations of this position are those of Giddens and Beck.

In his theorization of radical modernity, Anthony Giddens asserts that we are not beyond modernity; 'rather than entering a period of post-modernity, we are moving into one in which the consequences of modernity are becoming more radicalised and universalised than as never before' (1990: 3). The study of the formation process of modern society that Giddens (1985) develops in the course of his work is characterized by the particular importance attributed to the development of nation-states, thus integrating and correcting the Marxist conception of the centrality of social relations to production. The nation-state is examined in its dual capacity of goal-oriented community and bureaucratic-rational organization, able to pursue in an efficient way complex aims like industrialization, colonization, diplomacy and war.

The four institutional dimensions (or organizing principles) of a modern society are: (1) the capitalist system of production of commodities through wage labor in the context of competitive markets; (2) the industrial organization that systematically applies technology to the production of goods and services, transforms nature and develops the 'created environment'; (3) the administrative apparatus for coordinated control of the population in a determinate territory through surveillance techniques, information gathering and hierarchical supervision; and (4) the centralized control of legitimate violence in the context of the industrialization of war. The nation-state embodies the most mature development of these characteristics and therefore is identifiable to a large extent with modern society itself, representing the generalized political unit of a system of international relations.

According to Giddens, the discontinuity marked by the advent of modern society and its intrinsic dynamism derive from: (1) the separation of space and time (or *time–space distantiation*) and their recombination in forms which permit a precise definition of the spatial-temporal borders of social life; (2) the *disembedding* of social systems from their localized contexts of interaction; and (3) the *reflexive* ordering and reordering of social relations in the light of continual inputs of knowledge affecting the actions of individuals and groups (Giddens, 1990: 16–17).

Spatial-temporal distantiation and the disembedding of local contexts of interaction contribute to defining the specific condition of modern man, which is marked by the perception of risk, by the sensation of being part of a universe of events that we do not fully understand and that seem in large part beyond our control, by faith in abstract systems of specialist knowledge, and by the reflexivity of action.

The transformations that occur in the current phase of *high modernity* or radical modernity accentuate and radicalize these characteristics and can be summed up in the concept of globalization. The globalization process can be considered both an intrinsic trend and at the same time the consequence of modernization. We will examine here Gidden's theory with reference to the risk–trust concept pair, but we will refer to him again in the final chapter, with reference to the globalization process.

According to Giddens, as we will see also with Beck, in the mature phase of modernity, there is an intensification of risk. Risk is both objective (greater presence of risks connected to political relations and contemporary modes of production and living) as well as subjective (a more acute perception of the risks themselves).

New possibilities of global catastrophes (nuclear war, environmental destruction) universalize the risk – in the sense that it can affect anyone, regardless of class, ethnicity or gender – and the possible effects expand to a much broader population due to the interdependence of economic and political relations. In addition, risks are institutionalized in specialized organizations wherein risk is their functioning principle (such as stock exchanges, insurance companies, sporting activities, etc.). Finally, risks – in addition to deriving from planning errors and operative and control errors of abstract systems – are also partly unexpected consequences or unpredicted and unintended effects of actions consciously geared toward legitimate and shared aims, as in the case of environmental consequences, externalities of industrial activities, or the so-called ills of our society, caused by our ways of working or our lifestyles.

At the same time, subjective perception of risk is accentuated by the weakening of beliefs in religion and magic, the rise in educational levels (which increases awareness of dangers to one's health and safety), and the recognition of the limits of scientific-technical capabilities and abstract systems.

It should be noted that some of Giddens's arguments do not seem to concern specific traits of our epoch, especially when one considers the widespread plague epidemics of past centuries. Other arguments could even be overturned, in the sense that, for example, improved education and the weakening of superstition might increase – not decrease – faith in human abilities to control the environment. But, on the whole, Gidden's ideas (like those of Beck, whom we will discuss afterwards) are not lacking in empirical confirmations (like the numerous 'technical' accidents that in reality are not so much due to limits in scientific-technical or abstract system capabilities, but to the fact that it is real individuals with their limitations who control and manage these systems) and provide valuable insights in understanding the uncertain and erratic nature of contemporary societal life.

Closely connected to the concept of risk is that of trust, in the same way that safety and danger are connected. In radical modernity, the process is accentuated of removing social relations from their local contexts of interaction via the generalized employment of means of universal exchange, like money (which can transfer value from one context to another and therefore facilitate social relations distant in space and time) and abstract systems of scientific-technical and professional knowledge (which can be employed in a vast range of diverse contexts for solving specific problems).

The trust increases, therefore, that we must attribute to long-distance monetary transactions, to absent experts over whom we have no direct control and, in general, to abstract systems, whose operating principles are not all that clear to most people and require continual leaps of faith, but on which their daily lives are increasingly dependent. 'With the development of abstract systems, trust in impersonal principles, as well as in anonymous others, becomes indispensable to social existence' (Giddens, 1990: 120). People have to learn to get to know and rely on big impersonal organizations operating on abstract principles, in transportation and telecommunication, in financial markets and industries that involve technological risks (such as chemical or nuclear), in multinational corporations and vast communication networks and the armed forces.

In pre-modern cultures, the past is honored because it contains the experience of generations and tradition is a mode of integrating the reflexive monitoring of action with the time–space organization of the community. Reflexivity of modern social life has a different character: it consists in the fact that 'social practices are constantly examined and reformed in the light of incoming information about those very practices, thus constitutively altering their character' (ibid.: 38). In all cultures, social practices are altered in the light of new discoveries, but only with modernity has the revision of convention been radicalized and extended to apply to all aspects of human life, including technological intervention into the material world. The modern world is constituted in and through reflexively applied knowledge, but in late modern society we are increasingly aware that we can never be sure that any given element of knowledge will not be revised.

The society we live in is rendered *reflexive* due to the trust accorded to abstract systems of knowledge that present certain guarantees in their generalized application, and by the awareness of risk and the ability to reorganize and metabolize it, continually searching for information and analyzing it effectively (whether it is health consequences, frequency of accidents or financial market performance). Reflexivity is created by the separation of the thinking subject from the thought object, which makes possible both the control of emotive and irrational components of the personality as well as the comprehension and evaluation of the consequences of individual decisions.

In order to describe radical modernity in the age of globalization, Giddens (ibid.: 151) turns to the Juggernaut metaphor from Hindu mythology, one of the denominations of the all-powerful deity Krishna, a terrible animal endowed with an extraordinary and frightening destructive force who becomes the symbol of the collective power of humanity, which is at the same time a source of great risks and great creative opportunities. From this, the need for reflexivity is derived, or rather the capacity to ride and rein in the Juggernaut in order to minimize the risks and maximize the opportunities that modernity offers us.

In radical modernity there exists both the need and the ability to reflect on oneself, individual and collective choices, and the consequences of one's actions. The identification of reflexivity as a distinctive trait of contemporary society is shared by Giddens and Beck. However, while Beck concentrates on the reflexivity of society that manifests itself in social surveillance and in collective movements, Giddens mainly stresses the reflexivity of the individual who analyzes and reflects on his or her own actions and his or her own relationships with other individuals based on a constant flow of information. Even in traditional contexts (such as educating children or relationships between husband and wife and parent and child), consulting the advice of experts, reading books and listening to television programs progressively replace traditional practices and the authority of the elderly.

But knowledge is in continual evolution (also due to the pervasiveness and complexity of the changes that take place in contemporary society) and as it is often difficult to spread, this knowledge contributes to creating new inequalities of power and education and to instilling uncertainty in all those who cannot continually keep up-to-date and who, moreover, are no longer able to yield to the comfort of tradition. The reflexivity of social knowledge makes action more predictable but also more exposed to the effects of unexpected consequences.

It may be noted that this helps explain the success of radical traditionalist movements in countries involved in modernization processes imported from the outside. Such is the case of some Islamic countries, in which the fear of modernity's consequences provokes a retreat into the orthodoxy of religious tradition. In the contemporary age, therefore, modernity is radicalized and generalized. Both opportunities and risks grow, as does the capacity/necessity to reflect on them and the consequences of our actions. In many ways, Beck's formulation is similar.

Ulrich Beck and the 'risk society'

In Beck's opinion, the fundamental distinction to be made is between industrial society and modern society. Industrial society is for him a 'semi-modern' society, not so much for the persistence of feudal vestiges as for the institutions and behaviors that reject the universal principles of Enlightenment modernity. Beck, who is clearly influenced by Habermas's conception of modernity as an incomplete project, maintains that the current phase of Western developed society has changed both the global nature of risks and individuals' consciousness of them.

The concept of risk is at the center of his characterization of contemporary society. In modernization the nature of the risks that human beings are exposed to changes, in the sense that risks induced and introduced by modernization itself increase substantially, such as those connected with environmental pollution, the hazardous use of nuclear energy, agricultural fertilizers and principles employed in the industrial production of food products.

As long as modernity is expressed in the strict form of industrial society concerned with maximizing the flow of available material resources via technology and correcting inequalities through the welfare state, people are willing to accept negative consequences to their health and the health of the environment as necessary costs of economic and income growth. But contemporary society, defined as the *risk society*, has become aware of the danger of self-destruction inherent in the obtuse continuation of classic industrialization, and therefore requires less industrialization and more modernization. The nature of social conflict has consequently changed: the distributional conflicts over 'goods' (such as property, income, and jobs) that characterized industrial society have given way to distributional conflicts over 'bads', such as the risks of nuclear technology, genetic research, and the threat to the environment.

Just as the first process of modernization 'dissolved the structure of feudal society in the nineteenth century and produced industrial society, to-day modernization of the Western developed world is dissolving industrial society and creating a new modernity' (Beck, 1991: 10). We need to free ourselves from continually thinking of modernity within the categories of industrial society. Modernization within the horizon of experience of early modernity is being displaced by reflexive modernization. It is necessary to fully develop the potential for rational reflection and personal development that is contained within the modern project beyond and in contrast to its classic industrial design. We are not therefore witnessing the end but the beginning of modernity or at least its conscious expression, a modernity radicalized against the industrial paths and categories.

Positive knowledge and normative knowledge are fused and confused in Beck's interpretation. The analysis of trends under way of collective movements and *social surveillance* of the risks of industrialization is mixed with the exhortation to develop a conscious modernity. It is, however, an interesting theory and, in two fundamental aspects, consistent with the general line of this book, because it considers modernization to be an open process and anything but concluded and, following Habermas, a project in large part still to be realized, not a design that has exhausted its potential; and because it casts light on the links between modernization and globalization in the contemporary epoch.

Beck's theory raises an issue of crucial importance (which, however, is not explored deeply), and that is the dissimilarity between the development model of countries that have recently begun the modernization process and the model of already-developed countries. While in the latter, signs are manifested of what Giddens and Beck define as *reflexive modernization*, in the former, the traditional industrialist model oriented towards growth at any cost is still prevalent. Not that developed countries lack the tensions and conflicts between interests and mentalities connected to the two models, but these countries can 'afford' to devote resources to programs for labor protection and ecologically compatible development.

For countries at the beginning of modernization, growth instead entails enormous costs – from the destruction of Indonesian forests to the massive use of child labor – recalling the classic social ills of the English revolution. Thus, what Polanyi (1944) defines as 'the dilemma of the self-regulating market' still seems relevant, that is, the dilemma between the development of the market mechanism (which involves the risk of physically destroying humankind and transforming the environment into a desert) and the policies intended to oppose such development (which imply the risk of disorganizing economic life, placing society in danger in a different way).

In this regard, globalization plays a double and contradictory role. On the one hand, it stimulates competition between enterprises and country-systems and prompts the latecomers to concentrate their energies in this struggle. On the other, it nourishes the awareness of being part of a single planetary unit, in which survival depends on us all. But the relationship between globalization and modernity is much more complex and requires a more extended analysis, which is the topic of the next chapter.

5

Globalization and Modernity

Globalization is one of the most visible consequences of modernity and has in its turn reshaped the project of modernity. I have argued several times in this book that modernization is a global process, and that modernity must be reconceptualized in the context of globalization. The theme of globalization is central to re-examinations of modernity, especially those of Giddens and Beck, as it is in depictions of post-modern society and in studies of developing countries, that were analyzed in the previous pages. If one defines globalization as a long historical process as Robertson does (2001), such global processes as the growth of world religions, voyages of discovery, early map-making, or the spread of the Gregorian calendar, constitute key preconditions for the emergence of modernity. But, if one conceives of contemporary globalization as a quite distinct phenomenon – as I do in this book – globalization is indeed a consequence of modernity and requires a reformulation of the frame of analysis of modernization. This final chapter focuses specifically on the relationship between globalization and modernity.

First, I argue that globalization requires a theoretical rethinking of the analysis of modernity. Second, I briefly review the huge literature on the subject, giving my own view and analyzing key aspects of globalization that modify the frame of reference of modernization. Third, the question of multiple modernities and varieties of modernity is discussed, i.e. the fact that the global modern condition of contemporary world goes together with the great variety of cultural traditions and institutional arrangements. Fourth, the relationship between globalization and the nation-state is examined: since effective nation-building has been until now a necessary precondition of successful modernization, the extent and nature of the erosion of national sovereignty are therefore of the utmost importance in the analysis of modernization. And I will conclude with the question of global governance and its implications for modernizing countries.

Globalization as a visible consequence of modernity

Globalization modifies the frame of reference of modernization and requires a rethinking of the project of modernity in several ways. First, most studies of modernization have regarded societies as if they were separate entities, each with their own clear-cut national boundaries. Their focus has been on acquiring an understanding of a society's internal dynamics and structures, its distinctive cultural code, its specific mechanisms of integration, conflict and change, sometimes with an implicit comparative perspective, and more rarely with an explicit comparative approach. Today globalization implies not only the emergence of a new object of study, the world as such, but requires that more than in the past any study of social change in a specific country or region be framed in a global context, since each part of the world is increasingly interdependent on many others and the world as such is increasingly present in all of its parts. The contemporary world looks more and more like a laser beam hologram, where every point contains information about the whole, since each human being increasingly tends to consume information and resources coming from everywhere. Hence there is the need to shift the level of analysis to the global level and to take a world-system perspective in any study. The study of world society and its relations with national and local social realities should become the central theme of research. The higher the degree of interconnectedness of social relations at the world level, the greater the need to analyze the links between global social reality and multiple local social realities. 'Glocal' is an increasingly relevant neologism in our lexicon. At the cultural level we must analyze the many ways in which the unity and the diversity of the world combine and collide; at the social level, we should investigate the many manifestations of complementarity and antagonism in social action in the global arena.

Second, comparative studies of social change have mostly concerned Western developed countries and, when developing countries have been taken into account, they have often been studied as either traditional societies or incomplete cases according to the yardstick of the developed countries. Globalization makes the modern condition a global condition and at the same time fosters the dialectic interplay of different cultural traditions to an unparalleled extent. It raises the question of multiple modernities and of varieties of modernity and stimulates the need for good comparative research on the different cultural and institutional paths to and through modernity.

Third, globalization erodes the sovereignty of the nation-state, that has been the key institution and the basic element of structuration of modern society. Globalization implies a massive shake-up of the world order. It provokes an 'unbundling of the relationships between sovereignty, territoriality and state power' (Ruggie, 1993); affects the institutional encasement and implies a basic restructuring of the territorial nation-state (Sassen, 2000); and brings about a new mix of domestic and foreign policies (Rosenau's 'intermestic' affairs, 1997). It is within this framework that the basic normative questions of non-violent regulation of conflict, social justice, and individual freedom have been managed. With the erosion of sovereignty of the nation-state, a consequence of global interdependence, social structure has become less coherent than before. As Appadurai remarks, flows should be put at the center of the analysis alongside structures – flows of people, technologies, ideas, symbols, capital, etc. Global flows are fast increasing, and the values, institutions and practices needed to manage them lag behind. Economic relations and communications more and more are bypassing national frontiers, but they lack governance. This state of affairs has clear implications for modernizing countries: first, because, it puts pressure on, and redefines the role of, a key institutional actor in the development process; and, second, because different models of global governance have a very different impact on modernizing countries.

Finally, globalization raises the question of global governance, that is, the definition of a complex set of global norms concerning the entire world as a single system in various ways, i.e. planet Earth as an ecosystem; humanity as an endangered species, with the related concerns for the lives of future generations; the peoples of the world as a single constituency of individuals entitled to equal rights and responsibilities to whom decision-makers must be accountable; the world market as an economic space regulated by an international *lex mercatoria* which can guarantee the rights not only of investors, but also of workers, consumers and communities. The related question of globalization modifies the old sociological question asked by Simmel, 'How is society possible?' (that is, how cooperation can be fostered so that basic needs are met, social reproduction guaranteed and conflict regulated). This is still central, but now must be asked at the world level, in addition to the local, regional, group, and institutional levels. And it becomes a more difficult question, as more and more individuals are increasingly connected directly to the global level in institutions that lack both the representation and the accountability of national institutions, and since the very forces favoring a more interconnected world stimulate counter-forces that foster division and fragmentation.

The problems of legitimate power and conflict management and the question of the structuration of contemporary global society require institutions and normative elements as well as national governments, but the conditions that make possible democratic accountability and social cohesion at the national level are more difficult to reproduce in the global context. We should address our attention to patterns of cooperation and conflict at the world level, to the new forms of normative order for a complex multicultural world, and to the emergence of multi-layered types of governance through the institutional mixes of transnational actors (Martinelli, 2002). New forms of global governance are needed, i.e. the organization and the institutional regulation at the world level of social and economic life by the combined action of a plurality of actors who pursue strategies of various kinds (industrial exports, financial profit, national security, religious indoctrination, betterment of their own life chances, etc.) on the world stage in the context of basic human and social rights. Global governance can be conceived as a polyarchic mixed actor system, based on accountability, contextual universalism, multiple identities, and supranational democratic institutions.

A single system and a fragmented world

The social world in the twenty-first century is both a single system and a fragmented world. Globalization is marked by the tension between global economic and technological interdependence and social interconnectedness, on the one hand, and cultural fragmentation and political division, on the other.

The world can be conceptualized as a single system, but a world society does not exist yet, since there is no normative consensus reflected in commonly accepted institutions at the world level; and therefore global integration and governance should not be taken for granted.

Globalization is one of the most distinctive features of the contemporary world; one of the most rapidly spreading words both in scholarly lexicon and in daily language. The roots of the concept can be traced in different disciplines, in the studies of the French historical school, and particularly in Braudel (1967), in McLuhan's definition of the world as a global village (1964), in Wallerstein's world-economy approach (1974–89), in Cooper's notion of international interdependence (1968), in Robertson's seminal study (1984), as well as in the rich and diversified literature on multinational corporations and on the social consequences of the information and communication technologies.

The most interesting definitions of globalization define the process in several complementary ways, as 'time–space compression' (Harvey, 1989), 'action at distance' (Giddens, 1990), 'accelerating interdependence' (Ohmae, 1990), and 'networking' (Castells, 1998). We can define it as a set of related processes that involve a stretching of economic, social, cultural and political activity and interconnect the individuals, groups, communities, states, societies, markets, corporations, international governmental and non-governmental organizations in complex webs of social relations, intensifying their interdependence and increasing the consciousness of what is happening. Briefly, it can be defined as the growth of networks of worldwide interdependence.

Globalization is the result of a set of different factors, the most important of which are technological (the new ICTs), economic and financial (the restructuring of capitalist economy through the growth of multinational corporations, the consolidation of a world financial market, post-Fordist production, state policies of liberalization and deregulation), social and cultural (the creation of a global village through the spread of mass media, international migrations), and political (the collapse of the Soviet Union, the crisis of planned and protectionist economies, the rise of China).

Globalization has stimulated an intense debate among social scientists and produced a huge literature concerning its scale and degree of novelty, its driving forces, the various processes that take place under this general heading and their different dynamics, its positive and negative consequences for different peoples and social groups, its impact on nation-states and on the strategies of global actors, its historical trajectories. There is the risk that globalization will become a catchall word, that, by embracing too much, it will be scarcely useful at all. In order to avoid this risk we need both more empirically grounded comparative research and an effort of conceptual clarification. The impressive literature on globalization can be arranged in a conceptual space with reference to three major axes:

1. 'Hyperglobalizers vs skeptics', where the key distinction concerns the degree of novelty of globalization and its impact on nation-states.
2. 'Neo-liberals vs. neo-Marxist and radicals', where the key points are the balance between positive and negative impacts of globalization and its truly global or Western hegemonic character.
3. 'Homogenization vs. heterogeneity and hybridization', which focuses on the cultural dimension of globalization.

Hyperglobalists and skeptics

For those whom Held defines as hyperglobalists (Held et al., 1999), globalization is mainly conceptualized in economic terms. It is a borderless economy (Ohmae,

1990) where a growing number of countries are integrated and where global competition takes place (Porter, 1990). It entails a denationalization of economies through the establishment of transnational networks of production, trade and finance. Today globalization is an entirely new phenomenon, and an almost irreversible process. It implies a reconfiguration of the framework of human action (Albrow, 1996), which constrains the choices of states and individuals, pushing them to adopt neo-liberal economic strategies in order to compete in the global market. The world economy reshapes the traditional international division of labor between center and periphery and between the North and the South, and fosters new, more complex patterns of hierarchy and inequality, new 'winners' as well as 'losers' among countries and social groups within them, thus stimulating new forms of conflict and cooperation among transnational actors.

Hyperglobalists disagree strongly about the evaluation of the risks and opportunities of the world market for individuals, groups and peoples. On the one hand, neo-liberals are persuaded that globalization is not a zero-sum game, that its benefits are much greater than its costs, and that a new world civilization is emerging (Perlmutter, 1991). The best-known version of this interpretation is Fukuyama's thesis of the end of history: ideological conflict – which constituted the engine of historical movement – has virtually ended with the victory of capitalism and the liberal democracy. Fukuyama does not ignore the rise of new ideologies and new conflicts – such as those related to religious fundamentalism or aggressive nationalism – but sees them as partial and incapable of giving rise to new 'grand narratives' and of launching a global challenge. On the other, radicals and neo-Marxists portray a dark picture of growing inequalities, famines and wars, with the strongest economic actors trying to impose their world-wide domination and facing the opposition of global movements of struggle and liberation (Callinicos et al., 1994; Greider, 1997).

Both, however, share the view that globalization implies that the impersonal forces of world markets are now more powerful than states; that governments' major concerns are competing to attract investments and manage the social consequences of globalization for those who are marginalized; and that states are increasingly unable to control transnational flows of people, money and goods, and have to reduce their welfare policies because of the budget constraints imposed by global competition.

Many arguments of the hyperglobalizers remind us of the contradiction exposed in the 1970s by the theories of the overloaded government (Crozier et al., 1975), the legitimation crisis (Habermas, 1973), and the fiscal crisis of the state (O'Connor, 1973). Again, national governments are torn between the need to foster economic competitiveness and that of enhancing social cohesion, but this contradiction is framed in the new context of the challenges set by the global market.

The loss of autonomy of the nation-state is particularly relevant in a study on modernization, since the sovereign nation-state has been the key institution and the basic element of structuration of modern society. To the extent that globalization implies a massive shake-up of the world order and provokes an unbundling of the relationships between sovereignty, territoriality and state power, one of the basic premises of modernization is put into question and requires a theoretical reappraisal.

The hyperglobalist thesis of the demise of the nation-state is exaggerated. Globalization erodes national sovereignty, but the nation-states are still very important actors in the contemporary world. Their role is ambivalent: on the one hand, states are increasingly unable to control transnational flows of people, money and goods, and have to reduce their welfare policies because of the budget constraints imposed by global competition; on the other, their role has been redefined and even increased in order to strengthen the competitiveness of the 'country system' and to manage the social consequences of global competition (unemployment, outsourcing).

Furthermore, the hyperglobalist thesis can be criticized for not distinguishing between states with quite different power and influence, between different process of erosion and consolidation of states' roles. Limiting ourselves to a comparison between the European Union and the United States, we realize that while, in the case of the countries of the EU, their sovereign power has actually been reduced – both through their spontaneous ceding of portions of sovereignty to the institutions of the European Union and because of the constraints of the global market – the same situation does not apply to the USA, which is the hegemonic power and continues to exert unprecedented state strength.

The hyperglobalist perspective appears less convincing today than a few years ago, because the world economic system has become more fragile, less dependent on the global market and more dependent on state policies, as a consequences of a series of different events such as the 1997–98 Asian, Russian and Brazilian economic crises, the end of the long American stock exchange's boom in the summer of 2000, the September 11th terrorist attack, the financial scandals of American and European corporations such as Enron, Worldcom, or Parmalat. Close to the hyperglobalist pole are also those cultural descriptions of globalization which stress the increasing homogeneity of world values (rationalization, market competition, commodification, democratic rights), and of consumption patterns and styles of life (according to the 'McDonaldization', 'Coca-Colaization', or 'Disneyfication' of the world.).

At the other extreme of the conceptual spectrum are the *skeptics*. For them globalization, defined as a perfectly integrated world economy, is a myth. What is happening is not a novel phenomenon, but another wave of internationalization, i.e. of interactions among predominantly national economies, as has already happened in the past, in the sixteenth and seventeenth centuries and between the end of the nineteenth and the start of the twentieth century (Hirst and Thompson, 1996). Globalization is not 'a description of the present, but at best a prediction about the future' (Waltz, 1999).

In order to prove their point, the skeptics conceive of globalization in even stricter economic terms than the hyperglobalists. The indicators they select to prove their argument are mostly based on trade and finance flows and on their value as percentages of the GNP of various countries. They point out that trade and foreign investments are still concentrated in the most advanced capitalist countries and account for the continuing patterns of inequality and hierarchy in the world and for the marginalization of most 'third world' countries. But globalization is not just trade and finance.

The skeptics make a good point in arguing that what is actually taking place is the division of the world economy into regional financial and trading blocs (North America, the European Union, the Asia-Pacific region, Mercosur and the Andean Pact). Actually, more than 50 percent of foreign trade of European Union countries-which are among the most export-oriented economies in contemporary world-takes place among themselves. As a consequence of the 1994 North America Free Trade Agreement (NAFTA), the percentage of Mexican imports from the USA have grown from 79.4 to 88.7 percent, and that of Canadian imports have grown from 74.6 to 87.2 percent, whereas exports form Mexico and Canada into the USA have also grown from 28.3 to 36.3 percent. In Asia too, about 50 percent of exports takes place within the continent itself and regional markets are developing around the Japanese and the Chinese economy and to a lesser extent around the Asian countries of South-East Asia and the Indian peninsula.

And yet regionalization and globalization are not antithetical processes; the powerful growth of countries like China, India and Brazil fosters the growth of regional markets but contributes to the growing integration of the global market as well; it reduces the concentration of trade and investments in the more developed countries of the West and fosters new patterns of inequality, hierarchy and marginalization.

Skeptics also strongly disagree with hyperglobalists that the world market and global governance undermine national sovereignty, since they point out the continuing key role of governments (essentially of the most powerful Western states) in shaping economic relations. The forces of internationalization themselves depend on the regulatory power of national governments to ensure free trade. Multinational corporations are not multinational at all, since they have a clear home state and regional base. The skeptics' view is not exposed to my critique of neglecting the asymmetry of power and influence among nation-states, but some of them go too far, interpreting contemporary internationalization as the by-product of the US-initiated multilateral economic order since the end of the Second World War (Gilpin, 1987), or even as a new phase of Western imperialism with governments acting as agents of monopoly capital and MNCs (Callinicos et al., 1994; Hardt and Negri, 2000).

To this largely economistic perspective can be added Huntington's (1996) culturalist view of a world fragmented into clashing civilizations and radically opposed religious fundamentalisms and aggressive nationalisms, which go against the very possibility of a global civilization and democratic global governance. This view has been strongly criticized for over-estimating potential conflicts which have so far given rise to very limited actual clashes. After the September 11th terrorist attack on the United States, this view has become politically dangerous, since it corresponds to the declared objectives of the global terrorism of Islamic fundamentalist organizations; this view is strongly rejected by most major political, religious and moral authorities and by most Muslims.

My view of globalization

In between the opposite poles of hyperglobalizers and skeptics, optimists and pessimists, and homogenizers and heterogenizers, lies the perspective of those whom Held defines as 'transformationalists'. They conceive of globalization in broader and more complex terms as a multi-faceted process with multiple causes (economic, technological, cultural, and political). They are cautious about future developments and do not stress global integration, but rather the emergence of webs and networks of relations among individuals, groups, communities, states, international organizations and transnational actors.

According to this view, globalization reinforces old patterns of inequalities, but also forms new social hierarchies, which penetrate all regions of the world, thus recasting the traditional patterns of inclusion and exclusion. However, significant opportunities for the empowerment of individuals, communities and social groups also exist. Alongside the homogenizing impact of global corporations on lifestyles and consumption patterns, the transformationalists point out the increasing hybridization of cultural traits and the staunch defense of specific identities. They stress deterritorialization, but also the chances for a potentially greater role for national governments. And they point out the need for democratic global governance based on the principles of universal rights and responsibilities.

Placing myself on the map, I share much of the transformationalist view. I tend to be far from the extremes, but appreciate more the novelty of the phenomenon than its continuity with past. I consider globalization to be a multifaceted rather than a mostly economic process and I stress cultural heterogeneity and hybridization. I conceive of it as an open process that, as with any major social transformation, constrains action, redistributes costs and benefits, and reshapes patterns of inequality and opportunity, but whose net outcome differs for people according to structural constraints, individual decisions, and collective actions. As Stiglitz (2002) points out, the problem is not globalization, but the way it has been managed.

Globalization is a multi-faceted process with far-reaching consequences for the lives of all women and men, imposing constraints and opening opportunities for individual and collective action. The spatial organization of social relations is deeply transformed insofar as relations become more stretched and more intensively interconnected. Trans-continental and trans-regional flows and networks of activities, exchanges and power relations are generated, with major implications for decision-making processes. New patterns of hierarchy and inequality and of inclusion and exclusion cut across national borders. And new problems of social integration, global governance and democratic accountability arise, insofar as the sovereign power of nation-states is eroded and their role in world politics is reshaped. Globalization does not proceed in a linear and uniform fashion, but with accelerations and slow-downs, in unequal ways in various parts of the world, more rapidly in certain aspects with respect to others; it sparks very different responses from institutions and individual and collective subjects; it provokes opposing reactions, such as, for example, the rediscovery of local roots and the strengthening of ethnic and regional identities.

Globalization is not just a continuation of the process of internationalization, but also a qualitatively different process. Both processes contrast to a situation in which autonomous and to a large extent self-sufficient entities continue to exist in conditions of relative isolation, only coming in contact for war or trade. Both processes involve interdependence among activities and functions carried out in different places and belonging to different economic entities and governments, but it is an interdependence with a different degree of intensity.

Globalization is not just another phase in the long-standing cycle of openings and closures with free market and protectionist policies in the world economy. The world economy of the past 200 years was characterized by alternate phases of trade liberalization and protectionism. The past 50 years were witness to a strong internationalization process, in which every unit – while maintaining definite borders – is connected to the others by a series of interdependent ties (import and export of goods and services, migratory flows, cultural exchanges, mechanisms of collective decision such as accords, treaties and alliance pacts, international organizations, etc.). But this process has only recently transformed itself into a real globalization of the market and social relations. It is true, as pointed out by Bairoch (1996) among others, that just before the First World War capital and labor mobility across national borders was comparable to the present, that for OECD countries foreign trade as a percentage of GNP paralleled the 1913 levels only in the late 1970s and foreign investments as a percentage of GNP only in 1990. But the absolute value of capital movements, their speed, the number of investors, the range of financial options are now much greater. New also is the role of transnational corporations that organize production and sales on a global scale and decentralize entire phases of the productive process in various regions of the world, with the consequence that the percentages of foreign trade taking place within the same industry and within the same corporation are much greater than in the past. A further element of novelty is the creation of regional blocs – such as the European Union, NAFTA, Mercosur – where foreign trade and investments grow much faster (Zysman and Schwartz, 1998).

The difference between internationalization and globalization is not only a question of the intensity level of interdependence, but also a qualitative difference. The difference lies in the combined effect of the rapid growth in communications and information technologies (computers, telecommunications, and television) and in the increasing power of economic and financial transnational actors. Even more activities – not just the production and distribution of goods and services, but also the spread of material and symbolic communications – are organized on a world scale. The lives of individuals and the fates of communities increasingly depend on what takes place in distant places; they no longer depend only on what is spatially contiguous, but also on what happens in real time at any distance away. Markets, for example, tend to be not only spatially definite places but also world-wide networks in which buyers and sellers meet anywhere without ever having to meet physically.

The organization of activities on a global scale and the growing importance of temporal contiguity with respect to spatial proximity contribute to the weakening and redefining of borders, another distinctive element of globalization. Both national and local borders are weakened and redefined through processes of de-territorialization and re-territorialization. Whereas internationalization implies a limited and controlled erosion of sovereignty, insofar as each political entity autonomously decides whether to enter into relations of exchange with others, globalization implies a greater erosion of national sovereignty and a growing interconnectedness. In other words, with globalization, the borders between societies (which are identified less and less with nation-states) are opened and shifted, while the level of systemic interdependence grows among international, macro-regional (cutting across national territories) and sub-regional (cutting across regional territories) entities. Growing interdependence among peoples and states is shown by a variety of indicators, which range from the number and types of treaties to international governmental institutions, from imports and exports to levels of investments, from electronic communications traffic to measures of the ethnic, religious and linguistic composition of national populations, and from military alliances to environmental risks.

Global interdependence does not signify a reduction of the international division of labor among units that perform various functions, or of the hierarchical ordering of interdependent entities. On the contrary, even if globalization removes or weakens some access barriers to financial and commercial markets, to information and knowledge and provokes a certain degree of power and influence redistribution, it requires strategic centers of coordination and control – national governments and transnational corporations, as well as big metropolises and international organizations. Fueling processes of growing differentiation and specialization, globalization creates, in fact, new complex problems of systemic integration.

Globalization expresses the radicalization of the specific dynamics of modernization (Giddens, 1990): the interdependence and intensification of relations on a worldwide scale, so that locally occurring events are shaped by distant events and vice versa; spatial-temporal distantiation, in the sense that social relations no longer necessarily depend on the simultaneous physical presence of actors in a specific place; the uprooting of social relations from specific contexts of interaction and their reorganization in time and space through symbolic, universal means of trade and abstract systems of scientific-technical knowledge; and the reflexivity of individuals and social systems.

Globalization also modifies the frame of reference of modernization in that it transforms the social life of countries that began before this process and creates constraints as well as opportunities for countries that began after. In fact, it makes the corporations of developed countries more competitive, able to rely on the support of efficient institutional set-ups and consistent cultural orientations; but it also offers developing countries possibilities for learning new modernizing technologies and practices. In those countries it prompts new inequalities and new problems of social cohesion; but it also creates possibilities for social and individual emancipation. It threatens indigenous values and norms; but it also allows for creative adaptation and cultural hybridization.

The globalization process involves the profound transformations in societal life described by Harvey (1989) and Bauman among others. Modern society's institutions, facilitated by instantaneous communication, nourish relations among absentees and remove interpersonal relations from their local contexts of interaction, recombining them throughout time and space. The truth of experience no longer necessarily coincides with the location in which it takes place (Jameson, 1991). But, on the other hand, also in reaction to globalization processes, local contexts do not decrease in importance and actually take on increasing significance in defining individual identities. Consequently, that institution typical of classic modernity – the nation-state – is weakened in the face of the dual and opposing reinforcement of international and transnational relations and of local ties and identities.

These various tendencies toward the worldwide extension, impact and inter-connectedness of social phenomena and toward the erosion and reshaping of borders also foster a world-encompassing awareness among social actors of the interdependence of their activities and of their community of fate.

Globalization can be conceived of as an expression of our changed experience of time and space, where time is employed to reduce constraints of space and vice versa. Time shortens and space shrinks. Based on the growing speed of means of transportation, we could consider the dimensions of the world in the second half of this century to be one-fiftieth the size of the world in the sixteenth century, since the velocity of a jet airplane is fifty times greater than that of a sailing ship (Harvey, 1989). If the inhabitants of London participate in the same event at the same time as the inhabitants of Tokyo – whether it is a sporting competition or a financial trans-action – space has been drastically reduced by virtue of the compression of time.

Yet one should not draw the (false) conclusion that different locations have become interchangeable or even less comparable, from the (true) fact of the com-pression of time and space, and even the annulling of the distances made possi-ble by data communication. As Sassen (1991) effectively argues, in the current age the organization of economic activities is spread out territorially but inte-grated on a global level. Exactly from territorial dispersion emerges the need for a centralization of functions of control and management in the so-called 'global cities' (or better 'globalized') like New York, London and Tokyo.

These metropoles are at the same time decision-making and control centers of the world economy, privileged headquarters of financial firms and service sector companies that produce services for production (sectors that have come to the forefront of the economy), places of production and innovation for these service-oriented companies and, finally, markets for the buying and selling of innovative products that are produced by them. In recent years there have been predictions of the decay and obsolescence of big cities as a consequence of de-industrialization and the diffusion applications of information technologies (telecommuting, on-line shopping, etc.). It actually happened in reverse: globalization has re-established the centrality of large metropoles.

Globalized cities are, however, only one of the control mechanisms of the global economy. Multinational corporations and banks and world financial and commercial markets, even though based in these metropoles, have their own specificity. Transnational enterprises that organize their production in various countries, while continuing to keep well-defined headquarters in the most eco-nomically developed and politically strong countries (where they also benefit from the support of powerful nation-states (Martinelli, 1975)), must in fact also ensure that certain functions are carried out (such as guaranteeing the respect of contracts and property rights, the evaluation of real estate risks, arbitration of possible legal controversies) which can no longer be performed (partially or com-pletely) by national governments because they take place in the global market.

A world-system, not a world society

The study of the many dimensions of globalization provides sufficient theoretical and empirical elements for considering the entire world as a single system, and not only in economic terms. Since the sixteenth century the world can be conceptualized as a single economic system, but it is only in recent decades that most people have become aware of living in the same world, mostly by virtue of global media. This awareness can be conceptualized in various ways: we can conceive of planet Earth as an ecosystem; humanity as an endangered species, with related concern for the lives of future generations; the peoples of the world as a single constituency of individuals entitled with equal rights and responsibilities, and to whom decision-makers must be accountable; the world market as an economic space regulated by an international *lex mercatoria* that can guarantee not only investors' rights, but also the rights of workers, consumers, and communities.

However, considering the world as a single system does not imply that a world society exists. A society is a *de facto* network of social relations with mutual expectations, for which a *de jure* normative consensus – reflected in commonly accepted institutions – can be present at different degrees to be ascertained empirically. Following Lockwood's distinction between 'system integration' and 'social integration', we can argue that, at the world level, the growing economic interdependence and social interconnectedness are accompanied by persistently high degrees of political fragmentation and cultural heterogeneity.

The discussion about the existence of a world community is in a similar vein (Brown, 1995). The creation of one world, that is, the notion that the world is becoming more unified or integrated by common forces and practices, is a necessary condition for the emergence of a world community, but it is not a sufficient condition. If society is a cooperative venture for mutual advantage (Rawls, 1971), should we expect the emergence of a worldwide sense of community now that this cooperative venture is becoming worldwide in scope? This sense can be specified in terms of four basic types of consciousness: (1) the anthropological consciousness that recognizes unity in our diversity; (2) the ecological consciousness that recognizes our singular human nature within the biosphere; (3) the civic consciousness of our common responsibilities and solidarity; (4) and the dialogical consciousness that refers both to the critical mind and to the need for mutual understanding (Morin, 1999). Today a transnational civil society, an international public space, and a growing awareness of our common fate as human beings are taking shape, but a global communitarian culture is far from being achieved.

Skeptics argue that it cannot be achieved, since any sense of common identity and solidarity actually requires the existence of others with whom one does not identify, a distinction between them and us. Other scholars add that it is not even a desirable outcome. They argue that a more realistic portrait of the world today is as an association of communities founded on the rule of law but not united in any global project, or in other words, an international society as a practical association (Nardin, 1983). According to this approach the practical association of autonomous entities is not only a more realistic but also a more desirable option than that provided by global projects because the latter tend to be dominated by some powerful actor.

It is indisputable that we no longer live in a world of discrete civilizations, as at the time of the Han Empire and the Roman Empire, nor in the Westphalian order of an international society of states. Instead we live in a fundamentally interconnected global order, integrated by complex patterns of exchange, hierarchy and solidarity among multiple global actors, who are increasingly aware of their interdependence and common fate. But this does not mean we can take for granted the existence of a world society or a worldwide community. An underlying dissonance exists among growing integration and uniformity in economic and social relations and in infrastructural networks, on the one hand, and the persistent fragmentation of political institutions and growing pluralism of cultures, on the other. Tendencies toward homogenization co-exist and conflict with tendencies toward diversification and allow for at least a partially autonomous paths toward and through modernity.

Multiple modernities or varieties of modernity

The critique I made in the third chapter of the unilateral evolutionary model of modernization becomes even more pertinent in the contemporary global world. Modernity has gone global, but this goes together with the diffusion of multiple modernities. The extent to which multiple modernities are different and even alternative to each other or just varieties of a basic model is open to question and at the center of a most interesting contemporary debate.

There are different versions in the literature of multiple modernities. I will discuss the main arguments as they are set out in the most sophisticated formulations, i.e. those of Eisenstadt, Wittrock and Gaunkar. The advocates of the concept of multiple modernities proudly affirm that their approach not only goes against the view of the theories of modernization and of the convergence of industrial societies prevalent in the 1950s, but also against the classical sociological analyses of Marx, Durkheim and even Weber (at least in one reading of his work) since they 'all assumed that the cultural program of modernity as it developed in modern Europe and the basic institutional constellations that emerged there would ultimately … prevail throughout the world'. But, 'the actual developments in modernizing societies have refuted the homogenizing and hegemonic assumptions of this Western project of modernity' (Eisenstadt, 2000: 1). Besides taking a clear stand on the question of the convergence and divergence of modern and modernizing societies and on the identification of modernization and Westernization, the proponents of the multiple modernities approach argue that modernity is first and foremost a cultural program rather than a structural condition or an institutional reality and that 'the history of modernity is a story of continual constitution and reconstitution of a multiplicity of cultural programs'. This is related to the fact that the civilization of modernity as it first developed in the West 'was from its beginnings beset by internal antinomies and contradictions, giving rise to continual critical discourse and political contestation' (ibid.: 7). The first radical transformation of the premises of cultural and political order took place with the expansion of modernity in the Americas and now the crystallization of distinct patterns of modernity has spread to the whole world, since modernity has become a 'common global condition'.

Wittrock recalls two positions that have occupied a prominent place in contemporary discussions – both academic and non-academic – regarding the uniformity or diversity of modern societies. The first position is what he calls 'liberal historicism':

> in the wake of the collapse of the Soviet Union, liberal democracy and market economy, in the particular form that these institutional practices have come to exhibit in recent decades in parts of North America and Western Europe, are seen to provide the sole legitimate models of social organization. These forms will then come to be embraced, if with time lags, across the world. (2000: 53)

The proponents of the first position are not so naive as to assume that this type of global diffusion will entail a development toward cultural, or even linguistic, homogeneity, but think that there is no reason to expect any fundamental institutional innovation that would transcend these types of liberal institutional arrangements. To conclude, this position 'simply elevates the experiences of a single country to the status of a world historical yardstick' (ibid.: 54).

The alternative position, which stresses the multiplicity of modernities, 'focuses attention on the current array of cultural life forms and assigns each of them to a larger civilization entity'. It recognizes the Western European origin of a set of modern technological, economic and political institutions that have become diffused across the globe, although it seems to think that they spread more in the form of a set of ideals than as working realities. It affirms that 'these processes of diffusion and adaptation, however, do not at all mean that the deep-seated cultural and cosmological differences between say Western Europe, China and Japan are about to disappear', since 'in their core identities, these societies remain characterized by the form they acquired during much earlier periods of cultural crystallization' (ibid.: 55).

Wittrock argues that the latter position, although a valid critique of different convergence theories, is not a valid critique of his conception of modernity as a global condition, since modernity:

> is not so much a new unified civilization, global in its extensiveness, unparalleled in its intrusiveness and destructiveness; rather, modernity is a set of promissory notes, i.e. a set of hopes and expectations that entail some minimal conditions of adequacy that may be demanded of macro-sociological institutions no matter how much these institutions may differ in other respects.

In order to sustain this position, Wittrock reminds us that 'modernity from the very inception of its basic ideas in Europe has been characterized by a high degree of variability in institutional forms and conceptual constructions', and argues that:

> the existence of a common global condition does not mean that members of any singular cultural community are about to relinquish their ontological and cosmological assumptions, much less their traditional institutions; it means however that the continuous interpretation, reinterpretation and transformation of those commitments and institutional structures cannot but take account of the commonality of the global condition of modernity. (ibid.: 56)

I share both Wittrock's critique of what calls 'liberal historicism' – which can be seen as an updated version of the unilateral evolutionary model of modernization that I have criticized in the third chapter – and his main thesis that the global condition of modernity surely entails different paths toward and through modernity. But a few critical qualifications are in order, which imply a critique of at least the less subtle versions of the multiple modernities literature.

The European origins and the convergences of different paths toward and through modernity

First, it should be made clear that arguing for the existence of multiple modernities should not mean underplaying the fact that the contemporary global condition originated in the modernity of Europe and has been shaped by this historical experience. The existence of multiple modernities is a matter of empirical evidence; we should look at modernization from a transnational and transcultural perspective, and reject the view that modernization, once activated, moves inescapably toward establishing a certain type of mental outlook (scientific rationalism, pragmatic instrumentalism, secularism) and that certain types of institutional order (popular government, bureaucratic administration, market-driven industrial economy) are indifferent to the culture and politics of a given place. But it is also a matter of empirical evidence that modernity was born as a distinct European (Western) phenomenon – which shaped European identity as a cultural attitude of endless search and quest for knowledge, as going beyond the limit (expressed in such literary figures as Ulysses and Goethe's Faust), of individual freedom and religious tolerance, which crystallized into a set of specific institutions (market-led industrial capitalism, sovereign nation-state, research university). As Gaunkar argues:

> To think in terms of alternative modernities does not mean one blithely abandons the Western discourse on modernity. This is virtually impossible. Modernity has traveled from the West to the rest of the world not only in terms of cultural forms, social practices and institutional arrangements, but also as a form of discourse that interrogates the present. The questioning of the present, which is taking place at every national and cultural site to-day, cannot escape the legacy of Western discourse on modernity: Marx, Weber, Baudelaire, Benjamin, Habermas, Foucault. One can provincialize Western modernity only by thinking through and against its self-understandings, which are frequently cast in universalistic idioms (2001: 14–15)

The second critical qualification stems from the fact that I see greater elements of convergence in contemporary global modernity than some advocates of the multiple modernities' approach would admit; or, more specifically, I see greater similarities in most developing countries with older modern countries and with other modernizing ones than with their own past. The reason is twofold: on one hand, there is the continuous selection, reinterpretation, and reformulation of the imported ideas and institutional patterns of the original Western modern civilization by leaders, elites and collective movements producing innovations and showing an ambivalent attitude toward modernity in general and the West in particular. On the other hand, there are the different responses given to and the different strategies worked out to cope with the structural problems of modernization, such as industrialization, the opening of markets, social differentiation, urbanization and mass migrations. There are different national routes to modernization which are shaped by the structural location of a given country in the world system of economic and political relations (or, in other words in the global division of labor and distribution of power), by its specific genetic code, and by the strategies of those individual and collective actors – endowed with cultural and organizational resources – which are the key agents of modernization. In this sense different countries work out what we may call cultural and institutional equivalents to cope with common problems. The advocates of the multiple modernities' approach tend to neglect the global dimension and to over-emphasize local and national specificities, and tend to stress actors' cultural codes and under-estimate the structural context.

Most accounts of multiple modernities do not answer satisfactorily such relevant questions as: What *kinds* of diversity exist between different (modern) societies? How *profound* are the existing differences? And what are their future *prospects*? Are they more likely to persist, to withstand further social change ('globalization'), perhaps even to deepen as a result of (resistance to) it, or do we have reason to expect that they will diminish in the long run? Moreover, if we all experience the modern global condition, does this imply that all societies are equally modern now? Or is modernity a matter of degree? What does it exactly mean to be modern anyway?

Schmidt (2004) argues that since questions such as these have not been satisfactorily answered in the affirmative, they cannot justify the language of multiple modernities. Rather it would be more appropriate to speak of 'varieties of modernity'. According to him, the problem is

> whether Japan, China, India or whichever region or country one may consider – is so unique as to justify – or even warrant – the conceptualization of its institutional and cultural outlook in its own, and, what is more, even in civilizational terms – so different that something very important would be missed if Japan were treated as one of several members of a common family of modern societies. Is that really the case?

The question to be answered, however, is not as Schmidt frames it: 'Does contemporary Japan have more in common with pre-modern Japan than with, say, contemporary Canada or contemporary Germany?', because even if the answer is negative, it does not rule out the fact that Japanese modernity is strikingly different from, say, French modernity. Eisenstadt neatly addresses this question arguing that

> while a general trend toward structural differentiation developed across a wide range of institutions in most of these societies-in family, economic and political structures, urbanization, modern education, mass communication, and individualistic orientations-the ways in which these arenas were defined and organized varied greatly, in different periods of their development, giving rise to multiple institutional and ideological patterns. Significantly, these patterns did not constitute simple continuations in the modern era of the traditions of their respective societies. Such patterns were distinctively modern, through greatly influenced by specific cultural premises, traditions and historical experiences. All developed distinctly modern dynamics and modes of interpretation, for which the original Western project constituted the crucial (and usually ambivalent) reference point. Many of the movements that developed in non-Western societies articulated

strong anti-Western or even anti-modern themes, yet all were distinctively modern. There are multiple modernities also because there are different programs of modernity and different social actors who interpret them. (Eisenstadt, 1997: 55)

One can agree with two basic premises of my argument, i.e. that the breakthrough to modernization is a genuinely revolutionary process, radically transforming all aspects of life, and that today modernity is becoming global, and at the same time we can recognize the existence of multiple modernities Schmidt is right, however, to point out that much literature on multiple modernities does not clarify sufficiently what is being compared between two or more social entities (which need not be states) and it does not analyze in depth the basic questions about what are the existing differences between different (modern) societies, and how profound they are and how they are likely to evolve in the future (whereas the answers depend on what precisely one looks at). Some advocates of the multiple modernities approach do not even permit the posing of such questions as the very premises on which they rest imply that there must be greater variance across civilizational lines than across epochs in world history. But, given that almost everyone agrees that modern society – be it in the singular or in the plural – differs from pre-modern society – be it in the singular or in the plural too – the assumed differences between the newly discovered multiple modernities must be very profound indeed. For if they were not, then there would be no sound basis for speaking of modernities in the plural.

Defenders of the notion of multiple modernities might reply that I read too much into their accounts and that their aim is only to highlight a number of cultural differences between different parts of the world that are easily missed when approaching the whole world as one, which modernization theory seems to do. But while it may well be the case that modernization theorists have a tendency to under-estimate existing differences, we should also guard against over-stating them. In particular, we should be more specific about the exact nature of the differences that we claim to exist and about the reasons for their ascribed magnitude.

The arbitrary separation between the cultural and the other dimensions of modernization

The third critical qualification which I make to most advocates of the multiple modernities' approach is their tendency to focus mostly on cultural factors at the expenses of structural and institutional factors in the analysis of modernization, which in turn induces them to over-rate existing differences between countries and regions living the same experience of global modernity. An example of this way of reasoning is Taylor's distinction between acultural and cultural theories of modernity, where an *acultural* theory describes the transition to modernity in terms of a set of culture-neutral operations, which are viewed as 'input' that can transform any traditional society, whereas a *cultural* theory conceives modernity as a set of transformations defined by their position in a specific constellation of understandings of personhood, nature, social relations, goods and bads, virtues and vices, which are translated into specific languages and practices which are often mutually untranslatable (Taylor, 2001: 172–3).

A convincing target of Taylor's critique are those accounts of modernization which see Western modernity itself as a culture with a distinctive moral and philosophical outlook and which impose a false uniformity on the diverse encounters of non-Western cultures with the allegedly culture-neutral forms and processes on the basis of the belief that 'any culture could suffer the impact of growing scientific consciousness, any religion could undergo secularization, any set of ultimate ends could be challenged by the growth of instrumental thinking, any metaphysic could be dislocated by the split between fact and value' (ibid.: 173). But Taylor's thesis of the 'two theories of modernity' overshoots its target, insofar as it does not adequately problematize the unavoidable dialectic of convergence and divergence. Structural aspects of modernization such as industrialization, urbanization, social and geographical mobility, and modern institutions like the democratic nation-state, the liberal market economy, or the research-oriented university are closely linked to profound cultural changes in Western culture, and when they take place or are adopted in non-Western cultures, they cannot be fully separated from their cultural premises. Taylor stresses the unity of cultural and institutional aspects of modernity within each specific culture, but arbitrarily separates them whenever modern institutions spread to other parts of the world than those where they started. In this sense, Taylor's thesis of the 'two theories of modernity' is a step back with regard to his previous formulation in 'Nationalism and Modernity' (McKim and McMahon, 1997), because some major instances of the so-called acultural theory of modernity such as Weber's process of rationalization are not acultural at all Taylor is ambiguous in this respect since at first he states that 'in Max Weber's interpretation, rationalization was a steady process, occurring within all cultures over time' (2001: 174), while later on he acknowledges that Weber 'gave a reading of the Protestant ethic as a particular set of religio-moral concerns that in turn helped to bring about modern capitalism' (ibid.: 175).

This is not the view of all scholars identifiable with the multiple modernities approach. Wittrock's position is more balanced:

> modernity may be understood as culturally constituted and institutionally entrenched ... the institutional projects of modernity – be they a democratic nation-state, a liberal market economy, or a research-oriented university – cannot be understood unless their grounding in profound cultural changes is recognized. Ultimately, these institutional projects were premised on new assumptions about human beings, their rights and agency. These conceptual changes entailed promissory notes that came to constitute new affiliations, identities, and, ultimately, institutional realities. (2000: 36–8)

European modernity was not simply a package of technological and organizational developments; it was intimately linked to a political revolution, to an equally important transformation of the nature of scholarly and scientific practices and institutions.

Modernity can be defined in terms of a conjunction, with global implications, of a set of cultural, institutional and structural shifts which originated in a specific part of the world and then spread all over. As Collins argues (1999), a multidimensional model of modernization should take into account four variously related basic dimensions: bureaucratization, capitalist industrialization, secularization, and democratization.

Modernity had unavoidable, irresistible consequences, which Taylor himself admits: 'modernity is like a wave, flowing over and engulfing one traditional culture after another' (2001: 279). Recognizing this obvious fact does not amount to denying the existence of multiple modernities, since 'a successful transition involves a people finding resources in their traditional culture to take on the new practices. In this sense modernity is not a single wave.' However, precisely because the structural processes of modernity and the economic and political institutions of modernity are strictly connected to a specific modern culture that is different both from its predecessors' cultures and non-Western cultures, the extent to which they can take place or be adopted through a process of creative adaptation by non-Western cultures has definite limits.

It may be true that science and technology are neutral means that are applicable to different goals (D'Andrea, 2001); but if Western modernity corresponds to the absence of ethical limits to the technical dominion of nature, to what extent does the diffusion of modern science and technology imply deep changes in the value orientations of non-Western cultures? It may also be true that free market capitalism can be adapted to and co-exist with alternative political regimes and lifestyles, but, if this is the case, we will witness different varieties of capitalism rather than alternative multiple modernities, since differences in production regimes and in consumption patterns will have a limited range of variation. Moreover, if modernity corresponded historically with the beginning of the semantics of rights, with the forming of the concept of a core of individual freedoms (Bobbio, 1979) we can expect that the encounter with cultures based on community-based social cement will be very controversial and conflictual. Thomas McCarthy (2001) poses the crucial question of whether modern law, with its conceptions of basic human rights, belongs in Taylor's view and the answer is Rawls' notion of overlapping consensus (Rawls, 1993). It is a sensible but very abstract solution if only one considers the potential for conflict in husband/wife relations in mixed-ethnic communities and in such decisions as raising children by couples with different religious faiths.

Even the most controversial relation of all, that between modernity and democracy, requires a greater appreciation of the dialectics between convergence and divergence in non-Western modernizing countries. If, as Dahrendorf maintains, reinterpreting de Tocqueville, modernity involves two primary elements: the generalization of citizenship rights (or more modestly, the basic equality of status of all members of society) and the mobilization of people and their needs, demands and wishes, which is a precondition of economic growth, we should expect political struggles and regime changes in authoritarian states with open market economies (Dahrendorf, 1992: 16).

The hurried dismissal of previous theories of modernization

The fourth critical qualification has to do with the way most multiple modernities' advocates reject *in toto* the ideas of modernization theorists, and misunderstand their views. This book has tried to show that some of these ideas are still fruitful, if properly reformulated and updated in the light of globalization. Actually, as Schmidt remarks (2004), the literature on multiple modernities 'largely relies on an implicit notion of modernity which, when closely scrutinised, actually appears surprisingly close to that underlying much of the work of modernization theorists, only thinner', since to the extent that a theory of modernity is outlined at all, it is a self-proclaimed cultural theory, as in the accounts by Taylor (2001). Whereas modernization theory aims to capture the whole structure of modern society and all aspects of the dramatic change processes that give rise to its emergence, the literature on multiple modernities focuses almost exclusively on cultural factors and the ways these are believed to frame politics and the political order (as though modernity was identical to its polity or to the modern state).

The relationship between modernity and religion is actually an instance of mis-understanding. One of the main targets of the critique of classical modernization theory by multiple modernities advocates is the idea that modernization leads to secularization, a critique based on the empirical evidence concerning the contin-uing importance of religious beliefs and practices in global modernity. But for modernization theorists, secularization does not necessarily imply the complete vanishing or disappearance of religion. It only implies its gradual separation from many spheres of society in which its viewpoints can no longer claim paramount importance because the spheres (i.e., the economy, politics, the law, sciences, etc.) become structurally autonomous from religion and increasingly follow their own norms – an issue raised already by Max Weber in his notion of distinct 'value spheres'. And it implies that man and nature are less and less perceived as phe-nomena directly regulated by God's will or by some transcendent metaphysical principles as in the great religions and more and more as autonomous entities which can be understood by the human reason. The fact that most Americans believe in God does not mean the United States is not a modern society: it means that religion seems to interfere much less than in pre-modern contexts such as medieval Europe with American science, economics and politics.

In general, the contributions of modernization theorists are usually dismissed as theoretically obsolete and ideologically biased, without any effort to distinguish 'what is dead and what is alive' in those theories. There are, however, a few sig-nificant exceptions by authors who honestly recognize their debts, like Eisenstadt who recognizes the insights of Lerner and Inkeles on two basic components of the modern project, i.e. the awareness of a great variety of roles existing beyond nar-row, local, and familial ones and the possibility of belonging to wider translocal, changing communities (2000: 4). and Therborn's (1995) reference to Black's (1966) four different points of entry into modernity. But usually references are made even when recent writings are just new wine in old bottles. No doubt, the the classical theories of modernization of Marx, Weber and Durkheim (and other post-war modernization theorists) implicitly or explicitly exaggerate the degree of simultaneity of the different dimensions of modernization – assuming that although analytically distinct, they take place together; but the multiple moderni-ties' advocates exaggerate the degree of disjunction of such processes. In conclu-sion, I agree with those scholars who stress the co-existence of structural processes and cultural attitudes, like Gellner who argues that specialization, atomization, instrumental rationality, independence of fact and value, growth and provisionality of knowledge are all linked with each other.

The relevant point to make is that co-existence does not mean coherence. From its beginning in the West the civilization of modernity was beset by internal contradictions, giving rise to intellectual criticism and socio-political conflict. In the fourth chapter I discussed Berman's account of the tension between 'the modern promises of adventure, power, joy, growth, transformation of ourselves and the world and, at the same time, the modern threat of destroying everything we have, everything we know, everything we are', the conflict between instrumental rationality and communicative rationality as central in Habermas's theory of modernity, the revolt of the subject against reason in Touraine's account, as well as the contradictory mix of liberty and discipline in Wagner's interpretation of modernity. We can add here a few other formulations of the inherent tensions and conflicts of modernity. Castoriadis (1987) argues that modernity entails a central conflict between the 'radical imagination' – which presents the image of a self-creating society of autonomous individuals – and the 'institutional imaginary' of capitalism with its penchant for rational and instrumental mastery of human beings and objects. Delanty (1999) discusses the basic tension in modernity between autonomy of the subject and social fragmentation. On the one hand, modernity as a cultural project refers to the autonomy of the individual, the self-assertion of the individual and the progressive expansion of the discourses of creativity, reflexivity and discoursivity in all spheres of life. On the other, modernity entails the experience of fragmentation, in the sense that modernity as a social project destroys its own cultural foundations. And for Eisenstadt (2000) perhaps the most critical rift in both ideological and political terms was that which separated universal and pluralistic visions, between a view that accepted the existence of different values and rationalities and a view that conflated different values and, above all, rationalities, in a totalistic way.

The inherently contradictory character of the civilization of modernity fosters the perspective of multiple modernities in the sense that non-Western cultures can, at least to some extent, creatively select some aspects rather than others and develop original responses. Eisenstadt argues that 'the ideas of multiple modernities presumes that the best way to understand the contemporary world – indeed to explain the history of modernity – is to see it as a story of continual constitution and reconstitution of a multiplicity of cultural programs' (2000: 3).

But I stress once again that the multiplicity of cultural programs is limited and must be contextualized in the light of world economic and political relations that constrain the range of specific institutional responses which are given to the relatively similar structural changes that all modernizing countries have to face. In this respect, I consider the concept of cultural hegemony (in Gramsci's sense) relevant for the discussion of multiple modernities. In the contemporary world (even more than in the past), those countries/peoples that hold economic, political and military might exert a cultural hegemony as well and become a model to be imitated. The so-called 'soft power' – favored by the control of major global media – is often more important than the 'hard power' of military force. However, even this cultural hegemony is far from complete, not only because it is challenged by alternative cultural values, messages and visions but also because it is criticized from within; the contradictory character of Western modernity, its very nature of critical self-awareness and of democratic public discourse run contrary to the ideological indoctrination by the most powerful. Globalization favors global control, but at the same time it fosters global opposition (no-global and new-global movements, anti-Western political actors, etc.), as well as self-criticism and protest movements within the Western countries themselves.

A final critical qualification, which concerns only a few proponents of the multiple modernities approach, is that there is no need to link the notion of multiple modernities to that of postmodernity. Long ago, Amartya Sen (1966) criticized the peculiarly Hindu mix of postmodern enthusiasts – who ride the Western wave with a scrupulously anti-Western program – with pre-modern supporters of Hindu fundamentalism. Both are convinced that India must be preserved by the aggression of the so-called modern culture, because they are the victims of a serious prejudice, that of considering India as a culturally fragile country running the risk of losing its fundamental values under the impact of Western culture. They misread Indian history and forget that the country has been able to absorb influences of many kinds without giving up its own identity. And more recently, Gaunker (2001) persuasively argues that to announce the general end of modernity even as an epoch, much less than an attitude or an ethos, seems premature, if not patently ethnocentric at a time when non-Western people everywhere are beginning to engage critically with their own hybrid modernities.

In spite of these weaknesses, the advocates of multiple modernities make an important contribution by stressing the fact that there are as many roads to modernity as there are cultures. But because of the critical qualifications I have developed, I tend to share a mild view of the multiple modernities approach which is close to the varieties of capitalism perspective and which recognizes both the strength of the flowing wave of modernity and the possibility of creative adaptation along the lines of scholars like Gaunkar, Eisenstadt and Wittrock.

The dialectic of convergence and divergence

To think productively along the lines suggested by the idea of alternative modernities, we have to recognize and problematize the unavoidable dialectic of convergence and divergence. It is customary to think of convergence in terms of institutional arrangements and of divergence primarily in terms of lived experiences and cultural expressions of modernity. The idea of alternative modernities focuses on

> that narrow but critical band of variations consisting of site-specific creative adaptations on the axis of convergence… Creative adaptation is not simply a matter of adjusting the form or recoding the practice to soften the impact of modernity; rather it points to the manifold ways in which a people question the present. It is a site where people 'make' themselves modern, as opposed to being 'made' modern by alien and impersonal forces, and where they give themselves an identity and a destiny. (Gaunkar, 2001: 17–18)

Although empirical research along these lines is not extensive, some interesting contributions exist such as Hanchard's (2001) essay and Chakrabarty's (2001) essay. The former's essay, 'Afro-Modernity: Temporality, Politics and the African

Diaspora', studies the case of the African peoples' diaspora; often violently captured and removed from home, deprived of their languages, traditions and territory, forced to adopt the languages, religions and political ideas of their oppressors, they have succeeded in articulating a distinctive culture which often includes a vision of pan-African modernity. The latter's, 'Adda, Calcutta: dwelling and modernity', shows how creative adaptation, even when it succeeds as for the addas in Calcutta, succeeds only in exposing the tensions inherent into the process of learning to live with modernity.

Drawing on Lee's study of Shanghai in the 1930s and Chakrabarty's study of Calcutta in the 1940s, Gaunkar remarks that modernity is more often perceived as a lure than as threat, and people (not just the elite) everywhere, at every national or cultural site, rise to meet it, negotiate it, and appropriate it in their own fashion. Everything in sight is called modern: 'modern coffee house', 'Modern Age' the magazine for the 'modern woman', 'modern education', and so on. The Shangai modernist elite, especially writers, artists and political activists (including communists) eagerly consumed Western offerings; but they did so not in the mode of 'colonial minority' but in a cosmopolitan mode of dialogue and engagement, dazzled by and hungry for Western ideas, experiences and cultural forms, they remained certain of their identity as 'Chinese'. In spite of enormous differences with the contemporary modernization which involves a whole country and not limited minorities within a politically independent state, today the Chinese are also lured and dazzled by modernity while maintaining their Chinese identity. Other empirical evidence comes from research on the Africanization of Westernization which has taken place in various forms and degrees in post-colonial Africa (Bernardi, 1998).

Although cultural modernity is conventionally seen as both the machinery and the optic for the limitless production of differences, such difference always functions within a penumbra of similarities, and such similarities may be seen in the style of the *flâneur*, the mystique of fashion, the magic of the city, the ethos of irony, or the anxiety of mimicry, all ineffable yet recognizable across the noise of difference. What is common to these strings of similarities is a mood of distance, a habit of questioning, and an intimation of what Baudelaire calls the 'marvelous' in the midst of the ruins of our tradition, the tradition of the new. Whether these common intensities, which regularly find expression in popular media, especially film and music, will one day pave the way for an ethic of the global modern remains to be seen. And Gaunkar tentatively concludes that:

> just as societal modernization (the prime source of convergence theories) produces difference through creative adaptation or unintended consequences, so also cultural modernity (the prime source of divergence theories) produce similarities on its own borders...: everywhere, at every national/cultural site, modernity is not one but many; modernity is not new but old and familiar; modernity is incomplete and necessarily so. (2001: 23)

The existence of multiple modernities and varieties of modernity is explained by the different structural arrangements and cultural codes of modernizing countries and by the impact of the world economy and of the international division of power. But multiple modernities are possible also because globalization erodes nation-states' sovereignty, but not to the point of preventing governments from being proactive agents of development and modernization. In order to evaluate the role played by this key factor we now turn to the discussion of the question of the nation-state, another key aspect of the relation between globalization and modernization.

Globalization and the nation-state

Globalization is having an ambivalent impact on modernizing countries. On one hand, social and economic interconnectedness and the cultural impact of modernity as a global condition foster the modernization of less developed countries through the diffusion of symbolic, universal means of trade and abstract systems of scientific-technical knowledge; on the other, the erosion of national sovereignty and state autonomy limits the role of a key actor in the path toward modernity. In fact, effective nation-building has been and still is a necessary precondition of successful modernization. States play a key role in creating the institutional and legal framework favorable to development and in implementing policies aimed at controlling the social contradictions and political conflicts inherent in growth and modernization; and states' autonomy is necessary in order to resist attempts of economic exploitation and political domination by powerful global actors (other states, TNCs, etc.) within their territory and in international governmental organizations. The extent and nature of the erosion of national sovereignty are therefore of utmost importance in the analysis of modernization. We will discuss this question, first, in general terms and, then, with specific reference to a set of major state policies.

The institutional embodiment of political authority in modern society has been the nation-state, i.e., an impersonal and sovereign political entity with supreme jurisdiction over a clearly delimited territory and population, claiming a monopoly of coercive power, and enjoying legitimacy as a result of its citizens' support. As with other complex integrative institutions, the nation-state is not based on one principle only, insofar as it is both an organization and a community (real and imagined at the same time). It has developed historically through the growth of a civil bureaucracy, an army and a diplomacy, and through the formation of a nation as an imagined community (Anderson, 1991), resulting from the action of nationalist elites in the modernization process (Gellner, 1983) and capable of evoking primordial ethno-symbolic roots (Smith, 1983).

World system integration in the twentieth century has been the result of social integration at the nation-state level (including colonies wherever existed), an array of bilateral and multilateral treaties, and an increasing web of intergovernmental organizations. The so-called 'Westphalian order', starting with the peace treaty that ended the Thirty Years War and reaching its full articulation after the Napoleon wars, was based on a few principles: the formal equality of sovereign territorial states that recognize no superior authority, non-intervention in the domestic affairs of other recognized states, and consent as the basis of international legal obligation, plus the establishment of some minimal rules of co-existence (Cassese, 1986).

In the Westphalian order there are a few basic differences between the domestic and foreign realms: democracy within nation-states and non-democratic relations among states; the entrenchment of accountability and democratic legitimacy within state boundaries and the pursuit of the national interest (and maximum political advantage) outside of those boundaries; democracy and citizenship rights for those regarded as 'insiders' and the frequent negation of these rights for those on the outside (Held et al., 1999). In contemporary global politics, all these basic distinctions are becoming increasingly blurred. Today, the international society of states is becoming an interconnected global order, where people, goods, services, money, knowledge, news, images, beliefs, lifestyles, weapons, crime, drugs, and pollutants rapidly move across territorial boundaries.

The Westphalian and the post-Westphalian orders should be considered as ideal types of the international system rather than clearly defined historical phases. I agree with Krasner's critique in this respect: it is an instance of historical myopia to consider the Westphalian order as a model 'which describes a kind of golden age when states exercised an absolute authority within their borders', an order today violated by the forces of globalization. This order has been actually often violated because of asymmetries of power and diversity of interests of state actors and because of the weakness of regulating institutions. Those violations have taken various forms, from conventions (where rulers enter into voluntary agreements such as human rights accords) to coercion and imposition of the will of stronger states. Weaker states have seen their borders penetrated and experienced forms of limited sovereignty but even stronger states have not been immune to external influence.

Contrary to Krasner, however, I think that present globalization tends to erode the basis of sovereignty and autonomy of nation-states more than in the past. This is ironic, since the twentieth century was, among other things, the century of the proliferation of nation-states as the basic form of political organization. And it is paradoxical since the states of major Western countries have contributed to the creation of a context favorable to the financial and productive globalization through policies of market deregulation and free-trade doctrines, which in their turn have reduced the effectiveness of government policies (such as income policies) which were already compromised by the strategies of multinational corporations (Martinelli, 1975). Globalization tends to erode state capabilities at the very moment when government effectiveness is badly needed to manage the effects of the global market.

Predictions of the demise of the state are not new: just to take one example, Kindleberger already in 1969 affirmed that the nation-state had practically ceased to exist as an economic entity. These kinds of predictions have intensified recently: authors like Reinecke (1998) and Thurow (1999) maintain that states have lost the monopoly of internal sovereignty and soon will no longer be the key actor of international relations. Hyperglobalists of different ideological orientation – from Albrow (1996), who stresses the narrowing of choices of nation-states compelled to adopt neo-liberal economic policies in order to compete in the world market, to Strange (1996), who complains that the impersonal forces of world markets are more powerful than the states – have exaggerated the demise of the nation-state and should be criticized for not distinguishing among states with quite different levels of power and influence. More convincing is Rosenau's view (1997) which sees a global political system as characterized by the coexistence of a state-centric world-made of sovereign states – and a multi-centric world – made up of non-sovereign collective actors; this co-existence will last a long time, since there are not in sight political entities capable of replacing states as factors of social cohesion nor world institutions capable of institutionalizing the centralizing dynamics of the multi-centric world.

The erosion of national sovereignty and the developmental state

The erosion of state sovereignty and the decline of state autonomy are real, both as a result of the inescapable processes of global interconnectedness and of the conscious decisions made by certain governments to give away parts of their sovereignty to supranational institutions like the European Union. Those who think that the inter-state order is too entrenched and powerful to be in crisis forget that several global actors (financial markets, transnational corporations, collective movements, and churches) are already in a position to ignore many norms and obligations set by states. Among the many instances of sovereignty's erosion, we may here recall:

- the constraints set by international monetary institutions on the economic policies of national governments;
- the impact of transnational corporations' strategies on workers, consumers, and entrepreneurs of the countries where they operate;
- the permeability of national frontiers to illegal immigrants;
- the difficulties faced by authoritarian regimes in filtering or altogether banning the images and information of the 'global village';
- the problems of co-existence between different cultures in increasingly multiethnic societies.

However, the extent of the erosion should not be exaggerated. Recent political and financial crises have in fact favored new forms of government interventions. In the United States, the Sarbanes–Oxley law has introduced more severe controls on financial operations and anti-terrorism laws have introduced constraints on the free circulation of people and goods. The Commission of the European Union has strengthened anti-monopolistic controls and upgraded its fight against the so-called tax-havens. In China, progressive integration into the world market goes together with a huge sphere of state control. In the World Trade Organization, free market advocates like the USA and the EU are pursuing protectionist policies in steel and agriculture.

In order to evaluate the type and degree of a state's erosion induced by globalization we have to define more clearly the different meanings and definitions of sovereignty. Krasner (2001) identifies four main definitions: first, that focusing on the organization of authority within territorial boundaries, the regulation of economic activity and the maintenance of order by public entities; second, the control exercised by public authorities over trans-border movements; third, the right of certain actors to enter into international agreements; and, finally, the Westphalian institutional arrangement for organizing political life that is based on territoriality and autonomy. Constraints on the different versions of sovereignty often reinforce each other, but they can also be independent of each other. Violations concerning one dimension do not necessarily imply that sovereignty as a whole is eroded: for instance, poor control over trans-border movements of illegal immigrants can be compatible with strong state authority.

Keeping these distinctions in mind, I will examine how the scope and speed of global movements of people, capital, goods, services, information, messages, images, have made states less capable of implementing effective polices of economic growth and social cohesion, at the very time when they have a greater need to protect themselves from external destabilizing factors and to manage the greater ethnic and cultural complexity of their societies. But I will also show how the erosion is uneven among states and how opportunities exist for the 'developmental' or 'catalytic' state. More specifically, I will investigate the following:

1. to what extent national frontiers are permeable and difficult to control;
2. to what extent states are capable of deciding and implementing macroeconomic policies, as well as industrial and other supply-side policies;
3. to what extent states are able to raise the resources to implement extensive welfare and redistributional policies.

First, the erosion of state sovereignty is a general but uneven phenomenon, since states differ very much in terms of economic, political, military and cultural power. However, as the September 11th terrorist attack on New York and Washington dramatically showed, even the most powerful state in the world is unable to perform as basic a task of a sovereign state as the control of its frontiers. And how could it? In one year, 475 million people, 125 million vehicles, and 21 million import shipments come into the country at 3,700 terminals in 301 ports of entry. It takes five hours to inspect a fully loaded 40-foot shipping container, and more than 5 million enter each year. In addition, more than 2.7 million undocumented immigrants have simply walked or driven across the Mexican and Canadian borders in recent years. A terrorist can easily slip in, and it is easier to bring a few pounds of a deadly biological or chemical agent than to smuggle in the tons of illegal heroin or cocaine that arrive annually. The only way for the Customs Service and the Immigration and Naturalization Service to cope with such flows is to reach beyond the national borders through intelligence and cooperation within the jurisdiction of other states, and to rely on private corporations to develop transparent systems for tracking international commercial flows so that enforcement officials can conduct virtual audits of inbound shipments before they arrive. Thus custom officers work throughout Latin America to assist businesses in the implementation of security programs that reduce the risk of being exploited by drug smugglers, and cooperative international mechanisms are being developed for policy trade flows. The sovereign state adapts, but in doing so it transforms the meaning and exclusivity of governmental jurisdiction. 'Legal borders do not change, but they blur in practice' (Nye, 2002). In a similar vein, the Schengen Treaty for the free circulation of people in most member states of the European Union has made control of the frontiers more difficult, and it has accelerated strategies of intensified cooperation between the judiciaries and law and order agencies of the various states.

Second, in a global market of free-moving financial capital, once governments renounce trade protectionism and capital restrictions, the range of macroeconomic policy options is limited (Berger, 2000). Policy-makers may rely on monetary policy (the exchange rate and the interest rate) and fiscal policy. But even the use of these instruments is not discretionary for those countries that have linked their currency to the US dollar and/or have to maintain their borders open in order to keep the support of international financial institutions and to check the outflow of investors, even if interest rates soar and the currency falls. For the European Union countries using the Euro, the policy of competitive devaluation of the national currency is no longer available. This limited macroeconomic sovereignty is not only the inevitable consequence of global market constraints, but also the result of conscious policy decisions: many newly-industrializing countries are so focused on the need to attract foreign investment that they have given up using fiscal leverage; many developing countries have established free trade zones in which tax holidays are offered and normal regulatory requirements do not apply. Przeworski and Wallerstein (1988) and Scharpf (1991), among others, argue that this happens because globalization reduces the taxation of capital, which is mobile, and shifts the tax burden onto labor, which is less mobile. Even when governments want to tax foreign investment, transnational corporations can escape the burden of taxes through transfer pricing: the organization of production on a global scale allows the under- or over-charging by TNCs through internal transactions so as to artificially boost profits in low tax countries and reduce them in high tax ones (OECD, 1991; Cassou, 1997; Eichengreen, 1997). Other studies contradict this view. Garrett (1998), and Steinmo and Swank (1999) among others, point out that corporate tax burden (as a percentage of operating income) for the 17 largest and richest OECD countries has changed very little in the 1990s.

Over-emphasizing the structural constraints of macro-economic sovereignty risks obscuring the responsibility of political elites in developing countries. Options are limited, but they do exist: even if they share the need to attract foreign investment, governments have a choice, and differ with regard to the strategies they adopt: they can try to attract investments either through policies of low corporate taxation, low wages, limited guarantees for workers' rights, and scarce protection of the environment, or through the creation of good infrastructures, high investments in education and research, the development of an efficient public administration, or the fight against corruption. The mix of low taxes and low wages with poor labor and poor environmental standards is the way often preferred by corrupt elites.

Similar arguments apply to the problem of which industrial and other supply-side policies are available in a globalizing world. In the post-war decades, newly-industrializing economies and modernizing nation-states such as Japan, Italy, Spain, Korea, Singapore, Taiwan, could rely not only on capital control and trade barriers, but also on an array of policies to encourage specific industries: export subsidies, preferential credit, research and development grants, aid for the less developed areas, government procurement, or protection of domestic markets for key industries, etc. These industrial policies are more difficult in the contemporary world economy. A few examples are sufficient to prove this point: the rules of the global market make it difficult for states to help domestic industries in a way similar to that adopted by Germany or the United States in the nineteenth century. The complex supply chains that operate within transnational networks of production weaken the links between domestic producers and retailers. Local investors can choose to invest abroad if they can get higher returns, with the consequence that small firms in developing countries have difficult access to credit (with the notable exceptions of the 'bankers of the poor' like Yussuf and the enablers of new entrepreneurship like De Soto). Again, however, the choices for governments are limited but by no means lacking: investments in human capital and modern infrastructures are significant examples of socially compatible strategies of industrial development.

Even more controversial is the question as to whether globalization forces governments to renounce welfare and redistributional policies. The arguments of those who are convinced it does are the same as those which argue for the erosion of macro-economic sovereignty: that governments' fiscal policy is constrained by capital mobility, since taxes cannot be raised both in order to keep foreign investors and to avoid reducing the competitive advantage of domestic producers; that large budget deficits, without the possibility of exchange-rate devaluations, raise the prospect of inflation and higher interest rates, so that welfare expenditures must be cut and demand stimulation through deficit spending is not viable. For developed countries that had extensive welfare states the threat exists of dismantling it at least partially, for developing countries, the chances are that it will never develop and that competition between country systems will take the form of a race to the bottom in wages, social guarantees and labor-market regulation.

The pressures on welfare policies are real but they have been exaggerated. The thesis that attributes to globalization the primary responsibility for welfare cuts in European countries is not convincing. We should not forget that the primary source for these cuts were the 'fiscal crisis of the state' exemplified by huge state budget deficits of the 1970s (to which were added, for the Euro countries, the requirements set by the Maastricht Treaty). There are ways to combine strategies of growth and of higher competitiveness in the world market and strategies of keeping high levels of welfare protection through an effective combination of market, government and community mechanisms. For developing countries options are certainly more limited, but, again, choices exist for honest political elites committed to sound institution building and human capital development and determined to fight against growing wealth and income inequalities and to renounce the race to the bottom in the attempt to attract foreign capital.

A more threatening implication of globalization for modernizing countries is the impact on citizens' attachment to national authority, leading to a decline in the legitimacy of central governments. Here again the picture varies from one country to another. Several post-colonial countries, mostly in Africa, bear the consequences of frontiers traced according to the colonial powers' interests or partition agreements and with no regard to the country's historical heritage or ethnic and religious homogeneity. Other states are too weak to protect themselves from the interference of powerful global actors interested by natural resources. For those other countries where legitimate elites exist, the erosion of sovereignty by global forces is compensated for by citizens' demands for a more active state role in controlling international movements, negotiating agreements in international governmental organizations, coping with social and environmental problems.

The erosion of national sovereignty and power is only part of the picture and its extent has largely been over-estimated by the hyperglobalizers who argue for the demise of the nation-state. The other part of the picture is a reconstitution of state power, both in the developed countries and in the most powerful developing ones. In reality, because of the multifaceted impact of globalization, nation-states are undergoing a deep transformation, as their functions and powers are rearticulated and re-embedded in complex transnational, regional and local networks. Global flows stimulate a variety of adjustment strategies through national policies that require a rather active state – neither the neo-liberal minimum government nor the waning state of the hyperglobalizers, but the 'developmental' or 'catalytic' state. As an illustration of this continuous but changing governmental role we can cite the development of competitive industrial policies aimed at creating the most favorable conditions for foreign investment (friendly corporate law and fiscal policy, good infrastructures, flexible labor force, efficient public administration, etc.), while at the same time maintaining control over basic development strategies. We can therefore agree with Rosenau (1997) that the state is not reduced, but rather reconstructed and restructured, and with Keohane (1984) that sovereignty is less a territorially defined barrier than a resource for a politics characterized by complex transnational networks of competitive country systems and regional systems. Transnational forces increasingly challenge national sovereignty, but nation-states will remain key actors in global governance for a long time.

The varieties of capitalism and state sovereignty

We arrive at this conclusion through discussion of the literature on multiple modernities and on the varieties of capitalism. We have discussed the issue of multiple modernities in the previous section; what we need to stress here is that it constitutes an indirect proof of the continuing relevance of the nation-state even in a context of erosion of national sovereignty. In fact, if significant differences exist in the modernization of developing countries, they are due not only to their different cultural codes and in the ways they creatively adapt to the culture of modernity, but also to the different institutional configurations which systematically influence actors' behavior. A similar line of reasoning can be developed with regard to the literature on the varieties of capitalism. One of the key theses of the hyperglobalists is that the impersonal forces of the global market foster a growing homogeneity in the institutional design of modern economies. The advocates of the national varieties of capitalism, on the contrary, maintain that globalization has a quite different impact on the institutional configurations of different national systems. Different production regimes (Soskice, 1999), i.e. the set of rules and institutions regulating the industrial relations system, the educational and training system, the relations among firms, and corporate governance and finance, provide different responses to the challenges of globalization, according to a notion of comparative institutional advantage (Hall, 1997). The question is, for instance, whether a specific model of capitalism is made more or less vulnerable by global interdependence, whether the American market-led flexible model is more or less competitive than the continental European social market economy model. The answer is not univocal; the American model is appreciated for its more flexible labor market, better research institutions and closer relations between universities and firms, more developed financial markets and faster responses to the faults of corporate governance, but is criticized for adopting a model of corporate control too oriented to short-term stock values (Fligstein, 2001). By contrast, the continental European model of the social market economy is praised for trying to combine economic growth with social cohesion and environmental sustainability, but is criticized for its greater rigidity and smaller propensity for innovation. The discussion of the strengths and weaknesses in the performance of different models of capitalism is even more relevant for developing countries. Here too different routes to modernity are available and state policies play an important role, although limited by global interconnectedness.

Over-emphasizing the erosion of state powers risks obscuring two questions that are very relevant for global governance and the question of power and authority. The first question concerns the fact that most of the policies that can regulate and control market processes can be effectively implemented only at the national level. The processes of economic and financial globalization, and of social and cultural globalization as well, do not take place in a political vacuum; governments contribute individually and collectively to create the legal and institutional environment where constraints and opportunities for ordered economic and social activities are defined. The role of the judiciary in pursuing illegal market behavior – as in the Enron, Worldcom and Parmalat cases – and the role of welfare policies in reducing the inequality of opportunities and controlling undesirable outcomes of market processes – as in the unemployment provisions implemented by several advanced countries – are effective at the state level only, or at most, at the EU supranational level. As for the ability of states to raise the resources to implement extensive welfare and redistribution policies, governments are no doubt less able than in the past to adopt public investments programs and fiscal policies of deficit spending. But, in the face of those negative implications of globalization as the loss of jobs due to productive relocation, or increasing insecurity due to international terrorism and criminality, individuals ask for protection from their governments and consider them responsible for the outcomes. In this respect the nation-state is still very relevant, despite the changes.

Moreover, over-emphasizing the erosion of state power risks obscuring the fact that the erosion is uneven, since states differ greatly in terms of economic, political, military and cultural power and in terms of exerting the various dimensions of their sovereignty. When scholars speak of the demise of the state, what state are they talking about: the United States, Sierra Leone or Tuvalu? The key questions of world integration and global governance and of the contested hegemony of the United States in the present world system are blurred by this kind of over-simplification.

The relations of domination and cooperation between a core superpower, regional powers, and the various peripheral states (some with neo-colonial relations) should be accounted for in any discussion. After the collapse of the Soviet Union, the United States is the only superpower with the military and economic might required to foster world governance, but it does not have legitimate authority. Hence, the provocative proposal that all citizens of the world be given the right to take part in the election of the American president. The United States may have the power to exert leadership (although recent failures in the struggle against global terrorism and in Iraq cast doubt on it), but its leadership can hardly be considered as legitimate by, and accountable to, constituencies outside those of the hegemonic power and its allies. Global integration and global governance are key problematic questions.

Democratic governance at the world level

Globalization raises the question of global governance, that is the definition of a complex set of global norms concerning the entire world as a single system. But global governance can only be polyarchic, multi-layered and multipolar if it is to be effective, and it can only be democratic if it is to be accepted (Martinelli, 2004).

The creation of the global market develops the potentialities which were present from the start in capitalism as a world-system. However, the virtuous circle of democratization that took place within the context of the nation-state can hardly be reproduced at the world level. In the historical experience of the developed countries, markets, governments, and communities interacted in the formation of democratic governance and social integration. Capitalism developed predominantly within the context of national economies and societies. Sovereign states were able to tame and regulate the inherent vitality and tumultuous course of capitalist growth both through regulative and distributive policies. In the different capitalisms of Western Europe, North America, and Japan, different mixes of such policies took place: in the United States laws mostly aimed at preserving competition through anti-trust laws and safeguarding the rights of investors and consumers, whereas in the countries of Europe reformist policies were the result of the inclusion of the working class into the democratic polity and of the development of the welfare state. In other words, in Europe, labor parties 'exchanged' their loyalties to democratic institutions with the acquisition of political citizenship (voting rights) and social citizenship (welfare). In Japan's 'patronage capitalism' it was the mix of responsible leadership and employees' loyalty at the firm level which controlled the most negative effects of capitalist relations.

In contemporary global society, similar processes are much more difficult, since there is no equivalent of the nation-state at the world level which could implement anti-trust laws, labor and environmental laws, fiscal policies (like the Tobin tax on financial transactions) aimed at regulating capitalist relations; nor is there a world independent judiciary which can control and sanction illegal behavior. Nor is there a democratic polity at the world level, in which exploited or disadvantaged social groups could make their voices heard through their voting rights to political decision-makers competing for their support, and could exchange their loyalty to democratic institutions for equal rights of legal, political and social citizenship.

A united world state is not in sight and not even desirable. But democratic global governance is possible if it is conceived as a polyarchic, multi-layered and multipolar order, where the anarchy of sovereign nation-states and the hegemonic role of the United States are mitigated and controlled by three types of non-state actors: (1) international organizations around a reformed United Nations Organization; (2) community-type and the market-type associations of the world society; and (3) the supra-national unions such as the European Union. This is the outcome of diverse strategies in a polyarchic, mixed-actor system, and it focuses on democratic accountability, individual and community empowerment, multiple identities, contextual universalism, and supranational institutions.

Main obstacles to democratic global governance

Several political and cultural trends in contemporary world society have negative implications for achieving the project of democratic global governance. First, most powerful actors on the world stage usually address matters of common concern in terms of their own specific goals and interests, i.e., the interests of what they consider to be their constituencies (such as national interests for state powers, profits and capital gains for TNCs, and dogmatic beliefs for fundamentalist movements), with the result that old inequalities and hierarchies are consolidated while new ones are fostered, and basic human rights are violated.

Second, the strategies and behavior of international organizations, which by definition should have global constituencies, besides defending their bureaucratic survival are mostly weighted in favor of their most powerful members (such as the UN Security Council members or the members of the G8).

These first two tendencies lead to charges that global governance is a Western project (when not even an American project) designed to spread a kind of *pensée unique* of Western values, laws, and institutional arrangements, and to sustain the richest countries' primacy in world affairs.

Third, also as a consequence of the first two tendencies, inequalities among the peoples of the world do not reduce significantly and in some cases even increase. Poverty defined both as absolute deprivation below the subsistence level, and as lack of the capacity to exert one's own freedom to choose and to better the chances of individual and collective life, is a great obstacle to the development of democratic global governance and a breeding ground for fundamentalism and intolerance (in the sense of providing legitimation for violent reactions rather than a recruiting ground for militant activists).

The fourth tendency, closely related to the previous one, is the emergence of new forms of fundamentalism, aggressive nationalism, and tribalism, which construct people's identities upon primordial ties and dogmatic beliefs, and inhibit the growth of democratic citizenship, both at the national and the supra-national levels. In the contemporary world we are witnesses to numerous instances of the perversion of local identities, in terms of dogmatic closure, intolerances and prejudice, as a reaction to global trends. Fundamentalist religious faiths and dogmatic ideological beliefs deny the tension between the cultural message and the specific cultural code through which the message is spread, and pretend to monopolize the message, preaching irreducible truths. But in so doing they reduce the message's reach, tie it to a specific time and space, and make intercultural dialogue impossible. Fundamentalists and 'true believers' of different creeds live in a eschatological time, in a palingenetic world where any present project of reforms is devaluated in favor of future redemption.

The fifth negative tendency for democratic global governance is the declining participation in democratic politics and the reduced confidence in democratic processes and institutions in the developed countries with representative governments, as shown by many opinion polls. These weaken the appeal of democracy and make it more difficult to 'export' it beyond national boundaries and to developing countries with authoritarian regimes. The growing popularity of neo-populist forms of consensus formation, which appeal to many 'losers' in the globalization process, and the increasing reliance on technocratic elites, which appeals to many 'winners', both reduce the space for democratic participation and accountability. Neo-populist trends of local closure and xenophobic fear of different peoples and cultures have found renewed life among political entrepreneurs in several Western democracies, including France, Austria, Italy, and the Netherlands.

And, finally, the persistence of authoritarian regimes that repress civil rights and political liberties in many developing countries does not contribute to strengthening the voices in favor of democratic accountability at the global level. Authoritarian leaders of several developing countries reject any critique to their rule as undue foreign interference and attempts to impose Western hegemony. They also often counter the 'formal' rules of democracy with the 'substantial' democracy of their achievements for the well-being of their peoples. In fact, division of power, due process of law, the existence of multi-parties and electoral competition, freedom of speech and free information, are not examples of Western ethnocentrism, but essential ingredients of democratic life, which can be identified in different historical and cultural traditions and which must be generalized at the the world level.

Major favoring factors and building blocs of democratic global governance

And yet the project of democratic global is not impossible. Major factors favoring this project and counterbalancing the impact of its 'enemies' are the following:

1. The growing awareness of a common fate, i.e., of our common human and social rights, our common vulnerability to global environmental, social, and political crises, such as poverty and unemployment, disease and pollution, terrorism and ethnic cleansing, and the ensuing need to find common solutions and responses based on a culture of dialogue and cooperation.

2. The slow emergence of a transnational civic society and an international public space, with international scientific institutions playing a significant role, wherein all women and men learn to respect and try to understand others' values and beliefs without renouncing their own, but rather critically assessing and 'reinventing' them in a dialogue between civilizations. This intercultural dialogue requires two basic methodological assumptions: the weakening of the link between ethos and ethnos, between a given vision of the world and practical knowledge, on the one hand, and the belonging to a specific community of fate, on the other; and the spread of self-reflexive action and thought (although rooted in a specific culture with its norms, institutions and practices, more individuals today have more chances to be responsible actors in the making of social reality).

3. The diffusion of the notion of multiple citizenship through which different overlapping identities (local, national, regional, and cosmopolitan) can define different sets of rights and responsibilities. This notion does not imply that an emerging world community would require of its members an implausibly high level of cosmopolitan loyalty, over-riding all other obligations; but it does imply a sense of common identity through which we should not be indifferent to the suffering of others, but rather give the interests of others equal weight with our own or with those of our loved ones.

4. The growth of the cultural attitude of contextual universalism, i.e., the fertile and non-destructive encounter of cultures and the according of mutual respect among different cultural outlooks, along the lines developed by authors like Robertson (1992) and Beck (1997).

These trends, which are growing albeit very unevenly, can in turn reinforce existing processes of global governance and make possible new ones. Among the existing processes are: the harmonization of national laws in matters regulated by international agreements or resulting from court decisions taken in a different country; the strengthening of international regimes; the solutions to specific problems suggested by thematic networks; and the international standards of good practices.

Among the new institutional processes which constitute basic building blocs of global governance are the following:

1. the specification of rules of coexistence that are coherent with shared principles (starting with the UN declarations of universal human rights), and of procedures for making decision-making processes with global implications accountable;

2. the articulation of a cooperative ethos based on principles of transparency and accountability and the practice of periodical consultations with all actors involved in and affected by decisions with global implications;

3. the development of self-governing communities as alternative mechanisms of social and political organization at the world level, which will foster the empowerment of individuals and groups;

4. the strengthening of international regimes and supranational institutions of governance at the world level (through a transformed United Nations Organization) and at the regional level (through a reformed European Union and

similar political entities in the other regions of the world); these institutions must obtain greater authority, resources, and independence in order to avoid the political chaos that the unbundling of the relationships between sovereignty, state power, and territoriality may otherwise bring about;

5. the spread and consolidation of regional supranational unions such as the European Union, with mechanisms of reinforced cooperation in public policy and the pooling of resources for common goals through the voluntary ceding of some sovereignty by member nation-states.

All these elements can contribute to the advancement of democratic global governance in which sites and forms of power that at present operate beyond the scope of democratic control can be made more accountable to all those who are affected by their decisions. If this project advances we can expect that the complex modernization of countries like China and India will take place in a way which can both control the contradictions and conflicts of any process of deep transformation and contribute to a more peaceful world with greater individual freedom, social justice and respect for cultural diversity for all.

In a world where a growing number of basic aspects of the human condition tend to escape any form of political regulation in the name of the imperatives of productive growth and global economic competitiveness, and where democratic politics is confined to the national level of a few dozen nation-states, global governance amounts to a few 'watchers' (regulatory regimes, international courts, and scattered elements of an international *lex mercatoria*) that are often weak and not very legitimate (who will watch the watchers?), we need to strengthen both the values, rules and institutions of democratic global governance. For the first time in history, human beings are inserted in tendentially global social networks; productive systems and markets are coordinated at the world level; media images and messages reach masses of people all over the earth; informatics allows for interaction at a distance; and material and symbolic communications imply a compression of time and space. But there is no normative consensus that corresponds to all of this and is capable to fund widely agreed institutions of democratic global governance.

To conclude: analyzing the fundamental characteristics of globalization and its major implications for modernizing countries was a natural conclusion for this book. In the first part of the chapter I discussed globalization as a multi-faceted process, where tendencies toward homogenization and diversification co-exist and conflict with each other, allowing for at least a partially autonomous paths toward and through modernity. Multiple modernities and varieties of modernity take place in the contemporary world, as discussed in the second section, because of the different structural arrangements and cultural codes of modernizing countries and because of the position they hold in the world economy and in the international power system. Multiple modernities are possible also because, as argued in the third part of the chapter, globalization erodes nation-states' sovereignty, but not to the point of preventing governments from being proactive agents of development and modernization. The potentialities of relatively specific modernization projects, however, are more likely to be realized in a context of democratic global governance, outlined in the final section, rather than in a unipolar world-system.

The particular process of transformation of Western European societies that we call modernization in its original historical meaning has, in fact, encompassed the whole world, provoking a multiplicity of different responses and reactions that shape specific routes to and through modernity within a single world-system of interconnectedness and interdependency. Multiple modernities require a context of polyarchic, mixed-actor, multilevel democratic global governance. And democratic world governance requires the continuation and the extension to the whole world of the 'modern project', building on the institutions and values of human rights, peaceful regulation of conflict, people empowerment, multiple identities, and contextual universalism.

Bibliography

Adorno, T.W. and Horkheimer, M. ([1947] 1973) *Dialectic of Enlightenment*, London: Allen Lane.

Agarwala, S.P. and Singh, S.P. (eds) (1958) *The Economics of Underdevelopment*, Oxford: Oxford University Press.

Albert, M. (1991) *Capitalisme contre capitalisme*, Paris: Seuil.

Albrow, M. (1996) *The Global Age*, Cambridge: Polity Press.

Alen, J., Braham, P. and Lewis, P. (eds) (1992) Political and Economic Forms of Modernity, Cambridge: Polity Press.

Alexander, J.C. and Colomy, P. (eds) (1988) *Differentiation Theory and Social Change: Historical and Comparative Approaches*, New York: Columbia University Press.

Alexander, J.C. and Sztompka, P. (eds) (1990) *Rethinking Progress*, London: Unwin Hyman.

Almond, G. and Coleman, J. (eds) (1960) *The Politics of Developing Areas*, Princeton, NJ: Princeton University Press.

Almond, G., Flanagan, S.C. and Mundt, R.J. (eds) (1973) *Crisis, Choice and Change: Historical Studies of Political Development*, Boston: Little, Brown and Co.

Almond, G. and Powell, G.B. (1966) *Comparative Politics: A Developmental Approach*, Boston: Little Brown.

Amin, S. (1976) *Unequal Development: An Essay in the Social Formation of Peripheral Capitalism*, New York: Harvester.

Anderson, B. (1991) *Imagined Communities*, London: Verso.

Anderson, P. (1998) *The Origins of Postmodernity*, London: Verso.

Appadurai, A. (1996) *Modernity at Large: Cultural Dimensions of Globalization*, Minneapolis: University of Minnesota Press.

Apter, D. (1965) *The Politics of Modernization*, Chicago: University of Chicago Press.

Apter, D. (1968) *Some Conceptual Approaches to the Study of Modernization*, Englewood Cliffs, NJ: Prentice Hall.

Apter, D. (1987) *Rethinking Development: Modernization, Dependency and Postmodern Politics*, London: Sage.

Archibugi, D., Held, D. and Kohler, M. (eds) (1998) *Re-imagining Political Community: Studies in Cosmopolitan Democracy*, Cambridge: Polity Press.

Aron, R. (1969) *Progress and Disillusion: The Dialectics of Modern Society*, New York: Mentor Books.

Arrighi, G. and Silver, B. (1999) *Chaos and Governance in the Modern World System: Comparing Hegemonic Transition*, Minneapolis: University of Minnesota Press.

Bairoch, P. (1996) 'Globalization myths and realities: one century of external trade and foreign investment', in R. Boyer and D. Drache (eds), *The Limits of Globalization*, London: Routledge.

Baker, K. (1990) *Inventing the French Revolution*, Cambridge: Cambridge University Press.

Banfield, E. (1958) *The Moral Bases of a Backward Society*, Glencoe, IL: Free Press.

Baran, P.A. (1957) *The Political Economy of Growth*, New York: Monthly Review Press.

Baudelaire, C. (1962) 'Le peintre de la vie moderne', in *Curiosités esthétiques: l'art romantique*, Paris.

Baudrillard, J. (1981) *Simulacres et simulation*, Paris: Galilée.

Baudrillard, J. (1996) *La société de consommation, ses mythes, ses structures*, Paris: Gallimard.

Bauman, Z. (1989) *Modernity and the Holocaust*, Cambridge: Polity Press.

Bauman, Z. (1992) *Intimations of Postmodernity*, London: Routledge.

Beck, U. (1986) *Risikogesellschaft*, Frankfurt: Suhrkamp.

Beck, U. (1991) *Politik in die Risikogesellschaft*, Frankfurt: Suhrkamp.

Beck, U. (1997) *Was ist Globalisierung?*, Frankfurt: Suhrkamp.

Beck, U., Giddens, A. and Lash, S. (1994) *Reflexive Modernization*, Stanford, CA: Stanford University Press.

Bell, D. (1974) *The Coming of Post-Industrial Society*, London: Heinemann.

Bell, D. (1976) *The Cultural Contradictions of Capitalism*, New York: Basic Books.

Bellah, R. (1985) *Habits of the Heart: Individualism and Commitment in American Life*, Berkeley, CA: University of California Press.

Bendix, R. (1964) *Nation-Building and Citizenship: Studies of Our Changing Social Order*, New York: Wiley.

Bendix, R. (1967) 'Tradition and modernity reconsidered', *Comparative Studies in Society and History*, IX, 292–346.

Bendix, R. (1978) *Kings or People: Power and the Mandate to Rule*, Berkeley, CA: University of California Press.

Benjamin, W. (1982) 'Das Passagenwerk', in *Gesammelte Schriften*, vol. V, Frankfurt: Suhrkamp.

Berger, P. and Huntington, S.P. (eds) (2002) *Many Globalizations: Cultural Diversity in the Contemporary World*, New York: Oxford University Press.

Berger, S. (2000) 'Globalization and politics', *Annual Review of Political Science 2000*, 3: 43–62.

Berger, S. and Dore, R. (eds) (1996) *National Diversity and Global Capitalism*, Ithaca, NY: Cornell University Press.

Berman, M. (1983) *All that Is Solid Melts into Air: The Experience of Modernity*, London: Verso.

Bernardi, B. (1998) *Africa: Tradizione e modernità*, Rome: Carocci.

Beteille, A. (1991) *Society and Politics in India*, London.

Binder, L. et al. (eds) (1971) *Crises and Sequences in Political Development*, Princeton, NJ: Princeton University Press.

Black, C.E. (1966) *The Dynamics of Modernization*, New York: Harper.

Black, C.E. (1976) *Comparative Modernization*, New York: Free Press.

Blake, J. (1976) 'The changing status of women in developing countries', in J. Black, *Comparative Modernization*, New York: Free Press.

Bobbio, N. (1979) 'Il modello giusnaturalistico', in N. Bobbio and M. Bovero (eds), *Società e Stato nella filosofia politica moderna*, Milan: Il Saggiatore.

Bobbio, N. (1985) *Stato, governo, società*, Turin: Einaudi.

Bocock, R. and Thompson, K. (eds) (1992) *Social and Cultural Forms of Modernity*, London: Polity Press.

Boisvert, Y. (1997) *L'analyse postmoderniste: Une nouvelle grille d'analyse sociopolitique*, Paris: L'Harmattan.

Boli, J. and Thomas, G. (eds) (1999) *Constructing World Culture: International Nongovernmental Organizations since 1875*, Stanford, CA: Stanford University Press.

Bornschier, V. (1980) *Multinationale Konzerne: Wirtschaftspolitik und nationale Entwicklung im Weltssystem*, Frankfurt and New York: Campus.

Bornschier, V. and Heintz, P. (1979) *Compendium of Data for World System Analysis*, special issue of the *Bulletin of the Sociological Institute of the University of Zurich*, Zurich.

Boudon, R. (1984) *La place du désordre: Critique des théories du changement social*, Paris: Presses Universitaires de France.

Braibanti, R. and Spengler, J.J. (eds) (1961) *Tradition, Values and Socio-economic Development*, Durham, NC: Duke University Press.

Braudel, F. (1967) *Civilisation materielle et capitalisme*, Paris: Colin.

Brown, C. (1995) 'International political theory and the idea of world community', in K. Booth and S. Smith (eds), *International Relations Theory To-Day*, Cambridge: Polity Press.

Burawoy, M. et al. (2000) *Global Ethnography: Forces, Connections and Imaginations in a Postmodern World*, Berkeley, CA: University of California Press.

Callinicos, A. et al. (1994) *Marxism and the New Imperialism*, London: Bookmarks.

Campbell, C. (1987) *The Romantic Ethic and the Spirit of Modern Consumerism*, London: Basil Blackwell.

Cardoso, F.H. (1980) *As ideas e seu lugar: Ensaios sobre as teorias do desenvolvimento*, Petropolics: Editora brasileira de Ciencias.

Cardoso, F.H. and Faletto E. (1969) *Dependencia y desarrollo en America Latina*, Rio de Janeiro: Siglo XXI.

Cassese, A. (1986) *International Law in a Divided World*, London: Clarendon Press.

Cassou, S. (1997) 'The link between tax rates and foreign direct investment', *Applied Economics*, 29.

Castells, M. (1996–98) *The Information Age: Economy, Society and Culture*, 3 vols, Oxford: Blackwell.

Castoriadis, C. (1987) *The Imaginary Institution of Society*, Cambridge: Polity Press.

Castoriadis, C. (1993) *World in Fragments: Writings on Politics, Society, Psychoanalysis, and the Imagination*, Cambridge: Polity Press.

Cerase, F.P. (ed.) (1984) *Sviluppo capitalistico dipendente e regimi burocratico-autoritari*, Rome: Carucci.

Cerutti, F. and Rudolph, E. (eds) *A Soul for Europe*, vol. 2, Virginia: Peters leuven-Sterling.

Chakrabarty, D. (2001) 'Adda, Calcutta: dwelling in modernity', in D. Gaunkar (ed.), *Alternative Modernities*, Durham, NC: Duke University Press.

Chandra, B. (1981) *Nationalism and Communalism in Modern India*, Dehli:

Chase-Dunn, C. and Hall, T.D. (1997) *Rise and Demise: Comparing World Systems*, Boulder, CO: Westview Press.

Chiesi, A. and Martinelli, A. (1989) 'The representation of business interests as a mechanism of social regulation', in P. Lange and M. Regini (eds) *State, Market and Social Regulation*, Cambridge, MA: Harvard University Press.

Chirot, D. (1977) *Social Change in the Twentieth Century*, New York: Harcourt Brace.

Clapham, C. (1985) *Third World Politics: An Introduction*, Madison, WI: University of Wisconsin Press.

Cockcroft, J.D. et al. (eds) (1972) *Dependence and Underdevelopment*, Garden City, NY: Doubleday.

Collins, R. (1999) *Macrohistory: Essays in Sociology of the Long Run*, Stanford, CA: Stanford University Press.

Cooper, F. and Stoler, A.L. (eds) (1997) *Tensions of Empire: Colonial Cultures in a Bourgeois World*, Berkeley, CA: University of California Press.

Cooper, R.N. (1968) *The Economics of Interdependence: Economic Policy in the Atlantic Community*, New York: McGraw-Hill.

Crook, S., Pakulski, J, and Waters, M. (1992) *Post-modernization: Change in Advanced Society*, London: Sage.

Crozier, M., Huntington, S.P. and Watanuki, J. (1975) *The Crisis of Democracy. Report on the Governability of Democracies to the Trilateral Commission*, New York: New York University Press.

Daedalus (1998) *Early Modernities*, 127(3), summer, special issue.

Daedalus (2000) *Multiple Modernities*, 129(1), winter, special issue.

Dahrendorf, R. (1990) *Reflections on the Revolution in Europe*, London: Chatto and Windus.

Dahrendorf, R. (1992) 'Democracy and modernity: notes on the European experience', in S.N. Eisensadt (ed.), *Democracy and Modernity*, Leiden: E.J. Brill.

D'Andrea, D. (2001) 'Europe and the West: the identity beyond the origin', in F. Cerutti and E. Rudolph (eds), *A Soul for Europe*, vol. 2, Virginia: Peters leuven-Sterling.

Delanty, G. (1999) *Social Theory in a Changing World: Conceptions of Modernity*, Oxford: Blackwell.

Delanty, G. (2000) *Modernity and Postmodernity*, London: Sage.

Desai, A.R. (1966) 'Need for revaluation of the concept', in C.E. Black (ed.), *The Dynamics of Modernization*, New York: Harper.

Deutsch, K. (1961) 'Social mobilization and political development', *American Political Science Review*, 55: 493–514.

Devoto, F. and Di Tella, T.S. (eds) (1997) *Political Culture, Social Movements and Democratic Transitions in South America in the Twentieth Century*, Milan: Fondazione Feltrinelli.

Deyo, F. (ed.) (1987) *The Political Economy of the New Asian Industrialism*, Ithaca, NY: Cornell University Press.

Dore, R. (1973) *British Factory, Japanese Factory: The Origins of Diversity in Industrial Relations*, Berkeley, CA: University of California Press.

Dore, R. (1987) *Taking Japan Seriously: a Confucian Perspective on Leading Economic Issues*,

Dos Santos, T. (1970) 'The structure of dependence', *American Economic Review*, 60: 235–446.

Dube, S.C. (1966) 'Democracy and nation building in transitional societies', in J.L. Finkle and R.W. Gable (eds), *Political Development and Social Change*, New York: John Wiley & Sons Ltd.

Durkheim, E. (1960) *De la division du travail social: Etude sur l'organisation des sociétés supérieures*, Paris: Presses Universitaires de France.

Eco, U. (1987) *Travels in Hyper-reality*, London: Picador.

Eichengreen, B. (1997) *Globalizing Capital: A History of the International Monetary System*, Princeton, NJ: Princeton University Press.

Eisenstadt, S.N. (1961) *Essays in the Sociological Aspects of Political and Economic Development*, The Hague: Mouton.

Eisenstadt, S.N. (1966) *Modernization, Protest and Change*, Englewood Cliffs, NJ: Prentice Hall.

Eisenstadt, S.N. (1987) *European Civilization in Comparative Perspective*, Oslo: Norwegian University Press.

Eisenstadt, S.N. (1992a) 'A reappraisal of theories of social change and modernization', in H. Haferkamp and N.J. Smelser (eds), *Social Change and Modernity*, Berkeley, CA: University of California Press.

Eisenstadt, S.N. (1992b) *Democracy and Modernity*, Leiden: E.J. Brill.

Eisenstadt, S.N. (1997) *Modernità, modernizzazione e oltre*, Rome: Armando.

Eisenstadt, S.N. (2000) 'Multiple modernities', *Daedalus*, 129(1).

Elias, N. (1976) *Über den Prozess der Zivilisation*, 2 vols, Frankfurt: Suhrkamp.

Emmanuel, A. (1969) *L'échange inégal: Essai sur les antagonismes dans les rapports économiques internationaux*, Paris: Maspero.

Etzioni, A. and Etzioni, E. (eds) (1979) *Social Change*, London: Basil Blackwell.

Evans, P.B., Rueschemeyer, D. and Stephens J. (1985) *States Versus Markets in the World System*, London: Sage.

Evans, P.B. and Stephens J. (1994) 'Development and the world economy', in N.J. Smelser and R. Swedberg, (eds), *Handbook of Economic Sociology*, Princeton, NJ: Princeton University Press.

Featherstone, M. (1991) *Consumer Culture and Postmodernism*, London: Sage.

Featherstone, M., Lash, S. and Robertson, R. (eds) *Global Modernities*, London: Sage.

Finkle, J.L. and Gable R.W. (eds) (1966) *Political Development and Social Change*, New York: John Wiley & Sons Ltd.

Fligstein, N. (2001) *The Architecture of Markets: An Economic Sociology of Twenty-First-Century Capitalist Societies*, Princeton, NJ: Princeton University Press.

Flora, P. (1975) *Indikatoren der Modernisierung*, Opladen: Westdeutscher Verlag.

Flora, P. (ed.) (1999) *State Formation, Nation Building and Mass Politics in Europe: The Theory of Stein Rokkan,* Oxford: Oxford: University Press.

Florini, A., Kokusai, N. and Senta, K. (2000) *The Third Force: The Rise of Transnational Civil Society,* New York: Carnegie Endowment.

Foucault, M. (1966) *The Order of Things: An Archeology of the Human Sciences*, London: Tavistock Publications.

Foucault, M. (1997) 'What is Enlightenment?', in *Michel Foucault: The Essential Works,* vol. I, *Ethics*, London: Allen Lane.

Frank, A.G. (1967a) *Sociology of Development and Underdevelopment of Sociology*, New York: Catalyst.

Frank, A.G. (1967b) *Capitalism and Underdevelopment in Latin America*, New York: Monthly Review Press.

Frisby, D. (1985) *Fragments of Modernity: Theories of Modernity in Work of Simmel, Krakauer and Benjamin*, Cambridge: Polity Press.

Fukuyama, F. (1992) *The End of History and the Last Man*, London: Hamish Hamilton.

Furtado, C. (1970) *Economic Development of Latin America*, Cambridge: Cambridge University Press.

Galtung, J. (1971) 'A structural theory of imperialism', *Journal of Peace Research*, 2: 81–116.

Garrett, G. (1998) *Partisan Politics in the Global Economy*, Cambridge: Cambridge University Press.

Gauchet, M. (1997) *The Disenchantment of the World*, Princeton, NJ: Princeton University Press.

Gaunkar, D.P. (ed.) (2001) *Alternative Modernities*, Durham, NC: Duke University Press.

Geertz, C. (ed.) (1963) *Old Societies and New States: The Quest for Modernity in Asia and Africa,* New York: The Free Press.

Gellner, E. (1983) *Nations and Nationalism*, London: Basil Blackwell.

Gellner, E. (1995) *The Conditions of Liberty*, London: Basil Blackwell.

Gellner, E. (1997) *Plough, Sword and Book*, Chicago: University of Chicago Press.

Gereffi, G. (1994) 'The international economy and economic development', in N.J. Smelser and R. Swedberg (eds), *Handbook of Economic Sociology*, Princeton, NJ: Princeton University Press.

Gereffi, G. and Wyman, D. (eds) (1990) *Manufacturing Miracles: Paths of Industrialization in Latin America and East Asia*, Princeton, NJ: Princeton University Press.

Germani, G. (1971) *Sociologia della modernizzazione: L'esperienza dell'America latina*, Bari: Laterza.

Giddens, A. (1985) *The Nation State and Violence*, London: Polity Press

Giddens, A. (1990) *The Consequences of Modernity*, Stanford, CA: Stanford University Press.

Giddens, A. (1992) *Modernity and Self-Identity*, Cambridge: Cambridge University Press.

Giddens, A. (2000) *Runaway World: How Globalization is Reshaping Our Lives*, London: Routledge.

Gilpin, R. (1987) *The Political Economy of International Relations*, Princeton, NJ: Princeton University Press.

Gilpin, R. (2000) *The Challenge of Global Capitalism: The World Economy in the Twenty-First Century*, Princeton, NJ: Princeton University Press.

Goldthorpe, J. (1971) 'Theories of industrial society: reflections on the recrudescence of historicism and the future of futurology', *Archives europeéennes de sociologie*, 12: 263–88.

Goldthorpe, J.E. (1996) *The Sociology of Post-Colonial Societies*, Cambridge: Cambridge University Press.

Goodey, J.R. (1968) *Literacy in Transitional Societies*, Cambridge, MA: Harvard University Press.

Granovetter, M. (1992) 'Economic institutions as social construction: a framework of analysis', *Acta Sociologica,* 35: 3–12.

Greider, W. (1997) *One World, Ready or Not: The Manic Logic of Global Capitalism*, New York: Simon & Schuster.

Gurr, T.R. (1970) *Why Men Rebel*, Princeton, NJ: Princeton University Press.

Gusfield, J.R. (1967) 'Tradition and modernity: misplaced polarities in the study of social change', *American Journal of Sociology*, 72: 351–62.

Habermas, J. (1973) *Legitimationsprobleme in Spätkapitalismus*, Frankfurt: Suhrkamp.

Habermas, J. (1981) *Theorie des kommunikativen Handels*, Frankfurt: Suhrkamp.

Habermas, J. (1985) *Der philosophische Diskurs der Moderne*, Frankfurt: Suhrkamp.

Habermas, J. (1998) *Die Post-nationale Konstellation*, Frankfurt: Suhrkamp.

Haferkamp, H. and Smelser, N.J. (eds) (1992) *Social Change and Modernity*, Berkeley, CA: University of California Press.

Hagen, E. (1962) *On the Theory of Social Change: How Economic Growth Begins*, Homewood, IL: Dorsey Press.

Hall, P.A. (1997) 'The political economy of adjustment in Germany', in *Ökonomische Leistungsfachigkeit und institutionelle Innovation*, Berlin: WZB Jahrbuch, pp. 239–315.

Hall, S. and Gieben, B. (eds) (1992) *Formations of Modernity*, Cambridge: Polity Press.

Hall, S., Held, D. and Grew, T. (eds) (1992) *Modernity and its Futures*, Cambridge: Polity Press.

Hamilton, G. (1994) 'Civilizations and the organization of the economy', in N.J. Smelser and R. Swedberg (eds), *Handbook of Economic Sociology*, Princeton, NJ: Princeton University Press.

Hamilton, G. and Biggart, N. (1988) 'Market, culture and authority: a comparative analysis of management and organization in the Far East', *American Journal of Sociology*, 94: 52–93.

Hamilton, G. and Cheng-Shu Kao (1991) 'The institutional foundations of Chinese business: the family firm in Taiwan', in C. Calhoun (ed.), *Comparative Social Research*, vol. 12, *Business Institutions*, Greenwich, CT: JAI Press.

Hanchard, M. (2001) 'Afro-modernity: temporality, politics and the African diaspora', in D.P. Gaunkar (ed.), *Alternative Modernities*, Durham, NC: Duke University Press.

Hardt, M. and Negri, A. (2000) *Empire*, Cambridge: Cambridge University Press.

Harris, N. (1986) *The End of the Third World: Newly Industrializing Countries and the Decline of Ideology*, London: Penguin.

Harrison, D. (1988) *The Sociology of Modernization and Development*, London: Unwin & Hyman.

Harvey, D. (1989) *The Condition of Post-Modernity: An Inquiry into the Origins of Cultural Change*, London: Basil Blackwell.

Hefner, R.W. (ed.) (1997) *Market Cultures: Society and Morality in the New Asian Capitalisms*, Boulder, CO: Westview Press.

Held, D. (1995) *Democracy and the Modern State*, Cambridge: Polity Press.

Held, D., McGrew, A., Goldblatt, D. and Perraton, J. (1999) *Global Transformations*, Cambridge: Polity Press.

Higgins, B. (1959) *Economic Development. Principles: Problems and Policies*, New York: W.W. Norton & Co.

Hirschman, A. (1965) *Journeys Toward Progress*, New York: Doubleday.

Hirschman, A. (1970) *Exit, Voice and Loyalty*, Cambridge, MA: Harvard University Press.

Hirschman, A. (1971) 'Obstacles to development: a classification and a quasi vanishing act', in *A Bias for Hope*.

Hirst, P. and Thompson, G. (1996) *Globalization in Question: The International Economy and the Possibilities of Governance,* Cambridge: Polity Press.

Hollingsworth, R.J. and Boyer, R. (eds) (1997) *Contemporary Capitalism: The Embeddedness of Institutions*, Cambridge: Cambridge University Press.

Holt, R.T. and Turner, J.E. (1975) 'Crises and sequences in collective theory of development', *American Political Science Review*, 69: 979–94.

Hoogvelt, A. (1997) *Globalization and the Postcolonial World: The New Political Economy of Development*, London: Macmillan.

Hoselitz, B. (1960) *Sociological Factors in Economic Development*, Glencoe, IL: Free Press.

Hoselitz, B. and Moore W.E. (eds) (1963) *Industrialization and Society*, Paris: UNESCO-Mouton.

Huntington, S. (1965) 'Political development and political decay', *World Politics*, 17: 392–405.

Huntington, S. (1968) *Political Order in Changing Societies*, New Haven, CT: Yale University Press.

Huntington, S. (1996) *The Clash of Civilizations and the Remaking of World Order*, New York: Touchstone Books.

Huntington, S. (1997) 'Der Islam und seine Nachbarn', *Der Tagesspiegel*, 30 June.

Hurrel, A. and Woods, N. (eds) (1999) *Inequality, Globalization and World Politics*, Oxford: Oxford University Press.

Hutchinson, J. and Smith, A.D. (eds) (1994) *Nationalism*, Oxford: Oxford University Press.

Inglehart, R. (1997) *Modernization and Post-Modernization: Cultural, Economic and Political Change in 43 Societies*, Princeton, NJ: Princeton University Press.

Inkeles, A. and Smith, D.H. (1974) *Becoming Modern: Individual Change in Six Developing Countries*, Cambridge, MA: Harvard University Press.

International Social Science Journal (2001) 'Global governance and its critics', 170 (December): ???

International Sociology (2001) 'Rethinking civilizations analysis', 16(3) (Sept.): ???

Jaggers, K. and Gurr, T.R. (1996) *Polity III: Regime Type and Political Authority,1800–1994,* Inter-university Consortium for Political and Social Research, ICPSR Study 6695.

Jameson, F. (1991) *Postmodernism, or the Cultural Logic of Capitalism*, Durham, NC: University of North Carolina Press.

Jencks, C. (1977) *The Language of Post-Modern Architecture*, London: Academy Editions.

Jencks, C. (1989) *What is Post-Modernism?*, London: Academy Editions.

Johnson, C. (1966) *Revolutionary Change*, Boston: Little & Brown.

Jünger, E. (1930) 'Die totale Mobilmachung', in *Krieg und Krieger*, Berlin.

Keohane, R.O. (1984) *After Hegemony: Cooperation and Discord in the World Political Economy,* Princeton, NJ: Princeton University Press.

Keohane, R.O. (2002a) *Power and Governance in a Partially Globalized World*, London: Routledge.

Keohane, R.O. (2002b) 'Global governance and democratic accountability', in D. Held and M. Koenig-Archibugi (eds), *The Milliband Lectures*, London: London School of Economics.

Kerr, K., Dunlop, J., Harbison, F., Harbison, H. and Myers, C.A. (1960) *Industrialism and Industrial Man*, Cambridge, MA: Harvard University Press.

Kindleberger, C.P. (1958) *Economic Development*, New York: McGraw-Hill.

Kitschelt, H., Lange, P., Marks, G. and Stephens, J.D. (eds) (1999) *Continuity and Changes in Contemporary Capitalism*, Cambridge: Cambridge University Press.

Knobl, W. (2003) 'Theories that won't pass away: the never-ending story of modernization theory', in G. Delanty and E.F. Isin (eds), *Handbook of Historical Sociology*, London: Sage.

Kosellek, R. (1985) *Future Past: On the Semantics of Historical Time*, Cambridge, MA: MIT Press.

Krasner (2001)

Kroeber, A.L. (1923) *Anthropology*, New York: Harcourt Brace.

Krupp, H.J. (1977) 'Indikatoren der Modernisierung', in H.J. Krupp and W. Zapf (eds), *Sozialpolitik und Sozialberichterstattung*, Frankfurt: Campus Verlag.

Kumar, K. (1988) *The Rise of Modern Society: Aspects of the Social and Political Development of the West,* Oxford: Blackwell.

Kumar, K. (1995) *From Post-Industrial to Post-Modern Society*, Oxford: Blackwell.

La Palombara, J. (ed.) (1963) *Bureaucracy and Political Development*, Princeton, NJ: Princeton University Press.

Lash, S. (1990) *Sociology of Post-Modernism*, London: Routledge.

Lash, S. and Friedman, J. (eds) (1992) *Modernity and Identity*, Oxford: Basil Blackwell.

Lash, S. and Urry, J. (1987) *The End of Organized Capitalism*, Cambridge: Polity Press.

Latouche, S. (1989) *L'occidentalisation du monde*, Paris: Editions La découverte.

Latour, B. (1993) *We Have Never Been Modern*, Hemel Hempstead: Harvester Wheatsheaf.

Lee, L.O. (2001) 'Shanghai modern: reflections on urban culture in China in the 1930s', in D.P. Gaunkar (ed.), *Alternative Modernities*, Durham, NC: Duke University Press.

Lee, R.L.M. (1997) 'The limits and renewal of modernity: reflections on world development and Asia cultural values', *International Sociology*, 12(3): 275–94.

Leibenstein, H. (1957) *Economic Backwardness and Economic Growth*, New York: John Wiley & Sons Ltd.

Lerner, D. (1958) *The Passing of Traditional Society: Modernizing the Middle East*, Glencoe, IL: Free Press.

Lerner, D. (1968) 'Modernization: social aspects', in *International Encyclopedia of the Social Sciences*, New York: Macmillan.

Levy, M., Jr. (1966) *Modernization and the Structure of Societies*, 2 vols, Princeton, NJ: Princeton University Press.

Lewellen, T.C. (1995) *Dependency and Development*, London: Bergin and Garvey.

Lewis, W.A. (1965) *Politics in West Africa*, London: Allen & Unwin.

Lindblom, C. (2001) *The Market System*, New Haven, CT: Yale University Press.

Lipovetski, G. (1992) *Le crépuscule du devoir*, Paris: Gallimard.

Luhmann, N. (1998) *Observations on Modernity*, Stanford, CA: Stanford University Press.

Lyotard, J.-F. (1988) *La condition postmoderne*, Paris, Minuit.

Lyotard, J.-F. (1993) *Moralités postmodernes*, Paris: Galilée.

Machiavelli, N. (1975) *The Prince*, Harmondsworth: Penguin.

Machonin, P. (1997) *Social Transformation and Modernization*, Prague: Slon.

Mahajan, G. (1995) *Identities and Rights: Aspects of Liberal Democracy in India*, Delhi:

Maine, H and Sumner, J. (1861) *Ancient Law*, London: Murray.

Makler, H., Martinelli, A. and Smelser, N.J. (eds) (1973) *The New International Economy*, London: Sage.

Malinowski, B. (1945) *The Dynamics of Culture Change: An Inquiry into Race Relations in Africa*, New Haven, CT: Yale University Press.

Martinelli, A. (1968) 'In defense of the dialectics: Antonio Gramsci's theory of revolution', *Berkeley Journal of Sociology*, 13: 1–28.

Martinelli, A. (1975) 'Multinational corporations, national economic policies and labor unions', in L. Lindberg et al. (eds), *Stress and Contradiction in Modern Capitalism*, Lexington, MA: Lexington Books.

Martinelli, A. (1987) *Le soglie critiche dello sviluppo sociale*, mimeo, Milan: University of Milan.

Martinelli, A. (1994) 'Management and entrepreneurship', in N.J. Smelser and R. Swedberg (eds), *Handbook of Economic Sociology*, Princeton, NJ: Princeton University Press.

Martinelli, A. (2002) 'Markets, states, communities and global governance, presidential address: XV Congress, International Sociological Association', *International Sociology*, 2003, 2.

Martinelli, A. (2004) *La democrazia globale*, Milano: University Boccoli Editore.

Martinelli, A. (2005) 'The European identity', in E. Ben-Rafael (ed.), *Comparing Modern Civilizations: Pluralism Versus Homogeneity,* Leiden: Brill Academic Publishers.

Martinelli, A., Chiesi, A. and Stefanizzi, S. (1999) *Recent Social Trends in Italy 1960–1995*, Montreal: McGill-Queen's University Press.

Martinelli, A., Salvati, M. and Veca, S. (1989) *Progetto '89: Tre saggi su libertà, eguaglianza e fraternità*, Milan: Il Saggiatore.

Marx, K. (1970) *Capital*, 3 vols, London: Lawrence and Wishart.

Marx, K. and Engels, F. (1964) *The Communist Manifesto*, New York: Monthly Review Press.

McCarthy, T. (2001) 'On reconciling cosmopolitan unity and national diversity', in D.P. Gaunkar (ed.), *Alternative Modernities*, Durham, NC: Duke University Press.

McClelland, D. (1961) *The Achieving Society*, Princeton, NJ: Van Nostrand.

McKim, R. and McMahon, J. (eds) (1997) *The Morality of Nationalism*, New York: Oxford University Press.

McLuhan, M. (1964) *Understanding Media*, London: Routledge.

McLuhan, M. (1967) *The Medium is the Message*, London: Allen Lane.

Meier, G. (ed.) (1970) *Leading Issues in Economic Development*, Oxford: Oxford University Press.

Melucci, A. (1989) *Nomads of the Present*, Philadelphia, PA: Temple University Press.

Melucci, A. (1991) *L'invenzione del presente*, Bologne: Il Mulino.

Merritt, R.L. and Rokkan, S. (eds) (1966) *Comparing Nations*, New Haven, CT: Yale University Press.

Mendras, H. (1997) *L'Europe des Européens*, Paris: Gallimard.

Mestrovici, S.G. (1991) *The Coming Fin de Siècle*, London: Routledge.

Mongardini, C. (1993) *La cultura del presente: Tempo e storia nella tarda modernità*, Milan: Angeli.

Moore, B. Jr. (1966) *Social Origins of Dictatorship and Democracy*, Boston: Beacon Press.

Moore, W.E. (1963) *Social Change*, Englewood Cliffs, NJ: Prentice Hall.

Morin, E. (1999) *Les Sept savoirs necessaires à l'éducation du future*, Paris: UNESCO.

Murray, R. (1989) 'Fordism and post-Fordism', in S. Halle and M. Jacques (eds), *New Times*, London.

Mutti, A. (ed.) (1973) *Sociologia dello sviluppo e paesi sottosviluppati*, Turin: Loescher.

Myrdal, G. (1968) *Asian Drama: An Inquiry into the Poverty of Nations*, New York, Pantheon.

Nardin, T. (1983) *Laws, Morality and the Relations of States*, Princeton, NJ: Princeton University Press.

Nettl, J.P. and Robertson, R. (1968) *International Systems and the Modernization of Societies*, London: Faber and Faber.

Nye, J.S. Jr. (2002) *The Paradox of American Power*, Oxford: Oxford University Press.

O'Connor J. (1973) *The Fiscal Crisis of the State*, New York: St Martin's Press.

O'Donnell, G.A. (1968) *Modernizaciòn y autoritarismo*, Buenos Aires: Paidos.

O'Donnell, G.A. (1972) *Modernization and Bureaucratic Authoritarianism: Studies in South American Politics*, Berkeley, CA: University of California Press.

O'Donnell, G.A. and Schmitter, P. (eds) (1974) *Transition from Authoritarian Rule*, Baltimore, MD: Johns Hopkins University Press.

OECD (1991) *Taxing Profits in a Global Economy*, Paris: OECD.

Offe, K. (1984) *Contradictions of the Welfare State*, London: Hutchinson.

Ogburn, W.F. (1922) *Social Change: With Respect to Culture and Original Nature*, New York: Huebsch.

Ohmae, K. (1990) *The Borderless World: Power and Strategy in the Interlinked World*, New York: Harper.

Ohmae, K. (1995) *The End of the Nation State*, New York: Free Press.

Organski, A.F.K. (1965) *The Stages of Political Development*, New York: Knopf.

Parsons, T. (1937) *The Structure of Social Action*, New York: McGraw-Hill.

Parsons, T. (1966) *Societies: Evolutionary and Comparative Perspectives*, Englewood Cliffs, NJ: Prentice Hall.

Parsons, T. (1971) *The System of Modern Societies*, Englewood Cliffs, NJ: Prentice Hall.

Parsons, T. and Shils, E. (1951) *Toward a General Theory of Action*, Cambridge, MA: Harvard University Press.

Parsons, T. and Smelser, N.J. (1956) *Economy and Society*, Glencoe, IL: Free Press.

Pasquino, G. (1970) *Modernizzazione e sviluppo politico*, Bologne: Il Mulino.

Pellicani, L. (2002) *Dalla società chiusa alla società aperta*, Rubbettino: Soveria mannelli.

Peng Cheng, L. (1995) *Der chinesische Modernisierungsprozess den achtziger Jahren*, Berlin: WZB.

Perlmutter, H.V. (1991) 'On the rocky road to the first global civilization', *Human Relations*, 44.

Petras, J. and Zeitlin, M. (eds) (1968) *Latin America: Reform or Revolution?* Greenwich, CT: Fawcett.

Poggi, G. (1978) *La vicenda dello stato moderno*, Bologne: Il Mulino.

Polanyi, K. (1944) *The Great Transformation*, New York: Rinehart and Company.

Prebish, P. (1950) *The Economic Development of Latin America and its Problems*, New York: U.N. Department of Social and Economic Affairs.

Przeworski, A. and Limomgi, F. (1997) 'Modernization: theories and facts', *World Politics*, 49: 155–83.

Przeworski, A. and Wallerstein, I. (1988) 'Structural dependence of the state on capital', *American Political Science Review*, 91(3): 11–30.

Pye, L.W. (1966) *Aspects of Political Development*, Boston: Little Brown.

Pye, L.W. and Verba, S. (eds) (1965) *Political Culture and Political Development*, Princeton, NJ: Princeton University Press.

Randeria, S. (1999) 'Jenseits von Soziologie und soziokulturelle Anthropologie: zur Ortsbestimmung der nichtwestlichen Welt einer zukünftigen Sozialtheorie', *Soziale Welt*, 50(4): 373–82.

Randeria, S. (2002) 'Entangled histories of uneven modernities: civil society, caste solidarities and legal pluralism in post-colonial India', in Y. Elkana (ed.), *Unravelling Ties*, Frankfurt: Campus.

Rawls, J. (1993) *Political Liberalism*, New York: Columbia University Press.

Ribeiro, D. (1971) *El dilema de América Latina*, Buenos Aires: Siglo XXI Editores.

Riggs, F.W. (1964) *Administration in Developing Countries: The Theory of Prysmatic Society*, Boston: Houghton and Mifflin.

Robertson, R. (1984) 'Interpreting globality', in *World Reality and International Studies To-Day*, Genside, PA: Pennsylvania Council on International Education.

Robertson, R. (1992) *Globalization: Social Theory and Global Culture*, London: Sage.

Robertson, R. and Garrett, W. (eds) (1991) *Religion and Global Order*, New York: Paragon.

Rokkan, S. (1969) 'Models and methods in the comparative study of nation-building', *Acta sociological*, 12: 53–73.

Rokkan, S. (1970) *Citizens, Elections, Parties*, Oslo: Universitetsforlaget.

Rokkan, S. (1975) 'Dimensions of state formation and nation-building: a possible paradigm for research on variations within Europe', in C. Tilly (ed.), *The Formation of National States in Western Europe*, Princeton, NJ: Princeton University Press.

Rokkan, S., Saelen, K. and Warmbrunn, J. (1971) 'Nation-building: a review of models and approaches', *Current Sociology*, 19(3): 7–38.

Rorty, R. (1989) *Contingency, Irony and Solidarity*, Cambridge: Cambridge University Press.

Rose, M.A. (1991) *The Post-Modern and the Post-Industrial: A Critical Analysis*, Cambridge: Cambridge University Press.

Rosenau, J.N. (1980) *The Study of Global Interdependence*, New York: Nichols.

Rosenau, J.N. (1997) *Along the Domestic-Foreign Frontier*, Cambridge: Cambridge University Press.

Rostow, W. (1960) *The Stages of Economic Growth: A Non-Communist Manifesto*, Cambridge: Cambridge University Press.

Ruggie, J.G. (1993) 'Territoriality and beyond: problematizing modernity in international relations', *International Organization*, 47(1).

Rustow, D.A. (1967) *A World of Nations: Problems of Political Modernization*, Washington, DC: Brookings Institution.

Said, E.W. (1985) *Orientalism: Western Concepts of the Orient*, London: Penguin.

Sartori, G. (1968) 'Political development and political engineering', in J.D. Montgomery and A.O. Hirschman (eds), *Public Policy*, Cambridge, MA: Harvard University Press.

Sassen, S. (1991) *The Global City: New York: London: Tokyo*, Princeton, NJ: Princeton University Press.

Sassen, S. (2000) *Cities in a World Economy*, 2nd edn, London: Pine Forge Press.

Scharpf, F. (1991) *Crisis and Choice in European Social Democracy*, Ithaca, NY: Cornell University Press.

Schluchter, W. (1984) *The Development of Western Rationalism*, Berkeley, CA: University of California Press.

Schmidt, V.H. (2004) 'Multiple modernities or varieties of modernity?', unpublished paper.

Schurmann, F. (1966) *Ideology and Organization in Communist China*, Berkeley, CA: University of California Press.

Sen, A. (1966) 'Our culture, their culture: Satuajit Ray and the art of universalism', *The New Republic*, April.

Shils, E. (1960) *Political Development in the New States*, The Hague: Mouton.

Simmel, G. (1908) *Soziologie: Untersuchungen über die Formen der Vergesellschaftung*, Berlin: Duncker und Humblot.

Sklair, L. (1991) *Sociology of the Global System*, Hemel Hempstead: Harvester Wheatsheaf.

Skockpol, T. (1979) *States and Social Revolutions*, Cambridge: Cambridge University Press.

Smart, B. (1992) *Modern Conditions, Postmodern Controversies*, London: Routledge.

Smelser, N.J. (1959) *Social Change in the Industrial Revolution*, London: Routledge and Kegan Paul.

Smelser, N.J. (1968) *Essays in Sociological Explanations*, Englewood Cliffs, NJ: Prentice Hall.

Smelser, N.J. (1979) 'Toward a theory of modernization', in A. Etzioni and E. Etzioni (eds), *Social Change*, London: Basil Blackwell.

Smelser, N.J. and Swedberg, R. (eds) (1994) *Handbook of Economic Sociology*, Princeton, NJ: Princeton University Press.

Smith, A.D. (1973) *The Concept of Social Change: A Critique of the Functionalist Theory of Social Change*, London: Routledge.

Smith, A.D. (1983) *Theories of Nationalism*, London: Duckworth.

Smith, A.D. (1991) *National Identity*, London: Penguin.

Soskice, D. (1999) 'Divergent production regimes: coordinated and uncoordinated market economies in the 1980s and 1990s', in H. Kitschelt, P. Lange, G. Marks and J.D. Stephens (eds), *Continuity and Changes in Contemporary Capitalism*, Cambridge: Cambridge University Press, pp. 101–34.

Stavenhagen, R. (ed.) (1970) *Agrarian Problems and Peasant Movements in Latin America*, Garden City, NY: Doubleday.

Stepan, A. (ed.) (1973) *Authoritarian Brazil: Origins, Policies and Futures*, New Haven, CT: Yale University Press.

Strange, S. (1996) *The Retreat of the State: The Diffusion of Power in the World Economy*, Cambridge: Cambridge University Press.

Sztompka, P. (1992) *Dilemmas of the Great Transition*, Working paper Series No. 19, Harvard Center for European studies, Cambridge, MA.

Sztompka, P. (1993) *The Sociology of Social Change*, Oxford: Blackwell.

Taylor, C. (1997) 'Nationalism and modernity', in R. McKim and J. McMahon (eds), *The Morality of Nationalism*, New York: Oxford University Press.

Taylor, C. (2001) 'Two theories of modernity', in D.P. Gaunkar (ed.), *Alternative Modernities*, Durham, NC: Duke University Press.

Teich, M. and Porter, R. (eds) (1990) *Fin de Siècle and its Legacy*, Cambridge: Cambridge University Press.

Therborn, G. (1995) *European Modernity and Beyond: The Trajectory of European Societies 1945–2000*. London: Sage.

Therborn, G. (2000) 'Globalizations: dimensions, historical waves, regional effects, normative governance', *International Sociology*, 15(2): ???–???.

Thurow, L.C. (1999) *Building Wealth: New Rules for Individuals, Companies and Nations in a Knowledge-Based Economy*, New York: HarperCollins.

Tilly, C. (1973) 'Does modernization breed revolution?', *Comparative Politics*, 5(3): 42–7.

Tilly, C. (ed.) (1975) *The Formation of National States in Western Europe*, Princeton, NJ: Princeton University Press.

Tilly, C. (1978) *From Mobilization to Revolution*, Reading, MA: Addison-Wesley.

Tilly, C. (1993) *The European Revolutions 1492–1992*, ????

Tipps, D. (1973) 'Modernization theory and the comparative studies of societies: a critical perspective', *Comparative Studies in Society and History*, 5: 199–226.

Tiryakian, E.A. (1985) 'The changing centers of modernity', in E. Cohen, M. Lissak and U. Almagor (eds), *Comparative Social Dynamics*, Boulder, CO: Westview Press.

Tiryakian, E.A. (1991) 'Modernisation: exhumetur in pace', *International Sociology*, 6(2): 165–80.

Tiryakian, E.A. (2001) 'The civilisation of modernity and the modernity of civilisations', *International Sociology*, 16(3): ???.

Tocqueville, A. de (1945) *Democracy in America (1835–1840)*, 2 vols, the Henry Reeve text, edited by P. Bradley, New York: Vintage.

Tönnies, F. (1887) *Gemeinschaft und Gesellschaft*, Leipzig: Reislad.

Toulmin, S. (1990) *Cosmopolis: The Hidden Agenda of Modernity*, Chicago: The University of Chicago Press.

Touraine, A. (1974) *La Société post-industrielle*, Paris: Editions Denoëlle.

Touraine, A. (1992) *Critique de la modernité*, Paris: Fayard.

Trigilia, C. (1998) *Sociologia economica*, Bologne: Il Mulino.

Turner, B.S. (1990) *Theories of Modernity and Post-Modernity*, London: Sage.

Tuveson, E.L. (1964) *Millennium and Utopia: A Study in the Background of the Idea of Progress*, New York: Harper.

UNCTAD, *World Report*, various years, New York: United Nations.

UNDP, *Human Development Report*, various years, New York: United Nations.

Van Vucht Tijssen, L., Berting, J. and Lechner, F. (eds) (1995) *The Search for Fundamentals: Modernization and the Quest for Meaning*, Dordrecht: Kluwer Academic Publishers.

Wagner, P. (1992) 'Liberty and discipline: making sense of post-modernity, or, once again, toward a sociological understanding of modernity', *Theory and Society*, 21: 467–92.

Wagner, P. (1994) *A Sociology of Modernity: Liberty and Discipline*, London: Routledge.

Wagner, P. (2001) *Theorizing Modernity: Inescapability and Attainability in Social Theory*, London: Sage.

Wallerstein, I. (1974–89) *The Modern World-System*, 3 vols, New York and London: Academic Press.

Wallerstein, I. (1976) 'Modernization: requiescat in pace', in L. Coser and O. Larse (eds), *The Uses of Controversy in Sociology*, New York: Wiley.

Wallerstein, I. (1979) *The Capitalist World-Economy*, Cambridge: Cambridge University Press.

Wallerstein, I. (1991) *Unthinking Social Science: The Limits of Nineteenth-Century Paradigms*, Cambridge: Polity Press.

Waltz, K. (1999) *Globalization and Governance*, the 1999 James Madison Lecture.

Ward, B. et al. (1971) *The Widening Gap: Development in the 1970s*, New York: Columbia University Press.

Ward, R.E. and Rustow, D.A. (eds) *Political Modernization in Japan and Turkey*, Princeton, NJ: Princeton University Press.

Waters, M. (1995) *Globalization*, London: Routledge.

Weber, M. (1956) *Wirtschaft und Gesellschaft: Grundriss der verstehenden Soziologie*, Tübingen: Mohr.

Weber, M. (1972) *Gesammelte Aufsatze zur Religionssoziologie*, 3 vols, Tübingen: Mohr & Siebeck.

Wehler, H-U. (1975) *Modernisierungstheorie und Geschichte*, Göttingen: Vandenhoeck und Ruprecht.

Weiner, M. (ed.) (1966) *Modernization: The Dynamics of Growth*, New York: Basic Books.

Weiner, M. and Huntington, S. (eds) (1987) *Understanding Political Development*, Boston: Little, Brown and Co.

Wittrock, B. (2000) 'Modernity: one, none or many? European origins and modernity as a global condition', *Daedalus, Multiple Modernities*, 129(1): 31–60.

Wolf, E.R. (1982) *Europe and the People Without History*, Berkeley, CA: University of California Press.

World Bank (1997) *Global Economic Prospects and the Developing Countries*, Washington, DC: World Bank.

Yack, B. (1997) *The Fetishism of Modernities*, Notre Dame, IN: The University of Notre Dame Press.

Zapf, W. (ed.) (1991) *Die Modernisierung modernen Gesellschaften*, Frankfurt: Campus Verlag.

Zapf, W. and Flora, P. (1973) 'Differences in paths of development: an analysis of ten countries', in S.N. Eisenstadt and S. Rokkan (eds), *Building States and Nations: Models and Data Resources*, London: Sage.

Zysman, J. and Schwartz, A. (eds) (1998) *Enlarging Europe: The Industrial Foundations of a New Political Reality*, Berkeley, CA: University of California Press.

Index